DORSET PILGRIMS

· DORSET ·
PILGRIMS

THE
STORY OF
WEST COUNTRY
PILGRIMS
WHO WENT TO
NEW ENGLAND
IN THE
17TH CENTURY

FRANK
THISTLETHWAITE

Heart of the Lakes Publishing
Interlaken, New York
1993

Originally published in London by Barrie & Jenkins

American edition published in cooperation with
Family Society Tours
24 Murray Street
Norwalk, CT 06851

Library of Congress Cataloging-in-Publication Data

Thistlethwaite, Frank.
    Dorset pilgrims : the story of West Country Puritans who went
       to New England in the 17th century / Frank Thistlethwaite.
    294 p. cm
    Originally published : London : Barrie & Jenkins, 1989.
    Includes bibliographical references (12 p.) and index.
    ISBN 1-55787-099-3
    1. Puritans—New England—History—17th century. 2. Dorset (Eng-
       land)—History. 3. New England—History—Colonial period,
       ca. 1600–1775. I. Title.
    F7.T48   1993   93–27811
    974'.02—dc20   CIP

A *quality* publication by
Heart of the Lakes Publishing
Interlaken, New York 14847

CONTENTS

v

LIST OF ILLUSTRATIONS

MAPS AND PLANS

PRINCIPAL *DRAMATIS PERSONAE*

The Earl of Warwick *courtier and privateer*
The Rev. John White *Church of England rector*
John Winthrop Jr *colony governor*
Roger Ludlow *lawyer*
Major John Mason *regular soldier*
Matthew Grant *surveyor and town clerk*
The Rev. John Warham *minister*
William Hosford *ruling elder*
Henry Wolcott Jr *merchant*
John Hosford *farmer*
Benjamin Newberry *captain of militia*

PREFACE

I OWE IT TO THE PROSPECTIVE READER TO EXPLAIN THE CIRCUMSTANCES which led me to write this book.

As with many such undertakings it developed unexpectedly as the by-product of a modest and private intention. This was to write something for our children about their family history. One of my wife's direct ancestors happens to have been a member of a Puritan group who emigrated to New England in the 17th century. Many years ago I began in odd moments to find out what I could about him and I became interested in the community of which he became a fairly prominent member. This community was recruited largely from Dorset by a famous Dorchester clergyman called John White and was dispatched by him across the Atlantic to found Dorchester on Massachusetts Bay in 1630.

The history of this community came to have a particular attraction for me as a historian. These West Country people were a constituent group of the great migration from England which settled Massachusetts Bay in the 1630s. Whether they knew it or not, they were emigrants, and my special interest had come to be the history of migration. However, like most people in this field I had been concerned with the great European demographic explosion of the 19th century which populated the whole North American continent. For largely historiographic reasons to do with period specialization, the original migration to New England in the 17th century had been handled in

1

a separate context and according to different criteria. There were clearly marked contrasts and discontinuities between the two periods. The role of the 17th-century emigrant, whether to Massachusetts Bay or to Virginia, was different from that of his 19th-century successors, less clearly defined, understood or developed. The very word 'emigrant' first appeared in the language as late as 1754 and was applied to the Germans who emigrated to Pennsylvania. Our 17th-century subjects did not consciously think of themselves as moving from one country to another. They were simply Englishmen who had chosen to settle or 'plant' in a New England which was one of King Charles's dominions beyond the seas. It is not too far-fetched to think of them as predecessors of the 20th-century settlers of Southern Rhodesia or Kenya. They were colonial Englishmen and this distinction in itself is worth exploring. At the same time I thought it might be useful to approach the phenomenon of 17th-century New England from the broader angle of vision of a migration historian.

There was another special interest for me in this West Country group who settled Dorchester, Massachusetts. They were the most homogeneous of all those shiploads of emigrants who constituted the Great Migration. They not only came largely from one West Country locality, gathered themselves into a church there and settled together on Massachusetts Bay, but, like a hive of bees, they swarmed a second time. Within five years the greater part of the Dorchester people uprooted themselves once more and trekked through the New England wilderness to settle on its 'frontier', the Connecticut River. Here, in a single plantation, which they also called Dorchester before they renamed it Windsor, they persisted as that same close-knit West Country community. But they were already on the move. They were arguably the first example of that phenomenon of westward migration which was to become such a dominant theme in American history.

The fact that this was a West Country group is also of particular interest in the history of the founding of New England. When Samuel Eliot Morison wrote his brilliant *Builders of the Bay Colony* he gave pride of place among all those remarkable founding fathers to John White, the rector of Holy Trinity church, Dorchester, Dorset, that Puritan parson who, as the reader will discover, was the moving spirit behind the Puritan colonizing of New England. Recognizing the spiritual needs of the West Country fishermen off the New England shore, White conceived the idea of a farming–fishing settlement, organized the Dorchester Company and, when that failed, used the rump of it as the basis for a successor which, when taken over by men from the City of London and East Anglia, was transformed into the Massachusetts Bay Company. Morison did justice to White's pre-eminence and to that West Country whence came the first impetus for the settlement of Massachusetts Bay. Yet thereafter the West Country element in that epic became submerged by what was to become the dominant New England strain: that of the eastern counties and London, of the Winthrops, Congregationalism and the Boston ascendency, so that in time another Harvard historian could assert that New England might properly have been called New East Anglia. New England history has been as dyed in that Boston wool as ever was English history in its Whig tradition, and that rather different early West Country strain has tended to be ignored like a poor and inconvenient relation in a proud family. It seemed to me that it might be interesting to add a Dorchester counterpoint to the dominant New England theme.

I thought it also might be useful for an Englishman to look again at this case study from a perspective which embraced English origins as well as New England growth and development. Because of the unique role New England has played in the forming of American nationality, its history has been long and intensively studied and interpreted as a cradle of American values, always seeking the promise of the great events to follow, the Revolution and the Republic. The temptation to see it as an 'American' phenomenon from the start, a kind of Whig interpretation, was for an earlier generation inevitable. As a result the element of Englishness, of origins, tended to be at least foreshortened, used as a sort of permanent stage set, an unshifting backcloth, to what was regarded as an essentially American drama. It is true that within the last quarter-century a younger generation of scholars, using modern techniques of quantitative and sociological analysis, have produced a brilliant and sophisticated series of studies of New England towns. But they too, with notable exceptions, have taken English origins largely for granted.

Also, owing to the nature of these techniques, such studies, immensely valuable as they are in their quantitative analysis of social data, tend to be static in the pictures they present, still photographs rather than cinema film. For the historian of migration this is a limitation. The very nature of the migration process is movement, not the slow and perhaps imperceptible movement of societies over a generation, but the immediate and dramatic actions of travel and adventure, of trials and errors, of heady successes and miserable failures. Such subject matter demands in addition the use of another, more old-fashioned technique: that of narrative. Narrative is essentially a literary art and, at a time when history is in danger of being hijacked by the social sciences, its practice is neglected and indeed in some quarters despised. But I make no apology for my attempt to bring alive, to tell the story – the history – of this particular band of emigrants in narrative form.

For the social historian the art of narrative presents special difficulties because of the nature of the evidence. For the most part we are not writing about outstanding individuals whose influential careers may be traced from public archives and personal papers. We are dealing with collective groups of little-known or anonymous people, knowledge of whom must be gleaned from the impersonal data of social statistics, of births, marriages and deaths, wills and inventories, land grants and conveyances, court records, ship's manifests, passenger lists and the like and the lucky chance of a diary, a bundle of letters or a business ledger. This has been especially so for the historian of migration who has only truly come into his own since the perfection of the new statistical techniques for analysing such intractable data.

However, the reality underlying a particular migration story is not the undifferentiated mass of computerized statistics but the innumerable individuals and families who are often only partially and tantalizingly revealed by the historian's magnifying glass. In this study I have tried to tell the story in terms of individuals even at the risk of confusing the reader with a multiplicity of names of obscure people. Also, where the evidence supports it, I have written a particular episode round its principal protagonist. Thus the titles of nine of the fourteen chapters feature individuals (or in two cases a family and a group). In the first chapter I have introduced the reader to the Jacobethan globe through the personality of the Earl of Warwick who leads us from the glittering powerplays of the court, by way of the operations of buccaneers in the West Indies, to pin that tiny point on the map of New England where Puritan planters raised their flag, at the mouth of Connecticut River.

Finally, I hope it will be clear that I have written this book, not for the profession, but for the general reader. I believe it to be the important thing to do. Nowadays it is tempting for professional historians to write for our peers who together with our students constitute such an enormous teaching and learning public. But there is still a wider readership with a cast of mind to enjoy the story of the past and of people who themselves have a consuming interest in their family origins and the traditions they have inherited. History, as distinct from the great historical databank drawn on by social scientists, will only survive if historians continue to write as craftsmen for their fellow human beings. In the long run, society will not support us unless we do.

Among the many people who have helped bring this book into being I wish particularly to thank Professor Edmund S. Morgan, then of Yale University, who took the trouble to read an early and raw draft, and three colleagues at the University of East Anglia: Professor Robert Ashton and Professor A. Hassell Smith who brought their expert knowledge to bear on the English chapters and especially Dr R. F. Thompson who contributed to the final text his great knowledge of colonial New England, a belief in the book's theme and a talent for both scholarly and general editing which have greatly sustained me. I am also grateful to the colleagues and the members of my graduate seminar who helped me explore 17th-century New England during my tenure of a Hill Visiting Professorship at the University of Minnesota in 1986 and to Mrs Joan Peel on whose genealogical knowledge I greatly rely. The book has benefited immeasurably from their scholarly judgements and kindnesses. Its weaknesses and errors are my own.

I should also like to record my appreciation for the professional skill and patience of members of the staff of the Connecticut and Massachusetts Historical Societies, the Boston Public Library and especially, over many years, the Connecticut State Library in Hartford; also of the staff of the County Record office for Dorset (especially Mrs Margaret Holmes, County Archivist) and for Somerset and of the Cambridge University Library. I am also grateful to Mr H. A. Shelley for his expert draughtsmanship in drawing the maps.

My grateful thanks are owed to the Henry E. Huntington Library for electing me to a Visiting Fellowship in 1973, to the Nuffield Foundation for a research grant which helped support me at that time and to the Leverhulme Trust for its award of an Emeritus Fellowship in 1981 to enable me to write this book.

Finally, the book owes much to the imaginative and careful professionalism of my editor, Gila Falkus and of Philippa Lewis for the illustrations.

CAMBRIDGE, ENGLAND

FEBRUARY, 1989

INTRODUCTION: THE EARL OF WARWICK AND THE COLONIZING OF AMERICA 1600–35

O N SUNDAY, 24 JULY 1603, A COMPANY OF SIXTY NOBLES AND GENTRY IN full panoply, accompanied by squires and pages, rode out from St James's to the king's court at Whitehall. After parading round the tiltyard, they dismounted in St James's Park, went up to the gallery and into the royal presence. There, one by one, King James I dubbed them Knights of the Bath in honour of his coronation which was to take place the next day. Among them was a young sprig of the nobility, sixteen-year-old Robert, now Sir Robert, eldest son of the third Baron Rich of Leighs in Essex.

At the time he was knighted he was a Cambridge undergraduate. He was a golden boy, an outstanding member of the *jeunesse d'orée* of his time. A contemporary wrote that 'he had all those excellent endowments of body and fortune that give splendor to a glorious Court' and referred to 'a lovely sweetness transcending most men'. The Rich family belonged to the new order of aristocratic magnates whom the social upheavals begun by Henry VIII's Reformation seventy years before had brought to the fore. The founder of the family's fortunes, Richard Rich, of a London merchant family, rose rapidly by means of the Bar and the Reformation Parliament to become one of Henry VIII's most infamous hatchet-men and, in 1548, under Edward VI, lord chancellor. In his career he managed to double-cross an array of notables as disparate as Cardinal Wolsey, Bishop Fisher, Sir Thomas More, Protector Somerset, and his close colleague Thomas Cromwell. He was

6

instrumental as lord chancellor in putting through the Calvinistic reforms of Edward VI's reign, and then he ingratiated himself to Queen Mary by restoring the Old Religion and zealously persecuting heretics. He had a rapacious hand in dissolving the monasteries as a result of which he became the greatest landed magnate in Essex, converting Leighs Priory into his country seat. His grandson, Robert, the third Lord Rich, father of our youthful knight, therefore inherited one of the greatest fortunes in the land. Though considered by sophisticates to be coarse and uneducated, he was of sufficient wealth and position to be a worthy match for the Lady Penelope Devereux, daughter of the first Earl of Essex and sister of the Queen's favourite. This beautiful and talented young woman had as a girl been the object of Sir Philip Sidney's desire and the Stella of his celebrated sonnet sequence. Despite bearing Lord Rich seven children she cut a considerable figure at court until disgraced at the time of her brother Essex's execution and attainder in 1601. Restored to favour by James I, she once again became prominent in court festivities.

It was through her influence that her eldest son Robert began so spectacularly a career at court which led to his wider role in public life. He was a talented courtier. Like his mother, he took part in the masques which were so sparkling a feature of the Jacobean court. On Shrove Tuesday, 1609, there was a masque to celebrate Lord Hadington's marriage, text by Ben Jonson, sets by Inigo Jones and music by Ferrabosco. As a chronicler wrote: 'The attire of the masquers throughout was most graceful and noble, the colours carnation and silver enriched with embroidery and lace, the dressing of their heads, feathers and jewels; their performance so magnificent and illustrious that nothing can add to the seal of it but the subscription of their names.' Among the earls, barons and their eldest sons who were the principal players was young Sir Robert Rich. He was also a skilled performer of the martial arts and regularly took part in those combats in the tiltyard which so appealed to the King.

Yet for Robert Rich this was just gamesmanship. 'He used it but for his recreation', wrote contemporary Arthur Wilson, the dramatist and historian who, as his gentleman-in-waiting, saw him at close quarters. At the same time he was seeking more serious and public pursuits. After Cambridge he joined the Inner Temple and in 1610 he was elected Member of Parliament for Maldon, and thus embarked on a parliamentary career which would lead him to power and distinction among the leaders of the opposition to the autocratic government of Charles I. Our concern is with only one aspect of this achievement. As Wilson wrote, 'His spirit aimed at more publique adventures planting colonies in the Western World rather than himself in the King's favour.'

Robert Rich, who became Earl of Warwick on his father's death, not only personifies a cardinal theme of English history in the era of the early Stuarts but, as we shall see, became a key and influential figure at court in the colonizing of New England in general and particularly in that venture which is the subject of this chronicle. As president of the Council for New England and himself the patron of Puritans, he had a principal hand in launching the Massachusetts Bay Company and in issuing to a group of Puritan noblemen and gentry the patent which laid claim to the territory of Connecticut. In thus providing a link between the power and authority of the English court and those tiny outposts on the edge of the world he is the appropriate beginning to this story.

It goes back to his father. Not content with his landed wealth and powerful court connections, the third Lord Rich, like other Elizabethan magnates, augmented his fortunes by seafaring. For the previous forty years, with Catholic Spain in the ascendency and France weakened by religious war, the English were increasingly isolated from the Continent and, from the 1570s onwards, overtly at war with Spain and supporting the Calvinist revolt in the Netherlands. This was a time when a strong monarchy, a rising population, improved land and coastal transport, and the multiplying of money and credit, all stimulated more diverse industry – especially textiles and mining – and overseas commerce. English overseas trade had traditionally been chiefly with Channel and North Sea ports and the Iberian peninsula. The loss of Calais and the disruption of trade with Antwerp and the Channel ports had played havoc with these connections. Moreover, despite the explorations a century before by the Cabots and others, the English had been slow to exploit their strategic position at the gateway to the north Atlantic. West Countrymen had long before joined Bretons, Basques and Portuguese in fishing off the Newfoundland banks; but maritime expansion in the whole Atlantic basin appeared to be baulked by the hated papistical Spaniards, King Philip II, his dons and Inquisitorial clergy who controlled the shipping lanes to their vast and rich empire in South and Central America and, more immediately to the point, in the Caribbean. Until the power of Spain was neutralized, freebooting expeditions like those of Raleigh which attempted to establish English trading posts on the Virginia shore and the 'Wild Coast' of Guiana were bound to prove abortive. Meanwhile the navigational and mercantile skills, the religious and ideological zeal of the mariners and merchants of England were devoted to challenging the maritime power of Spain in the Atlantic. In those days of rudimentary navies expensively mobilized only for specific operations, the chief instruments of English sea power were armed merchantmen sailing on voyages whose object was part exploration, part trade but, above all, with 'letters of marque' or licences from the Queen, the capture of Spanish prizes. It was the heyday of the privateer. During the last years of Elizabeth's reign Lord Rich had built up one of the largest privateering fleets in England.

In 1604, the year after the young Robert Rich became a knight, the new king of England at last made peace with Spain and so, for twenty-one years, letters of marque were no longer issued against Spanish merchantmen; but this did not unduly hinder English seafarers. Some smaller men, ship's captains and the like, crossed the shadowy line from privateer to pirate, often raiding Spanish treasure ships and other foreign merchantmen from English settlements in the Caribbean which became notorious as pirate lairs. But Lord Rich and his fellow admirals in their more ambitious and respectable freebooting, trading, privateering ventures simply obtained licences from other friendly powers like the Dutch who were happy to share the booty of the voyage, and disposed of their cargoes in Continental ports. In 1616 Lord Rich sent out three ships with a commission from the Duke of Savoy to prey on the Spanish. At the same time his son, our Sir Robert Rich, under the same flag of convenience, sailed for the Red Sea where, but for the intervention of the East India Company fleet, and in an act of blatant piracy, he would have captured a ship belonging to no less than the queen mother of the Great Mogul with cargo valued at £100,000. (The resulting embarrassment kept young Robert in litigation with the East India Company for a decade or more.)

In 1618 Lord Rich died, having just become Earl of Warwick, and his son inherited both the title and his father's large-scale privateering enterprises. When after the death of James I in 1625 hostilities once again broke out with Spain, the second Earl of Warwick received a broadly drafted commission from King Charles I authorizing him 'to invade and possess any of the dominions of the King of Spain in Europe, Africa or America', sufficient excuse for three years of extensive privateering. In 1627 he had letters of marque for some eleven ships. He himself commanded a squadron off the Iberian coast in search of the Brazilian treasure fleet; unfortunately he became separated from his other ships, mistook the Spanish fleet for the treasure ships and, having sailed through the entire armada, only escaped by keeping his nerve in the confusion and a dense fog. He returned without booty but admired for his exploit. As a newsletter reported: 'He was never sick one hour at sea, and would as nimbly climb up to top and yard as any common mariner in the ship: and all the time of the fight was as active and as open to danger as any man there.'

In these years, however, Warwick increasingly turned his attention to the West Indies, whose islands and bays provided shelter for vessels engaged in trade with local Spanish settlements for such essentials as salt, and were within striking distance of the rich Spanish merchantmen. As early as 1612 he had become a member of a company set up to settle the newly discovered Somers or Bermuda Island, and in 1618 his ship *Treasurer* under Captain Elfrith made a notorious marauding voyage in those seas. At length, in 1630, in order to establish a base for such operations, he with his brother and others organized a company to effect a permanent settlement on the island of Santa Catalina off the Mosquito Coast, to be renamed Providence. In this he had already begun to transcend his role as admiral of privateers to become a principal influence in the English colonization of the North American littoral.

When James I came to the throne in 1603 there had been no English colonies on the American mainland; when his son was executed in 1649 there were upwards of 50,000 colonists settled up and down the North American seaboard and in the Caribbean from an England whose population was little more than four million. This astonishing phenomenon was the result of a combination of economic, religious and political forces which combined to give the reigns of the first two Stuarts a dynamic thrust towards colonization. With the ending of the long years of war with Spain in 1604 came the release of commercial energies looking for new outlets, especially in overseas trade. The very war itself, restricting trade with the Low Countries, had impelled the merchants of London and the outports to look further afield, and over the Tudor decades great monopolist companies had been organized under the Crown to trade with Muscovy, the Baltic, the Levant and the East Indies. A country's wealth, ran orthodox mercantilist wisdom, depended on foreign trade, with a favourable balance of exports over imports to provide treasure for capital investment. With the Spanish menace in eclipse, it was time to turn westwards across the Atlantic and, in increasing competition with the Dutch, to stake claims to the Caribbean islands with their tropical crops and those hundreds of miles of North American coastline separating Spanish Florida from the French settlements in the region of the St Lawrence. Here were abundant primary staple products, from fish to timber, naval stores and minerals (if not the elusive precious metals) – the raw materials of national wealth; and there was still the hope that among those uncharted bays and estuaries to the north-west might still be found a passage through to the Pacific Ocean and the riches of the East Indies.

The experience of Elizabethan explorers and freebooters, and especially Sir Walter Raleigh's tragic failure at Roanoke, had made clear that to establish trading settlements required the organization and resources enjoyed by the big regulated companies. In 1606, stimulated by Hakluyt's and other accounts of exploratory voyages, two groups of prominent seafaring knights and merchants, of London and West Country ports, obtained a charter from the Crown to establish twin companies to take that part of America 'commonly called Virginia' not in the possession of Spain or France, that is to say the middle Atlantic seaboard. Of these, the West Country (or Plymouth) Company quickly failed, but the London, now the Virginia Company, went ahead to establish settlements in the region about Chesapeake Bay. The first settlement did not prosper, suffering from the characteristic troubles of disease, inadequate planning of provisions, lack of accommodation and suitable colonists, and hostile Indians; but Virginia persisted and became England's first established mainland colony in North America.

Other colonizing ventures were to profit from her experience. Successful colonizing demanded technical knowledge, entrepreneurship, capital and labour. The first had been gradually acquired by explorers whose knowledge of seamanship, climate and topography had, over the years, sifted fact from fancy in a veritable corpus of travel literature and charts. Even so, the know-how required to survive a hazardous voyage and the hostile circumstances of the New World was still being acquired through the trials and errors of painful experience. Knowledge of the climate, which turned out to be temperate and fever-free; understanding the logistics of getting supplies across the Atlantic; the realization that hopes of quick profits from precious minerals and other exotics must be abandoned in favour of concentrating on practical subsistence crops and staples for trade; acknowledgment of the importance of selecting suitable, working colonists – all this expertise was only learnt as a result of bitter and sometimes mortal failures.

The necessary entrepreneurship was provided for the most part by that well-connected class, of which Warwick was so outstanding an example, of nobles, gentry and merchants with experience of mounting oceanic trading expeditions. Here the aristocratic element was vital. Such expeditions might have been privateering, but they were not private, and even the most buccaneering were undertaken with at least the tacit knowledge and interest of the Crown. When it came to establishing colonies, whether trading posts or settlements, it was assumed that these were English territory under the sovereignty of the monarch. They were political and territorial instruments and their promoters had to be such as had the ear and confidence of the king – for the most part grandees of standing at court and magnates in the country at large. As companies, they were in a sense an extension of the Privy Council and by their nature held a territorial and trading monopoly for which, incidentally, they usually paid a stiff price to the royal treasury. The granting of these monopolies to augment the royal revenues early became a contentious issue between James I and Parliament; but they were regarded as the natural device for colonization. For this purpose the organization of such companies had become more sophisticated since those Tudor times. The need to mobilize capital for expeditions involving squadrons of ships, continuous lines of communication and long lead-times before there was a return on the investment, led to the device of joint stock, whereby the company handled the subscribers' investment corporately, first for a single voyage and then for a number of years. Although not all colonizing companies functioned this way, the joint-stock company became the principal device for colonial settlement.

The mobilization of capital on a considerable scale was therefore the third cardinal factor in colonizing. The grandees with their court connections contributed their shares and enjoyed their profits and their losses. But their wealth usually consisted of lands and rents and hardly provided capital liquid enough for ambitious ventures. Such capital had to come from the rich and powerful mercantile fraternity, successors to the 'merchant adventurers' of Bristol, York, Hull, Exeter and other 'outports', and especially from the City of London, whose great companies and connections had subscribed backing for the regulated companies, and now in the boom times of the first Stuarts were poised to provide the credit and financial expertise for this new transoceanic, mercantile world. The connection between courtiers with access to royal influence and patronage and City merchants, intimate even to the point of family intermarriages, generated the intelligence, influence, wealth and power impelling the English colonization of North America.

To the south, the Spaniards had long before established an *imperium* of conquistadores and priests; the French, to the north, had their outposts for fishing and trapping; and the Dutch were building trading factories in all the seven seas; but the English were the first to establish colonies of permanent settlement in the New World. This needed not only entrepreneurs and capital, but labour on some scale – ordinary people, men, women and children, prepared to till the soil and make homes for themselves in an unknown American wilderness. It so happened that in England at the turn of the 17th century there were the motives and means to take advantage of such an opportunity.

An underlying motive for colonizing, then and for a long time to come, was a desire for land. In Elizabeth's day the population of England had grown apace and was outrunning the limited amount of good farmland. The enterprising were now converting moor, forest and waste and draining fenland at great expense and with limited results. This was also a time when the conditions of rural life were rapidly changing. A new generation of gentry and yeomen, concerned with growing crops for markets and investing profits, wherever possible raised rents to keep pace with the endemic inflation which underlay most aspects of Elizabethan life. In this period of economic and social turbulence some made fortunes but others, of all rural classes – gentry, yeomen, husbandmen and cottagers, landlords, tenants or day labourers – went under. In addition, the fluctuations of industry and trade, especially a depression in the textile industries under the early Stuarts, created unemployment in the small towns and villages where spinning and weaving were a vital supplementary income to farm wages. People drifted from their hamlets and villages in search of work, often into the towns which were overrun with the poor and indigent. There was a floating population, from younger sons of the gentry to cottagers, whose ties with the land and traditional habits had loosened and who were ripe for a more radical uprooting. As a result, there was a spirit of unease, of insecurity abroad and a conviction that England was becoming over-populated; and this was at a time when news of the fertile lands of the New World, conveyed by propagandist pamphleteering, was the talk of the town and the village. There were many in circumstances sufficiently discouraging and of a temperament sufficiently adventurous to be lured from their habitual existence and tempted to chance their arms across the Atlantic to win those fifty acres of freehold which were beyond the dreams of cottagers and artisans in Somerset or Suffolk. Such were the colonists whom the Virginia Company recruited for the first ship's companies who settled Jamestown.

It was through the Virginia Company that the young Sir Robert Rich first became seriously interested in colonization. In 1612 at the age of twenty-five he was made a member of it and its subsidiary, the Bermuda Company. Bermuda had been put on the map in 1609 when Sir George Somers was shipwrecked there and had returned to extol its beauties and fertility. Two years later the Bermuda Company had been given an independent charter with Rich as its principal shareholder and landowner. Thereafter, along with his privateering, Bermuda was a principal interest of his and he was responsible for importing the first negro slaves to work on his estate there. In due course he also came to be prominent in the affairs of the Virginia Company itself and deeply involved in its turbulent inner politics which, in 1623, led the King to revoke the company's charter and to take over Virginia as a royal colony. By this time, however, Warwick was beginning to shift his interests from Virginia to New England.

Now thirty-six, Warwick was a powerful and influential figure in colonial affairs. Personally, he had charm and an engaging intelligence and was expansive and generous with his associates. His daughter-in-law wrote that 'he was one of the most best-natured and the cheerfullest persons I have in my time met with'; and even Clarendon who was hostile to his politics conceded that 'he was a man of a pleasant and companionable wit and conversations, of a universal jollity'. Dominant and cool in keeping with his aristocratic bearing, he was aggressive, hard-headed, courageous and versatile in business. Unlike his younger brother who, as Lord Kensington then Earl of Holland, committed himself to a career at court, Warwick had by now outgrown court life and was probably out of sympathy with it. He would shortly emerge as one of the leaders of the Puritan party in Parliament in opposition to Charles I. For despite his worldly, swashbuckling, acquisitive style of life, Robert Warwick had grown up in a Puritan atmosphere and had been educated at Emmanuel College, Cambridge, which was at the forefront of the intellectually fashionable Puritan movement.

The Puritan opposition to the early Stuarts, like so much else in this story, had Tudor origins. The Elizabethan Church Settlement was designed to end the conflicts caused by the ambiguities of Henry VIII's Reformation and the alternating Protestantism and Catholicism of his successors. Matthew Parker and his colleagues, with great political tact, ingenuity and artistry, constructed a Protestant church for and of England which managed to contain these disparate strands of doctrine and liturgy within a single allegiance. But in the latter years of the 16th century the radical Calvinist mentality of Geneva came to sit more and more uneasily with the liturgy of the Elizabethan settlement. For some strenuous souls only a spiritual conversion to a state of grace could be the test of true religion, and groups like the Brownists came together as gathered communities or sects, predecessors of the Separatists who at the turn of the 17th century felt they could no longer practise their faith in England and migrated to the more congenial Calvinist Netherlands. But most people of this persuasion remained content to worship loyally within the Church of England while striving to purge it of papistical practices and simplify and purify its doctrines and liturgy in the spirit of the early church of New Testament times. Both sectaries and reformers came to be described as 'Puritans', a generic term which went beyond immediate issues of church doctrine. It stood for all the intellectual, spiritual and indeed aesthetic values of a whole generation who regarded themselves as 'modern'. They sought to discipline themselves to the learning of the Renaissance, the spirit of the Reformation and the responsible social values of a more urban and outward-looking style of living than that of the post-feudal world which they had inherited. Puritanism was especially fashionable among the educated classes, including an important and powerful element of the aristocracy, bred at the universities and the Inns of Court, and especially at Cambridge which sent forth a whole cadre of intellectual, educated graduates to raise the often ignorant and slovenly standards of the clergy in parishes throughout the land.

So long as Roman Catholic Spain remained the national enemy these fractures within the Church of England were contained; but with the waning of that menace and the growth of a High Anglican court party under Charles I and his Catholic queen the inherent opposition between Puritan and High Church parties became increasingly polarized. This especially concerned the position and authority of the bishops. The rise to power of the High Church William Laud, as Bishop of London and then Archbishop of Canterbury, signalled an outright drive against Puritan values in general and Puritan clergy in particular. Lines also became drawn in secular politics, between the court party upholding James I's notions of the divine right of kings and the aristocrats, knights of the shire and burgesses from the boroughs (especially the City of London) who constituted the Houses of Parliament.

Prominent among the opposition leaders in the House of Lords was the Earl of Warwick. In attacking the King's personal rule this group of peers made common cause with like-minded friends in the Commons such as Sir John Eliot and John Pym. Warwick supported the Commons in their struggle for the Petition of Right, refused to subscribe to the forced loan and made an eloquent speech against the King's bid to imprison without due cause. He would subsequently become a prominent figure in the Parliamentary cause. True to his interests and talents he became president of the commission governing the colonies under the Long Parliament and later as Lord High Admiral between 1643 and 1645 he would successfully command the Parliamentary navy.

More immediately relevant to this narrative was his active influence on behalf of Puritan ministers. One of the perks which his great-grandfather, along with others of his kind, had acquired at the Reformation was the right to present clergy to livings in the parishes of their extensive landholdings. Such livings, inherited or acquired by Warwick and other peers, like the Duke of Bedford and the Earl of Pembroke, were sufficiently extensive to block Laud's plan to achieve a fully Laudian parish clergy. Many of the great Puritan ministers survived as preachers because of this patronage. Perhaps the most powerful of them, Edmund Calamy, held one of Warwick's livings and described him as 'a great patron and Maecenas to the pious and religious ministry'. Even Clarendon, who thought Warwick a hypocrite, grudgingly admits it:

> He had great authority and credit with that people who, in the beginning of the trouble, did all the mischief; and by opening his doors and making his house the rendezvous of all the silenced ministers . . . and spending a good part of his estate . . . upon them, and by being present with them at their devotions . . . he became the head of that party and got the style of a godly man.

Warwick's leanings towards Puritan clergy were not limited to the patronage of his own livings in England. During the thirty years that he was governor of the Bermuda Company he selected as ministers for those islands clergy who, although professedly Anglican, were at heart non-conformists and set up a 'government of ministers' in Presbyterian fashion, eventually becoming schismatics. But this was only a minor aspect of the way he used his power and influence for the Puritan cause in the English colonizing of North America.

For among the ingredients making for successful colonization was religion. The lure of a landed freehold was powerful enough to attract the labour which made it possible to settle Virginia. But the unhappy early experiences of that colony with its motley band of settlers whose only motive was material betterment left something seriously lacking. And, if the less fertile and less climatically friendly region of the American littoral north of Chesapeake Bay was to be exploited, a motive was needed to release deeper and more sustained energies. With a fortunate conjunction of circumstances, which to its participants seemed like divine intervention, this was provided by Puritanism. For over a decade, from his influential position on the governing bodies of colonizing companies, Warwick was in a position to give a helping hand to directing Puritan energies towards colonial settlement.

After a failure in Maine the Plymouth Company remained inactive and indeed moribund. In 1620, however, it was reconstituted as the Council for New England with authority to develop the northern part of 'Virginia', that is to say all the territory between the Hudson River and the Gaspee Peninsula: that huge expanse stretching between 42° and 48° latitude which constitutes modern New England and Nova Scotia. Warwick was appointed to a seat on the new council. At this time those Separatists who twenty years before had left their native Lincolnshire for the religious freedom of the Netherlands were dissatisfied and restless with their life in Leyden and contemplating a more radical solution to their quest for a spiritual home. Like so many emigrants in the two centuries to come, having once uprooted themselves, they found it all the easier to contemplate uprooting themselves again, and the possibilities of America were being widely canvassed. At this time people were still thinking in terms of the Caribbean, and the year before a company had been formed to colonize Raleigh's old territory of Guiana. Warwick was the organizer and for some time had been in touch with the Leyden Separatists with a view to recruiting them for this venture. But it collapsed. Whereupon the Leyden people, with Warwick's help and backing from a group of London merchants, sailed in the *Mayflower* for their New World retreat, situated, they thought, to the north in the territory of the Virginia Company. However, the accidents of the voyage compelled them to land at what they called Plymouth in New England, outside the Virginia Company's patent but within the remit of the newly formed Council for New England. Once again it was Warwick, as a leading member of the latter, who came to their rescue and obtained for them a patent from the new council for the land on which they were squatting. 'It is a striking fact in Warwick's career', wrote Arthur Newton, the historian of this episode, 'that he was the only person of high rank and influence connected with all the bodies with whom the Leyden pilgrims negotiated before they could secure a home for themselves in the New World': that is to say, the

Guiana Company, the Virginia Company and the Council for New England; and ten years later it would be Warwick again, as president of the Council for New England, who would obtain for Plymouth Colony its second, and definitive, grant.

The fortuitous 'setting down', as the phrase went, of the Pilgrim Fathers in Massachusetts Bay rather than Virginia radically shifted the colonizing scene from its buccaneering, West Indian orientation to that of the north Atlantic fishing grounds. West Countrymen, along with French, Basques and Portugese, had been fishing off Newfoundland and Nova Scotia for nearly a century, and in 1610 some Bristol merchants had even tried to settle a colony on Newfoundland. More recently West Country ships were being attracted to the waters off the coast of Maine and it was the experience of fishermen whose home port was Weymouth, Dorset, that led to the first deliberate attempt to settle on the shores of New England. Weymouth was the port for Dorchester, eight miles inland and a county town with important mercantile connections overseas. Dorchester had come increasingly under the influence of its principal clergyman, John White. This remarkable man, a former fellow of New College, Oxford, was an able divine and an outstanding example of that generation of moderate Puritan reforming clergy. Since he will be the principal subject of the next chapter, it is sufficient here to note that from 1606, when he was inducted as rector of Holy Trinity, he had effected a single-handed reformation of public morality in Dorchester which extended from church worship to schooling and care of the poor. He also developed a concern for the spiritual needs of those Weymouth fishermen who were away from their parishes and family ties for half the year on their perilous calling. He became aware, too, that the effectiveness of that fishery left much to be desired. Since the season's catches had to be dried or salted for the long voyage home, the ships had to be double crewed to provide labour for the curing process at staithes set up on the New England shore. This was inefficient. Why not, thought this highly practical rector, transform those staithes into permanent shore settlements which could be manned throughout the winter as a service base for the seasonal fishing fleet and obviate the necessity for double manning? Moreover, such settlements might in time support wives and families and, more to his point, a minister to care for their spiritual needs.

After an exploratory voyage commissioned by a prominent Dorchester merchant, he organized the granting of a patent from the Council for New England and in 1624, after a public meeting in Dorchester (called by a local wag the 'Planters' Parliament') he launched what came to be known as the

Dorchester Company consisting of 109 members, mostly Dorset gentry and merchants and a strong element of Puritan clergy, the object of which was to establish a fishing 'plantation' in New England. Like so many pioneering efforts, this was a failure and in 1626 was wound up. White was not, however, a man to give up and leave in the lurch not only the company's creditors but a rump of settlers at Cape Ann on the north shore of Massachusetts Bay. By this time he had come to understand that his original idea of a fishing plantation was impracticable, if only because fishermen and 'landsmen' planters were fish and fowl; also the tide of governmental opinion was running so strongly against the Puritans that he and others were beginning to think seriously about establishing a colony specifically as a retreat where Puritans could practise their religion unmolested.

Realizing that such a project needed more ambitious organization and funding, he recruited a nucleus of West Country notables, including Sir Henry Rosewell, the Lord Lieutenant of Devon, and John Humphrey, Esquire, treasurer of the Dorchester Company, prominent enough to attract the interest of London merchants and to persuade the Council for New England to grant a new and more comprehensive patent. In 1628 that council appears to have been in abeyance; but its president was now our Earl of Warwick. With the council's great seal in his possession at Warwick House, off Holborn in London, he granted a patent for the New England Company, with more specific conditions, and territorial bounds four miles north of the Merrimac, four miles south of the Charles River, and west to the 'South Sea'. Whether he did this in his personal capacity as recipient of part of the council's earlier territorial division, or as president of the council without consulting the other council members, will never be known because the patent itself was spirited away and has disappeared. The act was, however, typical, both of Warwick's sympathy for the Puritan cause and of the high-handed way in which he took it upon himself to act: and the result in the end was a characteristic row.

The New England Company was constituted on a voluntary, unincorporated joint-stock basis with sufficient capital to start a plantation. Of its forty-one subscribers, twenty-five were merchants, most from the City of London and identified with other Puritan ventures, seven were gentry, mostly lawyers of the Inns of Court, and six belonged to the original Dorchester Company, including John White. They also included John Humphrey, who had been treasurer of that company. Humphrey, of Chaldon near Dorchester, was of the Dorset gentry and a Puritan friend of White. In 1630 he married Lady Susan, sister of the Earl of Lincoln who was of the same circle as the Earl of Warwick. Lady Lincoln was a daughter of Warwick's Puritan colleague in the House of Lords, Lord Saye and Sele. Lincoln's other sister, Arbella, was married to Isaac Johnson, also a member of the New England Company. John Humphrey succeeded in interesting his brother-in-law Lincoln in John White's colonizing venture; and it was Lincoln, together with his kinsman and steward Thomas Dudley, who was to provide, at Sempringham, a centre for that eastern counties group which, along with the London merchants, was to become so prominent in the New England Company and its successor, the Massachusetts Bay Company. It was owing to Humphrey that the Lincoln connection became associated with the enterprise.

The New England Company, having taken over the assets of the old Dorchester group, promptly dispatched the *Abigail*, one of the latter's ships, from Weymouth under John Endicott, a member of the new company and designated governor of the old Dorchester Company settlement, now at Salem; and other ships followed. Unfortunately these happenings came to the ears of an opponent of Warwick, Sir Fernando Gorges, who learned, to his annoyance, that they lay within territory which had been earlier granted to his son and where a scattering of his own servants were already settled. Realizing that their patent must thus be flawed and scenting trouble from the Gorges family, the members of the New England Company decided to go over the head of the Council for New England, whose president had so accommodatingly granted their patent, and apply to the King for a charter under the great seal. This they did and on 4 March 1629 when the charter passed the seals the New England Company was successfully transformed into the Massachusetts Bay Company. The circumstances whereby this came about are still obscure. Suffice it to say that of possible objectors Gorges was busy elsewhere, and of the two principal petitioners in favour one was Warwick, friend of the company's Puritan promoters.

With the granting of the charter, the company membership was revamped and extended to represent the rapidly growing Puritan interests of East Anglia and the Lincoln connection. In June, Warwick's Suffolk neighbour John Winthrop, squire and lawyer, like John Humphrey having been dismissed as attorney for the court of wards, was in a mood of profound depression about the state of the country. The passage by the Commons the year before of the Petition of Right had seemed at the time a triumph for the rights of the subject under the Common Law; but the King had responded by proroguing Parliament. In the new session that January matters had gone from bad to worse. The publication of a royal 'Declaration touching Public Worship', which seemed to Puritans to open the door to popish practices in religion, led to turbulent scenes in the Commons; and, when the King attempted to adjourn the House, the Speaker was forcibly held in his chair to enable defiant resolutions to be passed against Arminians and papists and the payment of tonnage and poundage. As a result, Parliament was dissolved and Eliot and eight other Members were arrested and sent to the Tower. It looked as if the King were preparing to rule the country personally. The appointment of Laud as Bishop of London and as president of the Court of High Commission was ominous news for Puritans. Abroad, the Protestant cause was everywhere on the run, from Denmark to La Rochelle, and absolutism and Catholicism seemed triumphant. It appeared only a matter of time before Laud and Charles's Catholic queen would bring England back to the Old Religion.

In a mood of despair, John Winthrop determined on the radical course and, with his brother-in-law Emmanuel Downing, rode up to Lord Lincoln's seat at Sempringham to identify himself with the project to emigrate to Massachusetts Bay. In July he was one of the twelve members of the company who met in Cambridge to pledge themselves to emigrate on the understanding that they should take the charter with them across the Atlantic. In other words, the government of the enterprise should be in the hands not of 'Adventurers' sitting as a court in London but of 'Planters', Assistants and freemen sitting as a general court in the colony itself. The full implications of this would take us beyond the scope of this narrative; it may, however, be ventured that this momentous decision, taken in private if not secretly, had the tacit approval of the Earl of Warwick who had been so influential in seeing that charter through the seals, just as he had on an earlier occasion approved a scheme for the local self-government of Virginia. It is clear from correspondence that the Massachusetts settlers were given considerable support by Warwick and his fellow colonizers then and later. Meanwhile Winthrop was elected Governor of the enlarged company to which he immediately gave a new and more radical thrust. John Humphrey was deputy governor, thus keeping the West Country connection; and on 29 March 1630, after a hectic winter of preparations and the expenditure of large sums of money, a fleet, with Winthrop on board the flagship *Arbella*, set sail for Massachusetts Bay.

The voyage of the Winthrop fleet bearing over 700 people across the north Atlantic and the consequent settlement of Charleston, Boston, Dorchester and a half-dozen or more other townships on the shores and rivers of Massachusetts Bay was a colonizing venture of a new and different order of magnitude from anything that had gone before. It was a far cry from the early privateering ventures which had first tempted the young Sir Robert Rich into the Atlantic world; but it was not to mark the end of his interest or endeavours in the field of colonizing.

The looming crisis in the affairs of England which caused John Winthrop to despair also induced a deep pessimism in the Earl of Warwick and his associates, who for the past few years had made so much of the running for the opposition in Parliament. Warwick himself and Saye and Lincoln in the Lords, and in the Commons its Leader Sir John Eliot, Warwick's cousin Sir Nathaniel Rich, and John Pym were part of the inner core of the party and through working together in the House and its committees had come to form a close-knit group whose activities extended beyond the politics of Westminster. The dissolution of Parliament and the clear determination of the King to rule on his own, the death in prison of Warwick's close friend Eliot which must have deeply affected them all, and the impressive example of Winthrop and company's expedition, turned the thoughts of Warwick and his friends towards establishing a colony of their own to which they might themselves emigrate should the worst ensue.

Warwick was not yet, however, convinced by Winthrop's decision in favour of New England, and still hankered after his familiar warm and sunny waters of the West Indies, and in the December after the departure of the Winthrop fleet he launched the company we noted earlier, with the object of establishing a colony on what came to be called Providence Island on the Mosquito Coast. Of its twenty original subscribers, five were members of Warwick's own coterie, including his brother Lord Holland and his cousin and man of business, Sir Nathaniel Rich; nine were members of the inner core of opposition and Members of the Parliament of 1628–9; they included, besides Warwick himself, Lords Saye and Sele and Brooke, and, above all, John Pym, who was emerging as the ablest organizer of them all; and finally there was a small group of Puritan squires from East Anglia.

However, this was not the only fall-back position envisaged by this group of disaffected Puritan notables who, perhaps influenced by Winthrop's example, turned their attention to New England. As Sir Fernando Gorges commented, these 'were so fearful what would follow [the dissolution of Parliament], some of the principal of those liberal speakers being committed to the Tower, others to other prisons – which took all hope of reformation of Church government . . . some of the discreeter sort . . . made use of their friends to procure from the Council for the affairs of New England to settle a colony within their limits.' Thus Warwick, whether as president of the Council for New England or under his own territorial share dating back to 1623, issued yet another patent, confirmed on 19 March 1632, for a grant of land stretching forty leagues west of the Narragansett River to a group of 'peers and gentlemen' who included the familiar names of Lord Saye and Sele, Lord Brooke, Lord Rich, the Hon. Charles Fiennes of the Lincoln connection, Sir Nathaniel Rich, Sir Richard Saltonstall, John Humphrey Esquire, deputy governor of the Massachusetts Bay Company, and John Pym. Once again Warwick, acting in his cavalier and lordly way, failed to consult the members of his council and there is doubt as to whether the patent was ever properly executed. There was another row with the Gorges faction who this time confronted Warwick and demanded that he deliver up the council's seal. Henceforward the court party, led by Gorges, took over the affairs of the council and Warwick played little part in its affairs.

In the next two years these notables were increasingly harried by the King's men. Warwick and Brooke were attacked on their estates by the vindictive enforcement of the forest laws, Pym was twice sued by the attorney general for breaking virtual house arrest in the country, Warwick lost his undivided lord lieutenancy and the first writs of ship money were levied. The time had come for these peers and gentlemen to take up their option of emigrating. There is no evidence that Warwick himself intended to emigrate; and the story put about by Royalist writers that Pym, Hampden and Cromwell actually embarked but were stopped on the King's orders is discredited. But with Pym and his associates the intention is clear.

Events crystallized with the return to England in the autumn of 1634 of John Winthrop the younger who, somewhat disenchanted with the way things were going in Massachusetts Bay, was hoping to organize a settlement somewhere else in New England. Seeking out his father's friends Lord Saye and Sir Nathaniel Rich, he helped shape the plans of what came to be called, after its two principal peers, the Saybrook Colony. The following spring Sir Richard Saltonstall sent twenty of his servants to stake out an estate up the Connecticut River, and Winthrop was commissioned to lead an expedition to establish a settlement at the mouth of the same river, to build a fort and 'such houses as may receive men of quality'. He arrived back in New England in late autumn and spent the winter at the mouth of the Connecticut where Lieutenant Lion Gardiner, an engineer officer who had served under Sir Edward Harwood in the Netherlands, supervised the construction of a fort.

A small settlement was thus precariously established; but as a base for the enterprise conceived by those English peers and gentlemen it proved to be yet another pioneering failure. It had been too long delayed. By 1635 Laud had become inquisitive about the Puritan colonies, demanding to see the Massachusetts Company charter, and suspicious of further departures, so that it was difficult to recruit colonists. By this time, also, the parties were becoming sufficiently polarized for Puritans to sense their duty was to take a stand at home. There was also uneasiness about the flaws in the so-called Warwick patent; and there was a problem over Saybrook's constitution, which limited voting and other civil rights to freemen in full church membership. English nobles and squires, brought up to govern in manors and villages where the parochial clergy knew their place, shied from the thought of control by such spiritual authority. In the event, only one of the peers and gentlemen actually turned up: George Fenwick, Esquire, who arrived in 1636 and later brought over his wife; after that poor lady sickened and died he returned to England, selling his land and other rights to Connecticut Colony. As for Saltonstall's 'estate' up the Connecticut River, his servants there were cold-shouldered by certain squatters who arrived overland from Massachusetts Bay, and were fobbed off with land on the upper frontier of the settlement and with a grant of 2000 acres on the east side of the river. The latter, grandiloquently entitled Saltonstall Park, was never developed. Saltonstall, to his bitter anger, was cheated of his investment. The time was already past when, in New England at any rate, patrician colonizers, however well intentioned, could establish a colony based on the English shire, with estates worked by servants or tenants and a parochial clergy. As for the Earl of Warwick, his future career lay at home, fighting for the Parliamentary cause in the English Civil War.

That pioneer band of settlers who in 1635 forestalled Sir Richard Saltonstall's men by squatting on his lush Connecticut River meadows had trekked across the New England wilderness from Massachusetts. Five years before, they had been part of the hegira organized by the Massachusetts Bay Company and led by John Winthrop which had sailed from Southampton to settle in New England. But they were a special and discrete part of that great migration. Most of them had crossed the Atlantic in one great ship, the *Mary and John*, which had sailed not in company with the Winthrop fleet, but alone; and her passengers had established themselves in a settlement of their own. For, unlike most of the Winthrop emigrants, who were East Anglians, these were West Country people voyaging from Plymouth and hailing from particular parts of Dorset, Somerset and Devon. It is this band

24

of emigrants who are the subject of this narrative.

The ship's company of the *Mary and John* named both their Massachusetts Bay and their Connecticut River settlements Dorchester (later they would rename the latter Windsor). There was a reason for this dedication. Dorchester was not only the county town of most of them; it was also the home and headquarters of the Rev. John White, who had recruited them and masterminded their whole enterprise. So its story begins, as did so much of the colonizing of New England itself, with the rector of Holy Trinity church, Dorchester. He will be the subject of the next chapter.

CHAPTER 1: JOHN WHITE AND THE WEST COUNTRY'S ATLANTIC HORIZON 1620–30

T HIS, THE TWENTIETH OF MARCH IN THE YEAR OF OUR LORD 1630 AND THE fifth year of the reign of King Charles I, had been dedicated to the merciful Providence of God; or so John White, rector of Dorchester, must have thought as he took leave of his departing flock of 'planters' and watched their *Mary and John* warping through the congested shipping of Plymouth Harbour, bound for the grey Atlantic and a remote New England landfall.

The *Mary and John*, a great ship of 400 tons burden, Thomas Squibb master, must have tied up in Plymouth Harbour a day or two before, having sailed round the coast from her home port of Weymouth, Dorset. Many of her passengers had probably embarked at Weymouth after journeying with their belongings from homes in the villages and country towns of west Dorset and Somerset. John White had most likely travelled with them, together with other notables, including Mr Roger Ludlow, the new owner of the *Mary and John*, who was one of two assistants of the Massachusetts Bay Company travelling with the party and providing its official leadership. The other assistant, Mr Edward Rossiter, a landed gentleman of Combe St Nicholas, Somerset, appears to have missed the ship at Weymouth and to have had to travel overland to Plymouth where he and his family embarked with other recruits from Devon, especially nearby Exeter. At any rate, by that morning the entire ship's company had been assembled and her manifest was complete.

It had been an emotional and spiritually charged day for these Puritans, mostly parents with young children, virtually the first families to entrust themselves to the unknown hazards of a north Atlantic voyage, and for John White, whose initiative and drive had conceived and launched the whole enterprise. As befitted such a Puritan occasion, it had been a solemn day of fasting, given over to preaching and prayer. In the morning, the ship's company had disembarked and walked up from the harbour through the thronged streets of the port to the barely completed Hospital of the Poor's Portion, a Puritan institution for indigent old people and 'for setting children to work'. Their host had been Matthias Nicholls, 'preacher of God's Word in the town of Plymouth', a Puritan colleague of White's from New College days and a family friend.

The morning's proceedings had begun in Puritan fashion with a sermon preached by John White, 'that worthy man of God'. In the afternoon the ship's company formally confirmed the nomination of the two 'Reverend and Godly Ministers of the Word' who were to lead them on their errand into the New World wilderness. This was a variant of the normal ceremony for the appointment of a clergyman to a parish living; but in the unique circumstances, with an eclectic, Puritan congregation that was also a ship's company, no bishop was likely to have been prepared to act, so the office was undertaken by the Dorchester patriarch and ecclesiastical colonizer, John White. The other departure from Anglican practice was the ordination of two ministers, a preacher and a teacher. The preacher was John Warham, recently curate of St Sidwell's by Exeter, the teacher John Maverick, rector of Beaworthy, also in Devon. In the words of young Roger Clapp who was one of the ship's company: 'These godly people resolved to live together . . . and the people did solemnly make choice of, and call those godly ministers to be their officers, so also did the Reverend Mr Warham and Mr Maverick accept thereof and expressed the same.' This day of fasting and solemn exercises of humble testimony and dedication proved a fitting send-off for the forty or so families, 140 people in all, who constituted what would be known, in honour of John White, as the Dorchester migration and who were by now settling in on shipboard as best they might, no doubt in anxious anticipation of the ocean journey ahead. They were to sail down the English Channel on the tide, perhaps that night or the following day.

Meanwhile, having said farewell to his intrepid company, John White made his way back on horseback from Plymouth through Exeter to his Dorchester home; but not to stay because he had to hurry on to the port of

Southampton in order to catch the *Arbella*, flagship of the fleet of emigrant ships under John Winthrop, governor of the Massachusetts Bay Company, which was also bound for New England and lay becalmed off Cowes. White's purpose, apart from saying farewell, was to present Winthrop with his own draft of a document entitled *A Humble Request* which he hoped would constitute a manifesto of the religious beliefs and purposes of the departing colonists and reassure the English ecclesiastical authorities that the departing Puritans remained loyal members of the Church of England and were not become subversive Separatists. For as we have seen, White had a principal hand not only in the venture of the *Mary and John* but in that whole great enterprise of the Massachusetts Bay Company and its precedessors which was to people New England.

When the *Mary and John* sailed for Massachusetts Bay, John White was in his fifty-sixth year and had been rector of Holy Trinity, Dorchester for some twenty years; it had been his first charge after leaving Oxford. Born at Christmas 1575, he was the son of the tenant of the manor farm of Stanton St John, just outside Oxford. This belonged to New College, Oxford and it was through the influence of an uncle, at that time warden of the college, that his father acquired the 'farme' of it. Young John was sent to Winchester and thence, in 1593, to that school's sister, New College. After taking his degree he remained there as a fellow until 1606 when he was appointed to the Crown living of Dorchester. In his time at Oxford, New College was known for its Puritan tendencies, which Laud had attributed to the study of Calvin's Institutes; and it is hardly surprising that the young John White should have been influenced by that fashionable theological discipline. In 1604 James I had instructed the Hampton Court conference of scholars and divines to compile a new translation of the Bible, and two of the translators were fellows of New College, one of them having taught White at Winchester. He had friends and associates who became known for their Puritan opinions. One, John Burgess, a pupil of Thomas Cartwright the Puritan divine, became White's brother-in-law; another probable kinsman, John Ball, wrote a *Treatise on Faith* which White was to use as a catechism; a third, Richard Bernard, who would become rector of Batcombe, Somerset, drew up a system of instruction for his parishioners which White adopted in Dorchester. Bernard's intimate friend John Conant, subsequently rector of Lincoln College, Oxford, was of the same school of thought and was to be a colleague of White's in his New England ventures; there was Dr Twise, a contemporary of White's at both Winchester and Oxford, who was concerned with events in the Palatinate and in New England, especially with converting the Indians; and there were the Nicholls brothers of New College, one of whom as we have just seen became a Puritan lecturer in Plymouth; the other, Ferdinando, was to be one of White's assistants in Dorchester and a more extreme Puritan than any.

These were heady times for young men about to take orders in the Church of England. For some, Puritan doctrines and practices were to take them further in the direction of the primitive church and against hierarchy, liturgy and ceremony, so that they sympathized with the Separatists who had fled episcopal persecution for Leyden and New England and, subsequently, with the more extreme sectaries of the Commonwealth. But not all were so extreme. John White, in particular, though Puritan, never parted from his identity with and loyalty to the Church of England or from his own sacramental dedication as a priest within it. This was fundamental to his role in the Puritan colonizing of New England. High-minded though he was, disciplined to a life of prayer, service and simplicity, he was no come-outer, and he assumed a role of dedicated leadership within the Church of England and to that West Country community of Dorchester to which he had been called. He remained a moderate Puritan, such as was congenial to his neighbour-to-be, the rector of Broadwindsor, Thomas Fuller, who was to write so vividly of the worthies of his generation and was a kindred spirit.

When White was instituted in 1606 he became rector of two churches, Holy Trinity and St Peter's, prominently situated within a stone's throw of each other towards the upper end of Dorchester's sloping High Street. The combined parishes in his charge comprised most of the area within the Roman walls of what was then, as it is now, the attractive county town of Dorset. A generation earlier Camden had praised it as 'a pretty, large town, with very wide streets and delicately situated on a rising ground, opening at the south and west ends into sweet fields and spacious downs.' In 1613, to quote what may well be White's own words, 'Dorchester (as it is well known) is one of the principal places of traffic for western merchants, by which means it grew rich and populous, beautified with many stately buildings and fair streets, flourishing full of all sorts of tradesmen and artificers, plenty with abundance revealed in her bosom, with a wise and civil government.' And twenty years later Thomas Gerard, though as a Dorset man no doubt prejudiced, was to describe it as having 'flourished exceedingly, so that now it may justly challenge the superiority of all this shire as well for quick markets and neat buildings as for the number of the inhabitants, many of which are men of great wealth.'

Although only a young man fresh down from Oxford, White had standing as a university divine and he found himself at the centre of the town's affairs. With his energy and force of personality he established an ascendency, both moral and practical, which was to span the thirty-six years of his time there and earn him the affectionate title of 'patriarch of Dorchester'.

In his young days Dorchester 'possessed anything but a pious and estimable reputation': but gradually he made his influence felt and a 'Puritanical or rather a "precise" tone' began to emanate from Holy Trinity and to pervade the town. Absences from church were inquired into and staying at home 'amending her stockings' was no longer a sufficient excuse. Coming late or leaving before the sermon could be punished by fine or even imprisonment. Holy Communion was celebrated more frequently and to larger congregations who were subjected to the Puritan discipline of exhortation and catechism the previous evening. The church itself was embellished with a new pulpit, communion plate, surplices and carpet for the communion table (an indication that White was no Puritan extremist). But his bent was eminently practical as well as moral, and within seven years of his incumbency he was vouchsafed an almost unique opportunity to exercise his talents for civic leadership.

In the early afternoon of 6 August 1613 a tallow chandler's workshop caught fire and in the warm summer wind flames spread quickly through the town while the men and women were in the fields for the harvest. As a result the town was largely reduced to charred rubble. Some 170 houses were destroyed, as well as two of the three churches, including Holy Trinity, and most of the public buildings, shops and merchants' warehouses with their rich stores of merchandise: 'shops of silks and velvets on a flaming fire, multitudes of linen and woollen clothes burned to ashes, gold and silver melted, and brass, pewter and copper, trunks and chests of damasks and fine linens with all manner of stuffs'. Although, marvellously, no lives were lost, the town was a disaster area: 'Dorchester was a famous town, now a heap of ashes for travellers that pass by to sigh at', and the King advanced £1000 towards its rescue. This was John White's opportunity to invoke the help of Almighty God in galvanizing the Dorchester people into rebuilding their town and community. In this he, together with the bailiffs, burgesses and merchants, succeeded dramatically. Within a few years and despite another fire in 1622 Thomas Gerard could report that 'it is risen up fairer than before'.

The fire was a purging experience and as the town rose from its ashes there was evident a new spirit of social responsibility which owed much to the patriarch's high-Puritan dedication to the urgent needs of the poor, the starved and famished, the homeless and the growing numbers of unemployed and feckless hangers-on which were characteristic of the times. As White later recalled, 'The whole Town consented to double their weekly rates for the relief of the poor, enlarged their churches and reduced the town into order by good government.' As a borough memorandum records: 'It is not unfit to be observed that before the former great fire . . . little or no money was given to any charitable uses . . . But when they saw by this sudden blast . . . the great miseries of many families that were in an instant harbourless, many men's bowels began to yearn in compassion towards them, studying how to do some good work for the relief of the poor . . . whereupon many of us, assisted by our faithful pastor, had many meetings.'

In the year after the fire were built the first of three sets of almshouses. In 1617 after many meetings of 'well affected persons' a subscription was raised to establish a hospital or workhouse for 'setting to work the poor children of the borough' in spinning and burling wool and for their instruction in religion. The latter took the form of learning the catechism of White's friend John Ball. Later, with money left over from this project, a brewhouse was built on hospital land to improve the quality of the town beer. Also in 1617 the Free School was rebuilt and an under-school established with, as master, one Aquila Purchase whom White was to recruit for New England. In the upper room of the Free School a library was established, with a widely ranging catalogue of titles from Foxe's *Book of Martyrs* to *Purchase his Pilgrims* and Speed's *History and Maps of England*. For twenty years, on the anniversary of the great fire, Pastor White preached a sermon linked to the Gunpowder Plot and the collection went to the hospital.

By 1630, when our emigrants took their leave of Dorset, the morale of their county town was riding high. In that year the borough purchased from the Crown a new corporation charter with a mayor and enhanced privileges and the trades organized themselves into livery companies: clothiers, ironmongers, fishmongers, shoemakers and skinners. More significant, White's Dorchester was becoming known for its Puritan character. 'No place in the west or indeed in any part of England was more deeply imbued with the rigid piety of the Puritans – a feeling which seems to have been strongly fostered by the ministry of the Patriarch of Dorchester'. Clarendon went on to describe the town as the most malignant in the country, the 'magazine whence the other places were supplied with principles of Rebellion'.

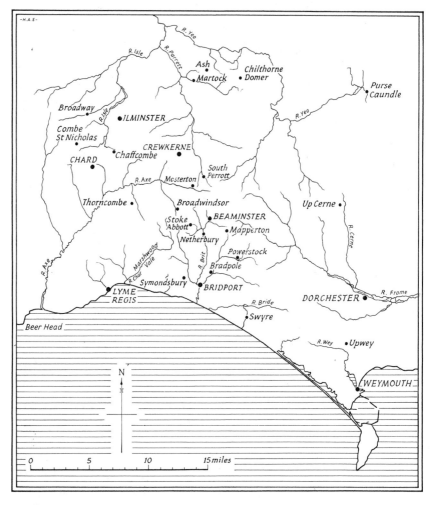

This attitude was taking a more specifically political turn. Of the
Members of Parliament imprisoned for resisting the King's order to adjourn
the House in 1629, three were West Countrymen associated with White:
Denzil Holles, the Member for Dorchester and described as the patriarch's
disciple, William Strode whose brother headed the list of New England
promoters at the 'Planters' Parliament' in Dorchester in 1623, and Sir John
Eliot who was probably influenced by White in preparing his *Project for New
England*. At any rate, on 7 May, according to a Privy Council minute, 'one
John White, Minister, preacher of Dorchester and Ferdinando Nicholls of
Sherborne', one-time assistant to John White, attempted to speak to Holles
from beneath his cell window in the Tower of London; they were discovered
by the keeper and ejected. The episode spotlights John White as Puritan and
as promoter of planting in New England.

*

When a Dorchester citizen looked up or down the street he saw beyond the houses an open vista of green downland; and in John White's time that downland was dotted white with sheep. In 1659 Edward Leigh recorded that 'within six miles compass round about Dorchester' there were 300,000 sheep. The Dorset downs were a prime wool-rearing district providing the raw material for the woollen-cloth industry of Dorset's towns and villages. Since its great fire Dorchester itself was in decline as a weaving centre; but from the shuttles of nearby Beaminster, Lyme and Bere and from farther off Sherborne, Shaftesbury and Sturminister, Gillingham and Wareham pack-horses and waggons carried along the winding country roads to Dorchester the broadcloths, the kersies and Dorset dozens which were her mercantile staples. As we have seen, Dorchester's warehouses were stocked with merchandise, notably woollen cloths and linen from the flax grown in the little Brit Valley between Beaminster and Bridport. The same very local rich, damp soil also grew the finest hemp in England, made into sacking and cordage, ropes and tackle in the rope-walks of Bridport which had had an ancient monopoly and still enjoyed a thriving manufacture for the fishing fleets sailing to Newfoundland.

Dorchester was no mere inland market town. She was an important entrepôt for 'western merchants' trading abroad. Only eight miles to the south lay the port of Weymouth whence Dorchester merchants exported their textiles and other wares across the Channel to France and Spain in exchange for wine and for 'rich stuffes' such as had been consumed in the great fire. Weymouth gave Dorchester a blue-water horizon. It was as much through her seaborne traffic out of Weymouth as by the carriers, waggoners and horsemen on their slow, dusty or muddy wayfaring up east over the downs to the Thames Valley and London that Dorchester kept in touch with the great world.

William Whiteway, member of a prominent burgess family and a family connection of White's, kept a diary throughout the 1620s and 30s in which he recorded immediate events, such as poor harvests, outbreaks of smallpox, a great cold which froze people to death on the highway, and a high wind which 'tore a coach all in pieces upon Eggardon Hill and beat out the brains of a serving maid in it', cheek-by-jowl with matters of state: Raleigh's execution, the rise of Buckingham, the settlement of Ulster and the plight of the Protestants in the Palatinate. He recorded the abortive negotiations with Spain over the royal marriage. The fleet sent to fetch a Catholic bride for Prince Charles from Madrid touched at Weymouth in

August 1623, and he described her flagship, the *Princess Royal*, as 'a vessel of wonderful bigness and beauty'. To local Puritans like John White the threat of a Catholic queen was of deep concern, as were the events in the Palatinate. As early as 1620 Dorchester raised the remarkable sum of £2000 for the relief of the Protestants there. The sufferings of the Thirty Years' War were brought home to Dorchester people by the arrival in 1626 of a party of German refugees who settled in their midst; and Protestant students from the Continent also appeared from time to time, attracted by John White's reputation. By this time the growing political crisis of Puritanism at home had turned John White's vision to seek a solution overseas.

In 1633 our friend Thomas Gerard noted that the port of Weymouth and its twin borough, Melcombe Regis, 'gain well by traffic into Newfoundland where they have had 80 sail of ships and barques'. The traffic of Dorset across the north Atlantic to the shores of Newfoundland and its Grand Banks in search of cod and ling was an important industry for the county involving considerable resources of ships and men, from Weymouth, Poole and Lyme. It already had a long history. The Newfoundland fishery was firmly established as early as 1574 when a fleet of some thirty ships sailed thither for the season's fishing, and the number increased rapidly in subsequent years. The trade was profitable and the merchants of Lyme in the reign of James I, 'being engaged in trade to Newfoundland acquired large fortunes and raised the town considerably'. The fishery was not without its difficulties and dangers. As we noted earlier, the operation was seasonal and involved setting up drying frames for the catches on the Newfoundland shores. To cope with this processing, the ships were double manned and at the height of the season there grew to be a considerable fishing and curing population on the Newfoundland shores, not only of English but of French and Dutch. There were jurisdictional disputes and inevitable problems of maintaining order between landsmen and fishermen; in the end the Privy Council had to invest the mayors of Weymouth and neighbouring ports, together with the Vice-Admiral of Dorset, with the admiralty power to administer justice in cases of crime and other offences in Newfoundland and at sea.

The Newfoundland fishery, based on Dorset home ports and involving nearly 3000 miles of hazardous navigation across the north Atlantic, was a remarkable business for the people of that small western county with a population of probably less than 60,000; and over the generations it bred in her men and women a knowledge and awareness of a wider, maritime world that was in striking contrast to their neighbourly parishes and rural, village occupations. By the 1620s the north Atlantic and the North American littoral were for them very much a part of an enlarged universe: dangerous, unfriendly no doubt, but already taken for granted; and the experience of it gave them understanding, skills and self-confidence to handle north Atlantic enterprise.

John White became conscious of the needs of this fishing fleet and the maritime community which made their living by it. He regarded them as a kind of extension of his own parish and spiritual charge and he had a special concern for the souls of the fishermen on the Banks. As he wrote, 'Being usually upon their voyages nine or ten months in the year they were left all the while without means of instruction.' He meant, of course, instruction in spiritual matters and he considered how best to improve their lot. He knew about the double manning of the ships and it occurred to him, as it occurred to others, that if a proportion of each ship's company could be left on the Newfoundland shore at the close of the fishing season and through the winter there might be established firm supporting bases for the fishing fleet the following year, and ultimately a colony raising foodstuffs for the fleet and living a more settled and Christian way of life, with a minister to care for their souls.

White wove this strand of thought with other strands into a rope of colonial policy strong enough for his purpose. Like other Puritan evangelists he had a concern for the souls, not only of Dorset fishermen in Newfoundland, but of the aborigines further west on the American main. Ever since the early Virginia settlements, the conversion of the Indians had been a strong colonial motive for the religious-minded. But the strongest strand of all was the idea of establishing a settlement on the American mainland dedicated to the living of a godly Puritan life. Although White strongly disapproved of Separatists, it was the example of the Leyden exiles and their settlement at New Plymouth in New England in 1621, together with the ever more legible writing on the Church of England wall threatening Puritanism at home, that impelled him to shape his own version of a Puritan colonial policy for New England. It took the best part of the 1620s for this remarkable West Country religious statesman to perfect his theory and practical plans but by 1630 both were maturing. The departure of the *Mary and John* was the culminating event of years of trial and error in colonial experiment under John White's leadership; it was also marked by the publication of his fully fledged treatise on Puritan colonial policy, *The Planters Plea*.

This piece of apologetics for 'planting' is only part of a large literature on the subject; but as a distillation of the ideas and experience that lie behind the Dorchester emigration it is especially illuminating. It begins, as do others of its kind, by dwelling on the current problems of employment, and especially the distortions whereby many are drawn into serving in 'luxury and wantonness to the impoverishing and corrupting of the most' and many others, brought up to skilled and useful trades, are under-employed or reduced to 'such a low condition as is little better than beggary' and to idleness and sin. His general conclusion is that 'we have more men than we can employ to any profitable or useful labour', especially skilled people in 'our towns and cities'. He then calls attention to England's special opportunity, as a seafaring nation,

> to transport our men and provisions by sea into those
> countries, without which advantage they cannot possibly
> be peopled from any part of the world . . . how useful a
> neighbour the sea is to the furthering of such a work . . .

and contrasts the relative economics of sea and land transport, where in the latter 'Planters . . . must needs spend much time and endure much labour in passing their families and provisions over rivers and through woods and thickets by unbeaten paths.'

The English, being so well placed, have a religious duty to undertake the planting of colonies, for 'the most eminent and desirable end of planting is the propagation of religion'. Having established this proposition, he turns to the advantages of North America, especially New England, where we had recently been sending 'yearly forty or fifty sail of ships of reasonable good burthen' to trade in furs and fish; and he recounts its advantages: the climate, 'the dryness of the air and constant temper of it'; 'the corn of the country'; the fertility of the soil for grain and cattle rearing. As a Dorset man, he emphasizes that it is 'naturally apt for hemp and flax especially', and it is abundant in fish, fowl and venison. He is aware that because of 'a three years plague' over a decade before, the Indian inhabitants have been decimated, that their cleared lands are to be had for the asking and at the Indians' friendly invitation. Mercantilist as he was, he emphasizes the advantages that such a colony would bring to the mother country, for 'it is to be desired that the daughter may answer something back by way of retribution to the mother that gave her being'. There were not only the fisheries and the fur trade, but products for shipbuilding – 'planks, masts, oars, pitch, tar and iron' – and, of course, for 'hemp, sails and cordage'. At this point he gets carried away by his enthusiasm when he mentions the wines which New England will produce, 'some as good as any that are found in France by humane culture'; and he finally returns to the overriding duty to civilize the natives:

> Withall, commerce and example of our course of living
> cannot but in time breed civility among them and that by
> God's blessing may make way for religion consequently
> and for the saving of their souls.

It already has a 19th-century ring about it.

As in similar tracts he then sets out in dialogue form to answer the principal objections to planting: the winter cold (the snow is no worse than in parts of Germany and there is plenty of fuel); the serpents and other wild beasts (again no worse than Germany); the mosquitoes (no worse than in fenny parts of Essex and Lincolnshire). More seriously, he answers the charge that the English are not natural colonists: 'We are known too well to the world to love the smoke of our own chimneys so well that hopes of great advantages are not likely to draw many of us from home.' He recognizes there is truth in this, but believes that personal interests will prevail with some and that their example will induce others to follow. But he devotes the greatest space to rebutting a charge that those who would go overseas are seditious people and Separatist in religion, determined to subvert the state and to separate from the Church of England. He denies this, challenging his accusers to produce evidence that the Massachusetts Bay people have any such subversive intentions; and making the distinction, vital to his own position on theology and church order, between Separatism and a refusal to conform to Laudian liturgy within the existing Church of England:

> ... there is great odds between peaceable men, who out
> of tenderness of heart forbear the use of some ceremonies
> of the Church (whom this State in some things thinks fit
> to wink at, and it may be would do more if it were
> assured of their temper) and men of fiery and turbulent
> spirits, that walk in a cross way out of distemper of mind.
> Now suppose some of those men that ... consider ...
> their contrary practice gives distaste to government, and
> occasions some disturbance unto the Church's peace,
> upon that ground withdraw themselves for quietness
> sake: Would not such dispositions be cherished with

great tenderness?

In conclusion, he summarizes the motives of 'our Planters in their voyage to New-England', making 'bold to manifest not only what I know, but what I guess concerning their purpose'. It is absurd to think that they are all of one mind. 'Necessity may press some; novelty draw on others; hopes of gain in time to come may prevail with a third sort; but that the most and most sincere and godly part have the advancement of the Gospel for their main scope I am confident.' And of these, he admits, 'some may entertain hope and expectation of enjoying greater liberty there than here in the use of some orders and ceremonies of our Church, it seems very probable.'

All this was apologetics for a *fait accompli*: not only the *Mary and John* but a whole fleet of emigrant ships were about to transport across the Atlantic by far the most ambitious colonizing expedition yet to be launched for North America.

In 1622 the recently formed Council for New England broadened its company terms to invite as subscribers not only 'persons of honour or gentlemen of blood' but 'western merchants', in order to attract capital and enterprise from those mercantile interests in Dorset and Devon engaged in trade with Newfoundland and New England. This came to White's notice and he seized the opportunity to interest one of his parishioners who was just one of these 'western merchants'. Richard Bushrod was a prosperous Dorchester mercer and merchant adventurer trading in furs and fish from New England, had been a Member of Parliament for the town and was to be so again. White prompted him to form a syndicate of local merchants and gentry. With Sir Walter Erle of Charborough, another local MP, as titular head, they obtained an indenture from the Privy Council to form a company to establish a settlement in New England. On 31 March 1624 they called the meeting at the Free School in Dorchester of interested people which became locally known as 'the New England Planters' Parliament'. Of the steering committee of sixteen there appointed, apart from three parsons, about half were local gentry and half Dorchester merchants. This was the nucleus of the Dorchester Company which before long numbered some 200 members. Of these fifty were Dorset gentry; a half-dozen gentry from Devon; more than thirty were merchants, mostly of Dorchester; at least twenty were clergy; there were four widows whose husbands had been gentry or merchants; there were a few Londoners and the rest were local men 'in a small way of business'.

The company lost no time in organizing its first voyage to New England on White's principle of combining fishing with settlement. The *Fellowship*, a small ship of 50 tons, was bought and sent out from Weymouth that very season to fish off Cape Ann on the north shore of Massachusetts Bay; but she arrived too late for profitable fishing and sold her catch for a poor price in Spain. The next year, the company added a Flemish flyboat of 40 tons, probably renamed *Pilgrim*; but she was badly converted and had to be retrimmed; so again both ships arrived late at the fishing grounds and this voyage made a trading loss, all the worse because of the cost of maintaining the company of landsmen left at Cape Ann over the winter. The third year they tried again with an additional ship, *Amytie*; but one of the ships sprang a leak about 200 leagues out and had to return to Weymouth for repairs, and because of the war with Spain the market for fish collapsed. This voyage also failed. At this point the adventurers sold off their shipping and stocks and dissolved the company. John White himself ruefully analysed the reasons for the failure. Apart from mishaps and mismanagement in fitting out ships and in the fishing strategy, he blamed the collapse of the market and the badly led and ill-disciplined landsmen left at Cape Ann. They failed to grow provisions according to plan and remained a drain on the company's resources. Above all, White faced up to the fact that the theory behind the scheme, to combine settlement with fishing, was unsound:

> Two things withal may be intimated by the way, that the very project itself of planting by the help of a fishing voyage can never answer the success that it seems to promise. First that no sure fishing place in the land is fit for planting nor any good place for planting found fit for fishing, at least near the shore. And secondly, rarely any fishermen will work at Land, neither are husbandmen fit for fishermen but with long use and experience.

However, he consoles himself by the philosophical reflection that

> experience taught us that as in building houses the first stones of the foundation are buried under ground and are not seen, so in planting Colonies, the first stocks employed that way are consumed, although they serve for a foundation to the work.

But John White was not one to be easily defeated. And there was the problem of his moral responsibility for the people, the 'landsmen' who, as an essential element in the Dorchester Company project, had been landed on the desolate shore of Cape Ann. Fourteen had been left in 1623, thirty-two the following year and there may have been scores more: the grandson of one of them mentions a figure of 200 and cattle. Although the company had paid them off in full and offered transport home, many undoubtedly were still there. Among them also was a significant group who were refugees from the uncompromising Separatism of Plymouth Colony. This group had established a temporary bivouac at Nantasket on the outer shore of what came to be called Boston Bay. They included a minister, John Lyford, a moderate Puritan, John Oldham, an experienced fur trader, and Roger Conant. Conant was one of three brothers of East Budleigh, Devon. He and his brother Christopher had made careers in London, the one as a salter, the other as a grocer, before joining the Plymouth Colony. The third brother, John, went to Oxford where, as we have seen, he was a contemporary and friend of John White, took orders and returned to the West Country as rector of Limington, Somerset. It was through John Conant that White had learned of the difficulties his brother Roger and the others had had with the Plymouth people. Whereupon White had taken the initiative on behalf of the Dorchester Company to write to Conant at Nantasket inviting him to settle at Cape Ann and to become the company's agent there. Conant had accepted. When, therefore, the company was wound up, Roger Conant was one of those who remained; and although he 'disliked the place' – i.e. Cape Ann – 'as much as the adventurers disliked the business' – i.e. the Dorchester Company – he clearly wished to stay and to establish a Puritan colony independent of the Plymouth influence. He looked about for a better place than Cape Ann and settled on Naumkeag, south-west of Cape Ann on the north shore of Massachusetts Bay. White encouraged him to found a new settlement there to be renamed Salem, and undertook to support this with a legal patent, men, provisions and trade goods for the Indians. To bring this about he recruited nine of the inner-core members of the old Dorchester Company under the old company articles, to be an instrument for the direct settlement of a Puritan colony. These were Dorchester merchants together with John Conant, Roger's brother. The new syndicate immediately set about organizing two small ships which were dispatched from Weymouth with cattle, fodder, beef, cheese and butter, soap and oil, beer and clothing for the infant colony.

But the undertaking was now too ambitious for this small, local group of merchants. They required a new patent under the Council for New England. For this they needed figureheads from among the gentry and they recruited five West Country notables of Puritan persuasion, three from Devon including Sir Henry Rosewell of Ford Abbey who gave his name to the patent, Simon Whetcombe of Sherborne and John Humphrey of Dorchester, both members of the earlier company. They also needed more capital and for this had to go to the City of London where, to begin with, some forty men – half a dozen or so gentlemen, mainly from the Inns of Court, a couple of clergy, two officers of the London trainbands and the rest merchants – subscribed to stock in the new venture, called for short the New England Company. This appointed a governor for Naumkeag, John Endicott, of unknown origins but a forceful personality, and dispatched him forthwith in the *Abigail* from Weymouth on 20 June 1628, with his commission and a cargo of supplies as befitted a governor including wines and spirits, arms and armour. Thereafter the operation transcended its West Country origins. Endecott's new commission was deemed a success and interest in the venture spread abroad 'in sundry parts of the kingdom', in White's words, and

> began to awaken the spirits of some persons of competent estates, not formerly engaged, considering that they lived either without any useful employment at home and might be more serviceable in assisting the planting of a colony in New England, took at last a resolution to unite themselves for the prosecution of that work.

These were the new men, gentry and merchants, 'the North Country men' from Lincolnshire and Suffolk, the Johnsons, Dudleys, Winthrops and the rest who during 1629 reshaped the New England Company into the Massachusetts Bay Company, the instrument under which the Winthrop fleet set sail in the spring of 1630.

Meanwhile John White, as an original stockholder and one of the two Puritan ministers among the first adventurers, remained an influential and respected figure. His *Planters Plea* was already circulating in manuscript among the promoters of the Massachusetts Bay Company in the summer of 1629; he was on the committee appointed to make the first allotment of land in New England to stockholders and there are grounds for believing he was of the inner group of 'old adventurers' with control over a special joint stock fund; he was present at a momentous meeting of the company's court in London on 19 August 1629 which voted in favour of the revolutionary proposal that the patent and government of the plantation be transferred from London headquarters to New England; when the financial interests of the adventurers (investors) and the planters (settlers) had to be reconciled, White was one of the arbitrators; and he was a member of a committee with the invidious job of estimating the true value of the company's joint stock after a heated debate in which it had been necessary for our Puritan minister to remind 'these pious gentlemen and traders' that the purpose of their enterprise 'was chiefly the glory of God'. It was probably his hand which ensured a continuing West Country influence with the election of Roger Ludlow of Maiden Bradley, Wiltshire, John Humphrey of Dorchester and Edward Rossiter of Combe St Nicholas, Somerset, as Assistants of the company.

It may be, however, that White felt himself increasingly crowded out by the personalities of the City magnates in London and the influx of new, radical men from eastern counties, keen to exert their authority in their new-found zeal for planting in New England and later given credit for the whole enterprise. He was also probably out of sympathy with the domineering personality of Governor Endicott and had a special concern for those 'old planters' like Roger Conant of Nantasket and Naumkeag who had to struggle to protect their rights.

What must have given the parson special cause for concern was the way in which church government in Salem was moving towards Separatist beliefs and practices under the influence of the Plymouth neighbours. The matter was brought to a head by the expulsion, under the direction of the governor, of two brothers, John and Samuel Browne of Roxwell, Essex, known personally to White. These had withdrawn from the Separatist-tainted church to worship according to the Book of Common Prayer and had accused the ministers of departing from the orders of the Church of England. The Brownes returned to England in the autumn of 1629 complaining to the Council for New England of their treatment. This must have distressed White because of the subversion of his plans for Salem as a non-conformist, moderately Puritan colony within a purified Church of England, and because of the West Country element in Salem, such as Roger Conant who may have taken part in the Brownes' protest. Worse, White had already begun to recruit entire families for Salem from the West Country to join the old planters and those who had sailed with Endicott in *Abigail*.

42

Some forty people sailed on the *Lyon's Whelp*, a 'neat and nimble ship', in April 1629 from Dorset and Somerset and 'specially from Dorchester and other places thereabouts', including the Sprague family of Fordington and of Upwey who were personal friends of White.

It seems probable that the *Lyon's Whelp* contingent were in a special sense under White's patronage. When the old planters were threatened with victimization he had, indeed, contemplated using his own land allocation, as an investor, to establish a colony of his own but had abandoned the idea when Conant, Oldham and company had received compensation. But with Salem going sour on him he may have returned to it. At any rate in the autumn and winter of 1629–30, after the momentous events in Cambridge and London which established the Massachusetts Bay Company and firmed up the plan for a multiple emigration to Massachusetts Bay the following sailing season, White, though playing his part in these events, appears in a measure to have kept his own counsel and back in Dorchester to have reverted to the idea of organizing a colony according to his own way of thinking and believing. He was concerned on the one hand to take the opportunity of the Massachusetts Bay Company's emigration plan to organize a new and more ambitious band of emigrant families from the West Country, while on the other to preserve not only their West Country character but their moderate non-conformity against the Separatist tendencies of Plymouth and Salem and, he may well have suspected, of the Winthrop party itself. And so, as he perfected his plans during that autumn and winter for a new Puritan swarming to the New World, commissioning a ship and sounding out suitable recruits for a Puritan ship's company of settlers, he appears to have thought in terms of a separate, autonomous venture sailing out of Plymouth, though under the general umbrella of the Massachusetts Bay Company and in association with what came to be called the Winthrop fleet. It is significant that John Winthrop made no reference to the enterprise in his diary even though, as we saw, White visited him on the *Arbella* at Southampton after seeing off the *Mary and John* from Plymouth. White also took care to ensure the Puritan orthodoxy of his emigrant flock within the Church of England by recruiting for it two ministers, properly ordained and with beliefs consonant with White's own.

He must also have thought his way through the problem of his emigrant band's destination in Massachusetts Bay. He had the choices of Salem, now from his point of view disaffected, of throwing in his lot with the eastern counties people or of keeping his distance from them. He appears to have chosen the third option. Among the planters of the *Lyon's Whelp* were some who, having fetched up at Salem, moved on to a new, infant settlement at the mouth of the Charles River (subsequently Charlestown) where the minister, Francis Bright, of the *Lyon's Whelp* contingent, was a moderate and congenial to the West Countrymen. Others, including the Sprague family, went from Salem further up the Charles River to what became Watertown. White determined that his chosen ship's company of the *Mary and John* should follow his friends the Spragues and should settle at Watertown.

As John White, a striking figure in his black gown, flat cap and white bands, waved fond goodbyes to his flock on the *Mary and John* in Plymouth Harbour that March day in 1630 he must have been confident that, God willing, his long-dreamed-of venture in Puritan living would grow into reality on the Charles River. But this was not to be. When that ship's company finally reached landfall in Massachusetts Bay they were to disembark willy-nilly and settle, not on the Charles River, but on a less hospitable neck of land. This settlement, which was to become the principal West Country outpost in New England, they would christen Dorchester in honour of their revered patriarch.

CHAPTER 2: THE UPROOTING 1630–35

IT IS TIME TO RETRACE THE STEPS OF THE *Mary and John* PASSENGERS FROM their embarkation at Weymouth in March 1630 and to make a journey of the imagination back in time to the spring of that year and by Dorset roads and lanes to the neighbourhoods from which these intrepid people were uprooting themselves. Apart from half a dozen families from Devon, they hailed from a restricted and well-defined part of west Dorset and south Somerset. The fifty or so heads of families in the *Mary and John* and in several later associated ships sailing from Weymouth to Dorchester on Massachusetts Bay came largely from a few clusters of towns and villages: Lyme Regis, Bridport and the Brit Valley in west Dorset, and Crewkerne, Chard and half a dozen satellite villages in south Somerset. Dorchester, which lay further to the east only eight miles inland up the well-travelled road from the port of Weymouth, provided its own quota, as might be expected of the county town which was John White's own headquarters; but even from Dorchester it was a mere twenty miles, a day's walk, up the Frome valley and over the downs to Crewkerne.

Through the medium of their rector's pulpit and study, and the commitment of some of their own merchants, Dorchester people had for a long time been made conscious of New England's high purpose (indeed some may have become bored by it and one Dorchester dame went so far as to accuse her parson of funnelling away money to that project which ought

45

by rights to have gone to the town poor). Only the previous spring, several families had joined a company of Dorset and Somerset people sailing from Weymouth in the *Lyon's Whelp* bound for Salem; and now in this spring of 1630 the town had lost six families and a couple of bachelors by the *Mary and John*, mostly important and interrelated merchant families, all recruited by the rector of Holy Trinity.

Leaving Dorchester by the High Street at the top of the town, past the gaol which was new in 1630, and climbing west on the old Roman road over downs which in that year were dotted white with grazing sheep, braced against the weather from Eggarden Hill to the north and Chesil Beach and the Channel to the south, travellers made their way over the tops, down to the estuary of the little River Brit and Bridport. Bridport, 'more old than fair' in the view of Gerard the chronicler, was a royal borough and a port, though with the silting of the estuary it had become somewhat decayed. Its fame and prosperity rested on making 'cordage or ropes for the Navie of England' and nets and fishing tackle. Until lately the town had a monopoly and still enjoyed an important trade, particularly with the Newfoundland fishing fleet. Its raw materials, hemp for the rope-walks and flax for rough clothing and sailcloth, grew abundantly in Bridport's backyard, cultivated in lynchets of the rich, damp, sandy soil up the little valley of the Brit where, according to Thomas Fuller, 'England hath no better than what groweth here betwist Beaminster and Bridport'. Bridport itself provided four families for the *Mary and John* and her successor ships and another important family, the Fords, derived from the pretty village of Simonsbury (now Symondsbury), only a mile and a half away on a minuscule tributary of the Brit called the Simene. Simonsbury, 'or as we now call it Symsbury', as Gerard wrote, would one day give its name to a settlement in Connecticut.

Simonsbury is just off the high road which, through good dairy and cider country and the fishing hamlets of Chideok and Charmouth, reaches the port of Lyme rising up its cliff above the Cobb and Lyme Bay. Lyme was a deep-water port with Newfoundland connections. It provided one important mercantile family for the *Mary and John*, that of William Hill, whose father had been mayor of the town and who himself had married into the important merchant community of Exeter. Lyme, on its salient thrusting into Devon, is the ultimate point of this coastal itinerary. Returning to Charmouth and then up the River Char past Whitchurch Canonicorum we pass on into Marshwood Vale. This was rough, steeply enclosed country on cold, heavy clay, remote and inaccessible in winter; it was largely pasture for dairying with plenty of game in the old forest and meandering roads linking ancient farmsteads. One of these was 'Coweleyes', the property of the Newberrys. Thomas Newberry was a younger son of a younger son of fairly prominent Dorset gentry. Like many a younger son he tried to make a living in London at the Bar but gave it up to return to live in the depths of the country in a house belonging to his father-in-law. In 1630 he was probably already contemplating a removal to New England, and with his family of seven children would sail from Weymouth in April 1634. Thomas himself, a stockholder in the Massachusetts Bay Company, would not long survive in Dorchester, Massachusetts, but his widow and their children would become one of the prominent first families of Windsor on the Connecticut.

From Marshwood Vale we return to Bridport and then up into the secluded Brit Valley which, in 1630, was terraced with flax and hemp. This was arguably the best land in Dorset, very deep, rich mould, yielding abundant harvests of grains as well as hemp and flax. In the next century land rents in this valley were twice the average for this part of Dorset. Its cider orchards were outstanding and cottagers were busy spinning wool as well as flax. Four miles upstream from Bridport lies Netherbury, to Leland 'an Uplandisch Town' on a hill with a strikingly dominant church, of which Thomas Fuller would become prebend the next year. Netherbury was a prosperous village, spinning wool and flax, making sailcloth and brewing cider by the thousand hogsheads. It had a well-endowed free grammar school. The largest parish in Dorset, its register entries include many whose names will be encountered in New England.

Only a little over a mile upstream from Netherbury, after skirting Parham, seat of the Strode family, we come at last to Beaminster itself, close to the source of the Brit which flows, as it did in Leland's day, 'under a little stone bridge of two pretty arches' and nestling under Beaminster Down. Beaminster is described by both Leland and Gerard as a pretty market town. In 1630 it had four main streets centring on an attractive square with a handsome pillared market house only recently built and much admired. The church had been enlarged in the Perpendicular style, with a fine tower built almost within living memory and an oak pulpit even more recent, carved with the fashionable Jacobean decoration. Beaminster was a place of importance in west Dorset. The justices met here for quarter sessions, staying at the White Hart, the principal inn and stopping place for carriers, higglers and an occasional coach. Apart from its market, Beaminster's chief activity was the cloth trade and its rows of weavers' houses were busy spinning wool from the renowned Dorset sheep on the nearby downs and weaving kersies and Dorset dozens for inland and overseas markets.

Beaminster had close relations with Dorchester, fifteen miles away, and reflected something of Dorchester's reforming morality. Like Dorchester it boasted a new almshouse, endowed by a rich cloth merchant of the town. There were signs of a growing Puritan disposition, and by the outbreak of the Civil War the town would be reported as being violently opposed to the King and the church hierarchy. Four Beaminster families – Hosfords, Hoskins, Pomeroys and Samways – would find their way to Dorchester, Massachusetts and thence to Windsor on the Connecticut River.

Leaving Beaminster to the north one climbs up over Horn Hill and down into the valley of the River Axe to the village of Mosterton, home of the Gallop family, passengers on the *Mary and John*, and thence, by a couple of roundabout miles, to South Perrott, home of the Gibbs and from which Giles Gibbs and family have probably left to join the same ship; and so, down and across the infant River Axe, to the county of Somerset and, two and a half miles further on, to Crewkerne.

Crewkerne was a thriving market town which specialized in weaving sailcloth. According to Gerard, it had 'a fair, sightly built church built in a cross with a bell tower rising up in the middle' and Leland records that it had 'a pretty town house in the market place', a grammar school and, once again, an almshouse of recent foundation. Crewkerne was an important resource for John White's recruiting. John Warham, White's choice as minister for the gathered church of the *Mary and John*'s ship's company, was born and bred there, though he came of gentle Dorset stock from nearby Maiden Newton. After coming down from Oxford he had apparently become a Puritan lecturer in the locality. He was clearly a considerable preacher. After he preached a farewell sermon in Crewkerne church the churchwardens were disciplined by the archdeacon's court for permitting it. At some point he was reputedly 'silenced or suspended' by his bishop for his subversive Puritan opinions but later given asylum by the more sympathetic Bishop of Exeter as curate of St Pedrock's. There he attracted to his congregation of Puritan-minded merchant families among others a young man, Roger Clap, who 'took such a liking unto [him] that he did desire to live near him', having 'never so much as heard of New England until he heard of many a godly person that were going there and that Mr Warham was to go also'. Warham's influence in that part of Somerset was clearly still strong, reaching beyond Crewkerne into its neighbouring villages. Those of his new flock who came from that vicinity knew and liked him well and were attracted to the prospect of emigrating to New England with him as their pastor. Altogether, from Crewkerne itself, from Chard and from neighbouring villages, a score or so of families and individuals were recruited for the *Mary and John* and subsequent ships to join his church in Dorchester on Massachusetts Bay. They included some of the more notable people in the enterprise.

Crewkerne contributed William Gaylord, whom Warham chose as the first deacon of his shipboard church that day of departure in Plymouth, and William Phelps, who became constable at Dorchester and magistrate in Connecticut. Five miles away, in the smiling vale sheltering below Windwhistle Ridge, lies the village of Chaffcombe, whose rector William Gillett contributed two young bachelor sons. A short walk from Chaffcombe brings one to Chard, an important cloth-weaving town which exported coarse cottons and woollens to Brittany, Bordeaux and La Rochelle. The largest of these groups of recruits came from here. The Cogans, a prominent family of merchants and clothiers, provided Boston, Massachusetts with its first shopkeeper and two daughters who married respectively Roger Ludlow, Assistant and owner of the *Mary and John* and principal colonizer of Windsor on the Connecticut River, and John Endicott, Governor of Salem, Massachusetts. A couple of miles north-west of Chard is Combe St Nicholas with another fine church standing high in the village. Here, in Ilminster and hereabouts, was the country of the Rossiters, country gentry of whom Edward, 'a godly man of good estate', an Assistant of the Massachusetts Bay Company, and his son Bryan, who was to practise medicine, were *Mary and John* passengers; and also from Ilminster came John Branker, an Oxford graduate who became schoolmaster and ruling elder in Warham's church.

Ten miles further still we come to the Vale of Taunton. Taunton Deane, with its rich, red earth which produces 'all fruits in great plenty', as Gerard put it, was renowned orchard and cider-making country. 'The paradise of England', John Norden called it. 'Where should I be born else than in Taunton Deane?' asked Thomas Fuller rhetorically. Its market town, Taunton, was a thriving and populous borough much praised by Gerard for the 'beauty of the streets and marketplace, having springs of most sweet water continually running through them', for its great church and its tower and ring of bells and, inevitably, for its almshouses. Taunton had a great market, especially for cattle; it was also an important cloth town. Some eight miles out of Taunton into the vale is the little village of Fitzhead, home of the Rockwell brothers, of whom William had been chosen by John Warham as deacon of his shipboard church, doubtless, like his fellow deacon Gaylord, in acknowledgment of his religious commitment and sterling qualities.

After Fitzhead, we have a short walk of a couple of miles by a back lane to our final destination on this excursion: the tiny, sequestered village of Tolland, home of the Wolcott family. The Wolcotts were clothiers from nearby Wellington who during the previous century had acquired lands, mills and a quarry in the manor of Tolland. Henry Wolcott, a man of affluent means, though in middle age had made a reconnoitring voyage to New England in 1628 and had then determined to foresake Somerset for the New World. Having disposed of the greater part of his family inheritance, he embarked with his family on the *Mary and John*. With his talents and energy Wolcott, along with Roger Ludlow, Edward Rossiter and Israel Stoughton, provided the leadership for the Dorchester enterprise, and would, together with Ludlow and Newberry, put up most of the money to found Windsor on the Connecticut. He was to be a principal magistrate of Connecticut Colony, the most prominent member of the Windsor settlement throughout his long life, and its richest citizen.

This journey through the highways and byways of the Dorset–Somerset border country on the track of New England planters has meandered through many villages and towns; but apart from a few outlying instances, the families concerned have been traced to a circumscribed area and this invites speculation. How did these families and individuals come to their Weymouth rendezvous in March 1630? To what extent were they in touch with one another beforehand as people with like motives? Did they come together spontaneously or were they organized from outside? We shall never have definite answers to such questions. We are dealing for the most part with people who left few, if any, family records beyond the register of their births, marriages and deaths, a few wills and inventories to illuminate their lives in England (their lives in New England are somewhat better documented), and a great deal has to be surmised.

The propinquity of these families and their villages and towns, the extent to which young men married girls two or three villages away, the inter-family connections which resulted, and the business travel to towns and ports, would lead one to suppose that many of these people knew or knew of one another and, stimulated by intelligence from New England, took steps to get in touch and concert their departure plans. It is hard to believe that the Fords, Ways, Capens, Purchases and Terrys of Dorchester, that county town which by our standards was still only a large village, did not know one another, or that the Hoskins, Hosfords and Pomeroys of Beaminster and Netherbury, the Denslows, Randalls and Ways of Bridport or the Gilletts, Rossiters, Brankers, Cogans, Strongs and Pinneys of the Chard–Ilminster neighbourhood did not at least hear through the local gossip what was afoot. John White's statement in *The Planters Plea*, of the *Mary and John* ship's company, that of 'about 140 persons . . . there were not six known either by face or fame to any of the rest' must be discounted. It has been plausibly suggested that he wrote thus to support his denial that his emigrants were an organized band of Separatists conspiring to subvert the Church of England. Yet the circumstances surrounding the sailing of the *Mary and John* and related ventures presuppose an organizing, external agent; and that agent must have been the patriarch of Dorchester in whose honour the emigrants named the place they founded on Massachusetts Bay.

John White was a man of energy and drive; and no doubt there came in and out of his rectory and vestry a daily stream of people who could be interested in and recruited for not only his good works in Dorchester but also his pious colonizing efforts. But although he masterminded the whole *Mary and John* expedition, he must have had agents to help him enlist his emigrants; and who better placed to act as such than his own professional colleagues, that network of parish clergy, many of whom shared White's convictions about theology, church order and the duty to save the souls of the heathen?

It will be recalled that among the members of the Dorchester Company were a score or so of clergymen, mostly in West Country livings, and no doubt many recruited by White himself. Of these, about a dozen held livings in our catchment area. In addition, another seven, not members of the company, were known for their Puritan leanings, their connections with White, or both. There was William Benn, rector of All Hallows, and Robert Cheeke, rector of All Saints and schoolmaster, in Dorchester itself. Edward Clarke, once one of White's assistants, member of the committee of the Planters' Parliament and brother-in-law of Dorchester's John Humphrey, the deputy governor of the Massachusetts Bay Company, was vicar of Taunton and in a position to make contact with such people as the Strongs, Rockwells and Wolcotts. There was William Tilly, rector of Broadwindsor, two miles or so from Netherbury and Beaminster, and his neighbour George Bowden, minister of Mapperton, only a couple of miles from Beaminster, both strong Puritans. Walter Newburgh, rector of Simonsbury, was not only a member of the Dorchester Company but married successively daughters of two of its chief adventurers, Sir Richard Strode and Mr John Browne of Frampton. The latter, Jane, survived the squire of Frampton to marry the Rev. John Stoughton, a prominent Puritan clergyman of Somerset and St

Mary, Aldermanbury, London, brother of Israel and Thomas, both important settlers at Dorchester, Massachusetts. Walter Newburgh may well have prompted the emigration not only of his cousin Thomas Newburgh but of the Ways, Randalls and Denslows of nearby Bridport. William Gillett of Chaffcombe may not only have contributed his own two sons but influenced John Hill of his own parish and the people of nearby Combe St Nicholas, Ilminster and Broadway. We have already noted the likely importance of John Warham's incumbency of Crewkerne. Richard Bernard, the rector of Batcombe, was an important Puritan friend of White's, a writer of controversial tracts, two of which, critical of 'the manner of our gathering our churches', he was to send over to John Winthrop in Boston. It was his system for instructing parishioners that John White adopted in Dorchester, and Batcombe was not only a mere stone's throw from Roger Ludlow's home at Maiden Bradley, but the parish from which Joseph Hull recruited his own emigrant congregation.

Joseph Hull was one of three clergymen apart from John White who deserve special attention as being all directly active in the colonizing movement. He lived at Crewkerne, and led a shipload of 106 persons to found Weymouth on Massachusetts Bay. The second was John Conant, rector of nearby Limington, Somerset; it was probably through him that White was put in touch with his brother Roger Conant who rescued the Cape Ann venture and virtually founded Salem. The third was Richard Eburne, vicar of Henstridge next door to Caundle Purse whence came William Hannum. Little is known of Eburne save the all-important fact that he was the author of *A Plain Pathway to Plantations* which he published in 1624, the year of the Planters' Parliament. This pamphlet is of the same genre as White's *Planters Plea* and others of the time. In the form of a dialogue between a thinly disguised Eburne and a merchant, it is vigorous and racy advocacy of planting in Newfoundland as a moral virtue in itself and as the only cure for the economic, social and moral ills of the country. Together with *The Planters Plea* it provides a valuable insight into the attitude of mind of that particular clerical generation in Dorset and Somerset.

Eburne was specific in his profile of the social composition for a successful colony in North America. First, there must be 'governors and rulers', people of 'better breeding and experience, gentlemen at the least'; but he qualified this by writing that if, as seems likely, not enough such come forward, then the organizers should go for 'others of a next degree unto gentlemen – that is, yeomen and yeomenlike men, that have in them

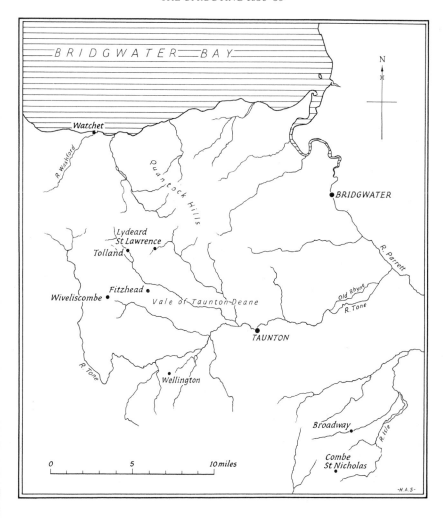

some good knowledge and courage . . . who may in defect of better men be advanced to places of preferment and government there and haply prove not altogether unworthy thereof.' Men of substance were essential. Men 'better stored in money and means than the generality' – that is to say with working capital – were needed to 'employ the poorer sort and set them to work'. Above all, he stipulated that the colony, however primitive its circumstances, must have a learned ministry; but then again, 'if scholars, that is graduates and men of note for learning cannot be had, it may suffice sometimes that such be invited to the ministry as are of mean knowledge so that they have good utterance and be of sound and honest life and conversation.' Indeed not much more could be expected 'in the infancy of a church where neither schools nor other means for learned and able men are yet planted. Better such than none.' In other words, though the colony must be governed by degree, by position or class – and no one in that day would assume otherwise – there was likely to be an element of levelling in which vigour and character would compensate for lack of breeding or position.

This passage is a revealing introduction to a consideration of the actual composition of the people whom White and his collaborators recruited for their New England venture. They were a strikingly eclectic group. Few individuals are completely unknown to us, whose families, towns and villages cannot be identified and whose social position at least roughly estimated. Of the fifty or so heads of families with whom we are becoming familiar, hardly any have left no trace of themselves. Broadly speaking our New England emigrants did not come from any social stratum lower than husbandman or artisan or higher than the minor gentry. The largest group, twelve families in all, belonged to that very broad class called yeomen, described by our local rector of Broadwindsor, Thomas Fuller, as 'an estate of people almost peculiar to England, living in the temperate zone between greatness and want'.

It was a large class, shading at the top into the gentry like the Hoskins of Beaminster and at the bottom into more humble husbandmen. Some of these were established families in their villages and towns, leaving land and chattels to their descendants and bequests to the poor with perhaps even a tomb in the parish church. Some were relatively poor. Others were younger sons who had to make their way in the world, like Humphrey Pinney of Broadway. A few, like Thomas Newberry of Marshwood Vale, were well off even by the standards of lesser gentry to which estate they might or might not aspire. Indeed, the line between yeomanry and gentry was shadowy and defined often as much by a man's 'port', his social ambition and style, as by a family listing in the Visitations of the Heralds, and many a younger son of a younger son like John Hill of Chaffcombe must reconcile himself to sinking from Esquire or Mister to Goodman. A dozen or so might be classed as minor gentry, some tinged with yeoman, merchant or burgess; or vice versa. As for the smaller group of county families with notable estates who dominated their neighbourhoods and provided the Crown with its justices and deputy lieutenants to govern the shire, probably only one figured in our company: Roger Ludlow, the owner of the *Mary and John*, who came from a distinguished landed family with legal connections on the border of Wiltshire.

However, even Ludlow did not think it beneath him to marry the daughter of a merchant, Philobert Cogan of Chard, although it is true the

Cogans were so well established that they were entitled to bear arms. The line between merchant and gentleman was as shadowy as that between gentleman and yeoman. It was common for daughters of rich merchants and burgesses like the Capens and the Hosfords of Dorchester to marry into the gentry; and the Wolcotts, clothiers who had acquired land, a grist mill and quarries in fee simple, were well on their way to becoming gentry.

In our emigrant band, the urban, merchant class was the largest, most cohesive and forceful in the whole enterprise. It was represented by some twelve families, mostly John White's parishioners in Dorchester, like George Way, who had been an adventurer of the Dorchester Company, and the Capens and Purchases with links overseas through Weymouth, but also others, from Lyme Regis, Chard and Exeter. They were interrelated, as families and in business. William Hill of Lyme and Nathaniel Duncan married daughters of Ignatius Jourdain, a prominent Puritan mayor of Exeter and a successful overseas merchant, once of Guernsey, then of Lyme Regis and now of Exeter and the City of London. John Cogan, one of the Chard clan, was also established, like the Jourdains, in St Sidwell's, Exeter and it was no coincidence that this was John Warham's parish. Hill and Duncan sailed in the *Mary and John* and Cogan three years later, all three with their families. Young William Humphrey, of another Lyme merchant family kin to White's friend John Humphrey of Charldon, was to become an important merchant in Windsor, Connecticut.

Equally significant were the professional people, the clerisy, gentry by courtesy: the clergy proper, the two ministers Warham and Maverick, both Oxford graduates; three sons of parsons, the two Gillett boys and Stephen Terry, John White's nephew; the surveyor George Hull whose two brothers were beneficed clergymen; and two schoolmasters, John Branker the Oxford graduate, and Aquila Purchase, who also belonged to the inner group of Dorchester merchant families.

Finally, there was a scattering of people with special skills – fullers, coopers, tanners and masons; and, not surprisingly for that Channel coast, there were six master mariners: John Gallop, Henry Way and John and Richard Rocket of the Bridport area, Elias Parkman of Sidmouth, and John Tilley, a black sheep of Chilthorne Domer who had first gone to sea and learnt to rough it at Cape Ann in 1623. All were to pursue their calling off the New England coast.

If our company were relatively homogeneous as a social class they were also essentially a community of families. Of the *Mary and John*'s adult passengers, only about twelve were single men (there were no single adult women); the rest, fifty-four in number, were twenty-seven married couples; and of those whose ages we know, the husbands range from a few in their twenties to nine who are well over forty, that is to say well over middle age for the time. Even more striking is the number of offspring; in that ship's company there were no less than seventy-two children. This was no band of young, unattached, swashbuckling adventurers such as had characterized transatlantic ventures hitherto. It was a well-knit company, among the very first, of emigrant families with children as hostages to their fortunes, sober in their commitment to a planting venture, hazardous as it might turn out to be. These gentry, merchants, yeomen, professionals, artisans, sea captains and their families formed an eclectic and yet cohesive group, significant for what it did not include – especially servants of both sexes – as for what it comprised. Its members were selected and, in a measure, self-selected for a very special purpose.

What was that purpose? Why did they go? Why did they leave their English hearths? John White himself noted that the English loved the smoke of their own chimneys too well to leave home; and Richard Eburne quoted the Latin tag: 'Fumus patriae alieno inculentior' ('the smoke of a man's own country is dearer in his eyes than the fire of another'). For these West Country people we may echo Thomas Fuller's question: 'Where should I be born else than in Taunton Deane?' by adding parenthetically, 'and where should I wish to bring up my children but in the Vale of Taunton, or the Axe or Brit valleys, or the close country between, the high country behind or the downland east towards Dorchester?' For this was a rich landscape, nurturing a country people as well-found and as prosperous as any in England.

In the 17th century, Somerset was the third or fourth most populous English shire and the people in its southern hundreds especially were sustained by a bountiful countryside. The valleys of Taunton, Wellington and the Axe sent barley, wheat and oats, orchard fruit and hops, beef and dairy products to commercial markets as far away as London. South and east, that district of Somerset and west Dorset within a radius of fifteen miles of Crewkerne whence came most of our emigrants was prosperous, mixed-farming country. Comfortable husbandmen living in small, enclosed farmsteads grew corn, reared cattle and sheep and kept dairy cows from whose milk their wives made renowned butter and cheeses for market. The coastal area between Lyme and Bridport was especially famous for its Dorset butter. Thomas Fuller's Broadwindsor and Netherbury were renowned for their cider and the Brit Valley for its hemp and flax. Although Dorset was less populous, its farm produce supported twenty-one market towns. Thomas Gerard wrote of the yeomen of nearby Martock of this time that they were

> seated in the fattest place of the earth of this county . . . which makes the inhabitants so fat in their purses . . . [They were] wealthy and substantial men though none of the best bred, which is the cause their neighbours about them are apt enough to slander them with the titles of clowns; but they care not much for that, knowing they have money in their purses to make them gentlemen when they are fit for the degree.

No doubt this was fair comment on neighbours of our Tilleys in the next village, Chilthorne Domer.

The key element in this rural economy, however, was wool. The raising of sheep for their wool was the important item in the cash returns of many a small husbandman and the sheep runs of the Dorset downs were big business. It was boasted that there were 300,000 sheep within six miles of Dorchester. By the end of the century Dorset would be producing the highest number of packs of shorn wool of any county in England, grown on the backs of Dorset's own breed of white-faced, short-woolled sheep, unique for their early lambing and their combination of hardiness and medium-fine fleece. Most of the best spun wool was sent to the weaving centres of Somerset and Wiltshire; but the rougher wools were worked up locally in the cottages of Beaminster, Bere, Lyme, Sturminster and elsewhere, into kersies and Dorset dozens, coarse woollen cloths which the merchants of Dorchester exported from Weymouth to St Malo for the peasants of Normandy and Brittany, poor people, it was said, 'of a base disposition', who would not 'go to the price of good cloth'.

Across the River Axe the weavers of Chard, Ilminster, Taunton, Wellington and Wiveliscombe were at the same business; but in Somerset the cloth industry dominated the rural economy in a way that was not true of Dorset and its prosperity or decline affected critically the fortunes of its populous towns and villages. Since the 1620s that industry had fallen on hard times.

The great expansion of the cloth trade in Tudor times had been followed by a slump beginning about 1620 which lasted on and off for a decade or more. Part of the problem was that the traditional English cloths were at a discount. The quality of the wool had declined and competition from abroad and changes in taste had lessened the demand for classic cloths woven from fine, short staple wool. The cloth industry of Wiltshire and Somerset, beautifully geared to the standard woollens, had suffered most. New products were in demand. Worsted cloths, more loosely woven from long staple wools and from mixtures of foreign wool, silk and cotton warps, the so-called 'new draperies', were in fashion for apparel and furnishing. This was the market which, with its Low Country technicians, East Anglia had captured and which the West Country, with the exception of Taunton's fine serges, shalloons and druggets made from Welsh and Spanish wools, had failed to exploit. The export trade itself had declined; Continental markets were disturbed by the breakdown of relations with Spain, by the futile war with Richelieu's France in support of the Huguenots of La Rochelle, and by those operations in the Low Countries and in Bohemia and northern Germany which were the beginning of what historians would call the Thirty Years' War.

The people of Somerset had been geared too closely to the woollen industry; and too many of her villages had become cluttered with cottages for weavers and their families who knew no other trade. With the slump, their masters the clothiers cut off wool supplies and orders, and they became a classic example of rural un- or under-employment. 'The glut of unsold worsteds and coarser stuffs in Blackhall Hall, London' spelled gloom and tension for the part of the West Country stretching in an arc from Ilminster, Chard and Taunton to Frome and the cloth-weaving areas of Wiltshire.

This depression was exacerbated by severe fluctuations in the harvests. Several bumper crops producing gluts and ruinously low grain prices alternated with crop failures like that of 1621 recorded by William Whiteway from his Dorchester window: 'This was a very cold and moist summer which ripened corn but slowly so that it began to rust at harvest which was very late, there being corn in the fields till the 10th of October.' It was followed by crop failures in 1622, 1629 and above all 1630 which brought famine prices, 'half-filled stomachs' and starvation to unemployed weavers. Even for those in work, wages lamentably failed to keep pace with prices so that 'the meaner sort of people . . . do live in great neediness and extremity'. Conditions were so bad that the Privy Council was concerned about industrial unrest by the unemployed who might 'raise Tumults and fall to uproars for their bellies' sake', like the uprising of 1621–22 when Whiteway wrote in his diary (June 1622): 'In this month was there a watch appointed in all highways . . . at every crossway, one by day and two by night perpetually to give notice if any tumult should arise for want of trade.' There were riots in protest against the export of corn to Bristol and magistrates acted to distribute corn equitably, prosecute corn hoarders and ration maltsters and alehouses. This uneasiness was increased by the violent rising of two years before, still endemic, of the people of Gillingham in Dorset against the threat to their livelihood by the King's decision to enclose the royal forest there.

Largely because of the cloth workers' plight, the pundits of the day were preoccupied with the fashionable diagnosis that the cause of the country's economic problems was over-population. When harvests failed, the landless poor took the brunt of the resulting poverty and famine, especially the cottagers in the clothing villages. Richard Eburne wrote his *Plain Pathway to Plantations* in Hendridge near Caundle Purse close to Sherborne and Yeovil at the centre of weavers' unemployment and distress. In his view, the region was no longer self-sufficient in food 'unless it be in an extraordinary year', the neighbourhood was over-populated and the only solution was emigration: 'Our land . . . swarmeth with multitude and plenty of people, it is time and high time that, like stalls that are overfull of bees or orchards overgrown with young sets, no small number of them should be transplanted into some other soil and removed hence into new hives and homes . . . The true and sure remedy is the diminution of the people.' This conclusion was echoed by his fellow colonial propagandist, John White: 'We have more men than we can employ to any profitable or useful labour . . . especially if there happen any interruption of trade.'

In addition to unemployment, poverty, and starvation, these were recurrent years of plague and other mortal sickness. Outbreaks of plague in London like that of 1625 led to the complete breakdown of markets and trade and there had been a particularly bad outbreak close to home, in Plymouth; and if not the plague there was always smallpox and sometimes typhus and 'famine fever'. In the parish of Martock where we have just noted fat farms and yeomen, forty-four people were carried off by these diseases in 1623, fifty-five the following year and as many as seventy-seven in 1625, the most severe plague year.

To what extent did such circumstances persuade our emigrant families to take the drastic step of uprooting themselves to begin life again in New England? This impression of a time and place of sunlit vistas streaked with ominous shadows of want, distress and unrest contrasts sharply with the image of that land across the Atlantic depicted by Eburne, White and their fellow propagandists, of a New England of plenty where the seasonal climate was familiar, where there was timber and fuel in abundance, where the forests teemed with game and rivers, lakes and ocean with fish, and where fifty acres of fertile land was to be had for the asking. In effect, here beckoned a land where transplanted English people might live in the social and economic circumstances they were used to but in much greater comfort and ease than in the more constricted circumstances of Dorset or Somerset.

As we have seen, most of our families were of the middling classes, yeomen, merchants and clerisy with a few gentry; none belonged to that nameless, landless class of cottagers and day workers, the poor, the indigent and the vagrant, who were most at risk and had least to lose by taking ship for the unknown. Yet the climate of the time may well have exerted a kind of lunar influence on that generation of West Country people. The tone of Eburne's and White's rhetoric suggests that they were conscious of the growing sprawl of over-crowded and unkempt cottages in the countryside, of the need for charities and almshouses for the poor and aged in the towns, of beggars and vagrants who must be moved on, of Protestant refugees from the Continental wars, of their own ragged troops returning from La Rochelle, billeted on the unwilling citizenry of Dorset towns. The shock of that catastrophic fire which consumed most of Dorchester and its wealth remained a vivid memory and a symbol of the transience of worldly possessions. The fat men of Martock might well be conscious that despite their rustic homespun they could buy themselves gentility should they have the mind for it; but the death of so many of their family and neighbours by typhus and the plague must have reminded them of their mortal state. This, the Jacobean scene, had a sombre hue, tinged with melodrama and tragedy like the plays of Thames-side, and, it could be, engendering an apocalyptic outlook, turning men's minds towards radical and final judgments. Perhaps we shall come nearer to answering our question of why they went by looking beyond the material to more deep-seated motives.

To White and his fellow proselytizers, as we have seen, the principal motive for colonizing in North America was religious: 'the most eminent and desirable end of planting colonies is the propagation of Religion.' Moreover, it was a high duty to which England had been called: 'this Nation is in a sort singled out unto this work, being of all the States that enjoy the libertie of the Religion Reformed, and are able to spare people for such an employment, the most Orthodox in our profession.'

In the 1620s the state of religious politics in England made that call ever more urgent. Discrimination against ministers of the reformed persuasion was not as marked in the West Country as in eastern England; but there was writing on the diocesan walls of Bristol, Exeter and Bath and Wells. John White's Puritan zeal had long been famous and to some people notorious, as to that widow Samays who accused him of robbing the Dorchester poor to further his cranky colonial enterprise. But he had so far kept out of the ecclesiastical line of fire, though events of the 1630s, especially when his papers were seized and he was called before the Court of High Commission, would ultimately drive him to a greater extreme. Although reformist in church doctrine he is still loyal to the Church of England and this would be a cardinal fact for the Dorchester settlement. He may have been protected in his Puritanism by his bishop, Arthur Lake, who had been his virtual contemporary at Winchester and New College and was an ardent supporter of his colonizing efforts. But Lake died in 1626 and was succeeded as Bishop of Bath and Wells by none other than William Laud, on his way to national eminence. It was Laud who had driven the Puritan-minded John Warham out of Crewkerne to seek temporary refuge under the more tolerant Bishop of Exeter before accepting his call to the New World. Warham himself had become sufficiently notorious to be lampooned in 'A Proper Ballad, called the Summons to New England, to the tune of the Townsman's cap', which began:

> Let all the Purisidian sect,
> I mean the counterfeit Elect

and ended:

> The native people, though yet wild,
> Are all by nature kind and mild,
> And apt already (by report)
> To live in this religious sort,
> Soon to conversion they'll be brought
> When Warham's miracles are wrought,
> Who, being sanctified and pure,
> May by the Spirit them allure.

By that time White's influence was pervasive and recognized as fostering the naturally Puritan temper of Dorchester and Dorset. It would not be long before Laud himself would complain that there were Puritans in nearly every parish in the county and Bishop Skinner of Bristol would feel impelled to exhort the clergy of Dorset to return to kneeling at prayers, using the cross at baptism and holding feasts and holidays, so Puritan had they become. No wonder Clarendon was to describe Dorchester as the most malignant place in the country.

This soil nurtured the emigrants whom White and his colleagues recruited and it is strong circumstantial evidence of a powerful religious motive for their uprooting. This seems to have been popularly accepted. That November of 1630, in a deposition before the Dorchester magistrates, a Thomas Jarvis of Lyme Regis said that 'all the Projectors for New England business are Rebells and those that are gone over are Idolators, captivated and separatists'.

It is possible to be certain of the religious convictions of only a minority of our ships' passengers. Apart from the two parsons, Warham and Maverick, their two deacons Rockwell and Gaylord, and Ludlow and Rossiter, Assistants of the company, there were only a few whose religious convictions are explicitly recorded. One was young Roger Clap who in his old age was to describe in a memoir how as a youth he persuaded his parents to let him live with a Huguenot family in Exeter so that he could sit at John Warham's feet; there was Henry Wolcott who underwent a marked conversion to Puritan beliefs and whose plan to shift his family and fortune to the New World implies a powerful Puritan commitment; and there are a number of others in similar circumstances, such as Stephen Terry, the Gillett brothers and George Hull, sons and brother respectively of Puritan parsons, and Thomas Newberry, cousin of Roger, rector of Simonsbury. For the rest, the evidence is more circumstantial. Not all who took part in those farewell services in Plymouth would pass the rigorous process of self-examination and public declaration which would come to be the test of full church membership in Dorchester or subsequently in Windsor; and there were clearly a few odd men out, like the reprobate John Tilley.

Yet when all is said and especially bearing in mind the homogeneous character of those fifty or so families, their earnest commitment, their responsibilities for children, the hazardous nature of the enterprise, and also the high rate of success they would achieve in establishing themselves in New England, we can hardly doubt that a Puritan religious conviction was a dominant motive for most of them or that John White's own assessment, recorded at the very time of their departure, is sound:

I should be very unwilling to hide any thing I think

might be fit to discover the uttermost of the intentions of our planters in their voyage to New-England, and therefore shall make bold to manifest not only what I know, but what I guess concerning their purpose. As it were absurd to conceive that they have all one mind, so were it more ridiculous to imagine they have all one scope. Necessity may press some; novelty draw on others; hopes of gain in time to come may prevail with a third sort; but that the most sincere and godly part have the advancement of the Gospel for their main scope I am confident. That of them some may entertain hope and expectation of enjoying greater liberty there than here in the use of some orders and ceremonies of our Church it seems very probable.

CHAPTER 3: THE VOYAGE

W E DO NOT KNOW HOW LONG IT TOOK THE *Mary and John* TO RAISE anchor and manoeuvre out of Plymouth Sound round Rame Head into open Channel. There exists no account of this voyage. However, there are diaries kept by passengers on other voyages bound for Massachusetts Bay, notably Francis Higginson's for the *Talbot* the previous season, John Winthrop's for the *Arbella* three weeks after the *Mary and John*, Richard Mather's for the *James* in 1635 and John Josselyn's for the *New Supply* in 1638. These provide plausible evidence of the experience of the ship's company of the *Mary and John* and of the later sailings for Dorchester, Massachusetts.

In 1630 the voyage from England across the north Atlantic might be perilous but was scarcely an unknown adventure. For a century or more West Country seamen had been navigating Atlantic waters, to Newfoundland to fish and latterly to New England both to fish and to plant. The masters, officers and seamen were professionals, for the most part committed to north Atlantic sailing, and during the season there was a fair amount of traffic. The previous spring at least six ships with a total of 350 passengers as well as cattle, armaments and provisions had sailed from the Thames alone and these were only the precursors of the great migration of the 1630s when some 200 ships transported more than 20,000 settlers to New England. The home ports of many of these ships were indeed on the

Thames, or even further up the North Sea, at Ipswich or Yarmouth; but most hailed from the West Country, from Southampton round to Bristol. In 1634 William Whiteway noted in his Dorchester diary that 'this summer there went over to [New England] at least 20 sail of ships and in them 2,000 planters' from the ports of Weymouth and Plymouth alone. Sailing from western Channel ports could shorten the voyage considerably. It took *Talbot* and her sister ship *Lyon's Whelp* two weeks and *New Supply* ten days to make the complicated passage from Gravesend by way of anchorages in Margaret Bay and Dover Roads round to the Isle of Wight; and *James* hung about for over a month before sailing from Bristol, only to put in successively to Minehead, Lundy Island and Milford Haven before finally losing sight of land over five weeks later.

Apart from problems of cargo loading and government clearances, such delays were caused by the limited sailing capacity of the ships of the time. A square-sail rigged ship was at its best with a following wind or at least on the quarter and could not normally sail nearer to the wind than seven points. Consequently she must wait, sometimes for weeks, for a favourable wind. *Mary and John* was fortunate in sailing from a port as far west as Plymouth and she may have got away quite quickly down Channel, though the ultimate length of her voyage, over ten weeks, does not suggest this.

One cause of *James*'s slow start was the reluctance of her crew to part company with *Angel Gabriel* who, though slower, was 'a strong ship furnished with fourteen or sixteen pieces of ordnance'; for there was always a risk in coastal waters of attack from hostile privateers like those on the prowl from Spanish-held Dunkirk. *Talbot* 'saw six or seven sail of Dunkirkers wafting after us; but it seemed they saw our company was too strong for them', and the bark *Warwick*, 'a pretty ship of about eighty tons and ten pieces of ordnance', never made her rendezvous with Winthrop's squadron, having been, it was supposed, captured by a Dunkirker off the Downs. Four days out from the Scillies, *Talbot* was threatened by 'a Biskainer ship, a man-of-war . . . but finding us too strong for him durst not venture to assault us'; and *James* had a similar scare from what was rumoured to be a Turkish pirate. *Arbella*'s look-out saw eight sail astern which it was supposed were Dunkirkers, whereupon her captain 'caused the gunroom and gundeck to be cleared, hammocks taken down, ordnance loaded and powder chests and fireworks made ready, our landsmen quartered among the seamen and twenty five of them appointed for muskets . . . [He also] took down some cabins which were in the way of our ordnance . . . The Lady Arbella and the other women and children were removed into the lower deck . . . All things being thus fitted, we went to prayer upon the upper deck.' But fortunately, 'when we came near we conceived them to be our friends'. Hostile interference had to be looked for not only from foreign vessels. The long arm of the English Crown was felt in the shape of officers on behalf of the Privy Council checking the papers of suspect passengers at the port of embarkation, and in officers of the king's navy who exercised their right to impress sailors for the fleet; *Talbot* lost two of her seamen that way and *New Supply* two of her trumpeters.

Such dangers receded as the *Mary and John* sailed down the English Channel, past the Lizard and out towards the open Atlantic. Without a log we cannot plot the course of that ship's voyage but there is no reason to doubt that Captain Squibb followed the route to be taken three weeks later by *Arbella*. This was the northerly course, keeping roughly to between 46° and 48° latitude. It may be that *Mary and John*'s passengers saw their last of England 'at the Land's End, in the utmost part of Cornwall', or as far west as the Scillies; but it must have been an emotional moment when, as one of them wrote, they 'so left our dear native soil of England behind us'. It must have been especially poignant for the Dorchester people because, unlike *Talbot* or *Arbella* which were sailing in company, *Mary and John* was sailing on her own.

The Dorchester people were fortunate that their ship was relatively commodious. At 400 tons, she was large for her day, in the current phrase, 'a great ship'. Only a score or so of ships in the entire merchant fleet were over 400 tons. With only 140 passengers, *Mary and John* was, moreover, not unduly crowded, a less 'close' ship, as the phrase went, than many in the Winthrop fleet. She would have carried a crew of between forty and fifty seamen and, as a 'strong' ship, was probably armed with upwards of twenty guns. There is a hint in John White's *Planters Plea* that the organizers had originally envisaged a smaller ship but, presumably because more volunteers came forward than had been anticipated, Roger Ludlow had bought this 400-tonner. Her passengers were therefore not subjected to greater discomfort or hardship than was normal for the time.

There were miseries enough, all the same. These small ships tossed and rolled or, as they said, 'daunced' in the waves even in sheltered water, and once in 'the tossing waves of the western sea' people unused to ocean sailing were quickly prostrate with seasickness. The misery experienced by the seasick between decks on *Mary and John* may be imagined, with the vomiting, primitive sanitation, lack of air and confined space. Some of the grander passengers like the Ludlows, Rossiters, Wolcotts and Warhams may have had separate cabins, but most made do dormitory-fashion. On *Arbella* for instance the single men 'were very nasty and slovenly, and the gundeck where they lodged was so beastly and noisesome with their victuals and beastliness as would much endanger the health of the ship', whereupon, 'after prayer', a rota was drawn up to keep the gun deck clean.

But, although conditions were primitive, life at sea was disciplined, sociable and shipshape, especially once the passengers had found their sea legs and could be up on deck in fair weather. On *Arbella* the children and others 'that were sick and lay groaning in the cabins, were fetched out, and having stretched a rope from the steerage to the mainmast, we made them stand, some of one side and some of the other, and sway it up and down till they were warm, and by this means they soon grew well and merry.' The officers, like their successors down to this day, organized deck games: 'Our captain set our children and young men to some harmless exercises, which the seamen were very active in, and did our people much good, though they would sometimes play the wags with them.' Soon their minister was preparing a sermon 'sitting at his study on the ship's poop'; and observing the Mother Carey's chickens (storm petrels), 'a little bird like a swallow', following the ship.

They were all fascinated by the fish and sea mammals. There were porpoises 'pursuing one another and leaping some of them a yard above the water'; there were carvel or Portuguese men o' war, like 'a ship with sails'; there were sunfish, flying fish, swordfish, 'having a long, strong and sharp fin like a sword blade'; there were shoals of mackerel, and bonitoes 'leaping and playing about the ship', and codfish, 'most of them very great fish, some a yard and a half long and a yard in compass', which the sailors assured them were good to eat. Even more exotic were the grampus, 'leaping and spewing up water about the ship', a turtle, 'a great and large shellfish swimming above the water near the ship', and sharks, 'a great one, with his pilot fish or pilgrim upon his back'. Above all, there were whales, 'huffing up water as they go, their backs ... like a little island'. One passenger spotted 'two mighty whales ... the one spouted water through two great holes in her head into the air a great height and making a great noise with puffing and blowing; the seamen called her a soufler ... [The whale's spout makes] the sea to boil like a pot, and if any vessel be near it sucks it in.'

The *Mary and John* passengers quickly settled to a shipboard routine. With such Puritan leadership the first matters to be organized were the religious exercises. She had sailed the day before Palm Sunday and no doubt seasickness prevented much in the way of devotions during Easter week; but by Easter Day, 28 March, they would have recovered enough for Masters Warham and Maverick to have celebrated fittingly. Thereafter, their ministers in turn 'preached and expounded the Word of God every day during the voyage'. The Sabbath was observed with prayers, psalms and sermons morning and afternoon, with catechisms on Tuesdays and Wednesdays; and 'solemn days of fasting'. Fasting at sea was a novelty for the crew, one of whom said 'that this was the first sea-fast that ever was kept and that they never heard of the like'; and one of the ministers noted with approval that the captain set the eight and twelve o'clock watches with a prayer and a psalm and that the prayer was 'not read out of a book' but improvised Puritan-fashion. He also took an unchristian satisfaction in the fate of 'a notorious wicked fellow' who 'mocked at our days of fast, railing and jesting against Puritans' and who 'fell sick of the pocks and died'.

Not all the passengers were saints or postulants for saintliness, and *Mary and John*, like the other ships, must have had her delinquents, to be dealt with by summary nautical discipline. Men involved in fights were 'put in the bolts' or made to walk the deck with hands bound behind them. During a fast, which was presumably too much for them, two landsmen broached a rundlet of spirits, for which they were laid in the bolts all night, and next morning the chief culprit was whipped in the open and both were kept on bread and water for the day. For stealing lemons from the surgeon's cabin a young servant was whipped naked at the capstan with a cat o' nine tails, and another servant was ducked at the main yard-arm three times for being drunk on his master's stolen spirits. Drink seems to have been a problem, particularly with the young, for Winthrop 'observed it a common fault in our young people, that they have themselves to drink hot waters very immoderately' – even girls, like the maidservant who, 'being stomach sick, drank so much strong water that she was senseless'.

There were severe punishments for a miscellany of offences: a man was put in bolts until he apologized for being rude to John Winthrop; a servant was strung from a bar for two hours with a heavy basket of stones round his neck for bribing a child into letting him have the child's supply of biscuits. But such delinquency seems to have been exceptional, and Winthrop considered that the *Arbella*, for one, had 'many young gentlemen . . . who behaved themselves well and are conformable to all good orders'. This was the small change of shipboard life which made day-to-day living vivid: there was the maid who fell down a grating by the galley and would have gone through into the hold but for the carpenter's mate who, 'with incredible nimbleness', managed to catch her; or the great dog which fell overboard and could not be recovered; or the birth of a child; or the flame called St Elmo's fire, 'the bigness of a great candle which settled on the main mast and was commonly thought to be a spirit'. More serious was real sickness and the threat of epidemic disease, above all smallpox or even the plague; but there is no evidence of any serious disease on *Mary and John*.

There must have quickly developed an easy social life among her company. Captain Squibb invited passengers of note to supper, when they did themselves well on boiled and roast mutton and roast turkey washed down with good sack in the comparative luxury of the captain's quarters. For the most part the passengers shared memories of growing up in the same neighbourhoods, and many were families of similar ages, with small or teenaged children. Altogether there were seventy-two children on board; and for them especially this must have been a formative experience, thrown together as they were, at close quarters on deck and between decks, playing games and making their own amusements. For the rest of their lives, in Dorchester and then, for so many of them, in Windsor on the Connecticut River, they were to share the secret freemasonry of children and young people who have gone through an enclosed universe of experience together. No wonder so many subsequently married one another. For example, the young bachelors Aaron Cooke, Roger Clap and John Strong were all to marry daughters of Thomas Ford of Simonsbury; and Humphrey Pinney would marry the daughter of his fellow passenger George Hull when they were settled in Dorchester. To have been youthful passengers on these ships must have forged a bond as intimate as any set of school or family relationships.

Although the northern course may have been the most expeditious, it was not without its rough weather even in that favourable season of spring and early summer. *Arbella* suffered a storm only three days out from the Scillies which 'split her foresail and tore it in pieces' and a wave washed their fresh fish tub overboard. Thirteen days out *Talbot* was hit by a terrible storm when waves smashed over the deck and the crew had difficulty securing the long boat; it was fearfully dark and 'even the mariners' maid' (whoever she may have been) was afraid. As for the passengers, they were terrified by the wind and crashing waves and 'the noise [of the sailors] with their running here and there, loud crying one to another to pull at this and that rope'. However, it did not last many hours, 'after which it became a calmish day'; and one of the diarists recorded that his 'fear at this time was the less when I remembered [that] . . . it seldom falls out that a ship perisheth at storm if it

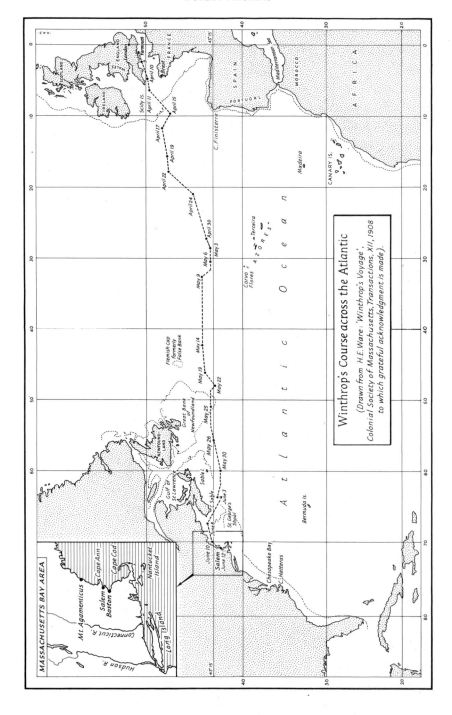

Winthrop's Course across the Atlantic

(Drawn from H.E.Ware: 'Winthrop's Voyage',
Colonial Society of Massachusetts, Transactions, XII, 1908
to which grateful acknowledgment is made).

have sea-room', which was sound reasoning. On 10 May when *Arbella* was in the meridian of the Azores, that is about half-way across the Atlantic, she was hit by another great storm with such high seas that they had to lower the mainsail. This was followed by heavy rain; the wind shifted and they tacked and 'stood into the head sea', making no headway but riding out the storm. Ten days later still *Arbella* breasted yet another head wind and sea and her tossing spritsail was plunged so deep into the waves that it split in pieces just at the moment when her captain emerged from his cabin to give orders to take it in. It was fortunate that the sail did split, because 'otherwise it had endangered the breaking of our bowsprit and topmasts at least', and then, 'unless the wind had shifted we had no other way but to have returned to England'.

These were the times when passengers began to appreciate the qualities of their captains. Some of them were men of mark, well connected and with shares in ships and plantations. Authoritarian and perhaps overbearing, they were forceful and versatile in command. We have seen how they cleared the decks and manned the guns to fight an enemy privateer, dispensed summary justice, played host and concerned themselves with the ship's company morale. In stormy weather, the passengers became especially conscious of the captain's controlling authority. Once, *Arbella's* Captain Milborne, 'so soon as he had set the watch, at eight in the evening called his men and told them he feared we should have a storm, and therefore commanded them to be ready upon the deck, if occasion should be; and he himself was up and down the decks all times of the night.' On another occasion, in heavy and murky rain, the captain was on deck all night 'and was forced to come in, in the night, to shift his clothes'.

A ship's captain on the north Atlantic run in the 17th century had to be both intrepid and skilled. He had to handle his clumsy vessel in high seas, driving winds, calm and fog; he had to be a master of navigation at a time when the science was little developed; instruments were primitive – observations were made and positions calculated by the 'cross-staff' or early quadrant. It is remarkable how the captains managed to keep such consistent courses. For example Milborne, after sailing south-west from the Scillies to about the 47° meridian for a week, kept to a course of between about 45° and 43° all the forty-five days' voyage to Cape Sable. Charts were inadequate, the English being a century behind Antwerp in the art of line-engraving, which was the means of reproducing them. In consequence the captains had to rely heavily on their own experience and memory, on trial and expensive error and on oral tradition. They cherished their own channels and courses as vital trade secrets and their dog-eared charts were the most highly prized of any shipmaster's possessions.

North Atlantic storms were formidable; but given sea room, courage and good seamanship they could be handled. Most to be dreaded was fog. As *Mary and John* approached the waters off Newfoundland, the weather changed, the wind dropped and, although it was early summer, it became clammy and cold and the landsmen shivered and wished for warmer clothes. With the cold came fog. All the ships of which we have logs encountered 'very thick foggy weather'. Passengers had the eerie experience of sailing for days in deadening silence through a white misty wall. Ships sailing in consort beat drums to avoid collision and for all there was the nightmare of icebergs. For they were now off Newfoundland and in the path of drifting ice broken off the Greenland icecap: strange, white islands looming through the fog of which they were in part the cause. 'We saw a mountain of ice shining as white as snow like a great rock or cliff', wrote one diarist and another described 'an island of ice . . . three leagues in length, mountain high in form of land with bays and capes like high clift land and a river pouring off it into the sea. Here it was as cold as in the middle of January in England and so continued till we were some leagues beyond it.'

However, the western ocean off Newfoundland had its compensations: the waters of the Grand Banks, those fabulous fishing grounds which had first tempted English seamen across the Atlantic. By this time the crew had begun to take soundings, first 40 fathoms, then 35, then 24 and then they were directly over the Banks. And so they cast their hooks and lines overboard and took in cod 'as fast as they could haul them up into the ship', sixty-seven cod with a few hooks in less than two hours. They were especially thankful for this at a time when, with 250 leagues still to sail, they were short of victuals, as they were probably also short of hay for the cattle and of water which had to be rationed.

By now *Mary and John* had been sailing her solitary course for upwards of six weeks without sight of land or sail; but off Newfoundland there were signs that they were not too far from land. *Arbella* saw a ship but the unfriendly vessel would not respond to her signal and made off in a surly and suspicious manner, evidently a Frenchman, they thought, from off the Grand Banks; and *James* saw 'abundance of fowl . . . swimming in the sea as a token of nearness of land'. Eventually, they sighted land. *Arbella*, the mist breaking, suddenly saw the shore, as they supposed south-west of Cape Sable at the southern tip of Nova Scotia, latitude 43¼°. On *Talbot* they 'had all a clear and comfortable sight of America' on 24 June, dead on course, seven or eight leagues south of Cape Sable, and, as a further token for their thanksgiving, 'saw yellow gilliflowers on the sea'; and *James*, after being frustrated for several days 'with foggy mists and winds', sighted land at about eight o'clock on a Saturday morning, in this case further south-west, off Menhiggin Island, Maine. After forty-two days out from Land's End in the case of *Talbot*, fifty-six from the Scillies for *Arbella*, forty-seven from Milford Haven for *James* and fifty-four from the Lizard for *New Supply*, they had at last made a North American landfall. It must have been a moment charged with emotion.

Cape Sable was, however, a long way from Massachusetts Bay and a deal of tricky sailing lay ahead off that New England coast notorious for its fogs and storms and treacherous shoals. Passengers might be beguiled by the distant sight of 'fine woods and green trees . . . and these yellow flowers painting the sea' into believing that they were already home and dry in their 'new paradise of New England', but, as one diarist exclaimed, 'how things may suddenly change'. Having tacked about to obtain sea room and in a vain attempt to make the harbour of Cape Ann, there came a 'fearful gust of wind and rain, thunder and lightning', heralding a furious storm which *Talbot* had to ride out as best she could with sails lowered. *James* had a similar experience. Having anchored overnight off the Isle of Shoals so as to reach Cape Ann next day, they, too, were hit by 'a most terrible storm of rain and easterly wind, whereby we were in as much danger as I think ever people were. For we lost in that morning three great anchors and cables and the sails were rent asunder and split in pieces as if they had been rotten rags'; they came within an ace of being driven on to the rocks. It was clearly a frightening experience, and 'when news was brought unto us into the gun room, that the danger was past, O how our hearts did then relent and melt within us and how we burst out into tears of joy amongst ourselves in love unto our gracious God'. *New Supply*, also within two leagues of Cape Ann, similarly ran into a storm, lost sight of land and 'fearing the lee-shore all night . . . bore out to sea'. However, for all three ships this proved to be the last kick of the Atlantic Ocean, a reminder of her savage power and a memory of perils overcome.

Thereafter, it was plain sailing and no doubt a mounting excitement as familiar signs of land and human activity began to multiply. Off the Isle of Shoals *Arbella* saw a ship at anchor and 'five or six shallops [sloops] under sail up and down'. After her terrifying storm, *James* had a 'marvellous pleasant day, for a fresh gale of wind and clear sunshiny weather . . . and had delight all along the coast, as we went, in viewing Cape Ann, the Bay of Saugust, the Bay of Salem, Marvil Head, Pullin Point and other places'. *Arbella*, too, had 'now fair sunshine weather and so pleasant a sweet air as did much refresh us, and there came a smell off the shore like the smell of a garden' and 'there came a wild pigeon into our ship and another small bird'. At Cape Ann, some of the *Arbella* people went ashore and gathered 'store of fine strawberries'; four of the *Talbot* men 'went and brought back again ripe strawberries and gooseberries and sweet, single roses'; and Higginson continued to marvel at the many islands 'full of gay woods and high trees . . . and flowers in abundance, yellow flowers painting the sea'. On the Friday, *Arbella* was stood to, within sight of Cape Ann, and on the Saturday, 12 June, they arrived off Naumkeag (Salem). Here the Governor, Mr Endecott, came aboard to welcome them and took them ashore where they supped on good venison pasty and good beer. *Talbot*, even with a pilot, had found the entrance to Salem's spacious harbour 'curious and difficult' and *Arbella* failed altogether to sail up the narrow channel and had to be warped in. As her passengers disembarked, they were saluted by Captain Milborne with a parting volley of five guns.

As the emigrants disembarked, lost the feel of the ocean swell and found their land legs, there was a general sense of thankfulness. *Talbot*'s diarist the year before had noted that 'we rested that night with glad and thankful hearts that God had put an end to our long and tedious journey through the greatest sea in the world'; and he and his fellow passengers had congratulated themselves on a short and speedy voyage – 3000 English miles in six weeks and three days – 'comfortable and easy for the most part' and, though crowded, largely free of disease save for a few cases of scurvy towards the end. Six years later the *James*'s voyage was thought to be 'very safe and healthful' with 100 passengers, 23 seamen, 23 heifers, three sucking calves and eight mares, 'yet not one of all these died by the way', an achievement which was attributed to good exercise and the excellence of the diet. This was in tragic contrast to her consort, *Angel Gabriel*, which was driven on to the rocks near Pemaquid, and was a total loss including her cargo; moreover, some of her passengers, having survived this disaster, were drowned on the same day in the wreck of the ship which had picked them up only a few hours before.

In 1630 *Arbella* came through comparatively unscathed; but other ships of the Winthrop fleet fared less well; in one, fourteen passengers died from smallpox, another arrived with 'many of her passengers . . . near starved' and two lost most of their cattle as a result of heavy seas when the animals 'shut up in the narrow room of those wooden walls where the fierceness of the wind and waves would often fling or throw them on heaps to the mischiefing and destroying [of] one another'. As for *Mary and John*, she had arrived on Sunday 30 May, the first of all that fleet, as John Winthrop was shortly to discover.

Three days after landing in Salem harbour, Winthrop set out to prospect for somewhere to settle or, as he wrote, 'to find out a place for our sitting down', staying with a hospitable old planter on Noddle's Island at the mouth of the Mystic River. During the course of this reconnoitre, he learned that *Mary and John*, of whose departure from Plymouth John White had told him while *Arbella* was still lying off the Isle of Wight, had indeed already arrived in Massachusetts Bay and that her passengers were bivouacking at a place round a neck of land to the east of the Charles River. On Thursday 19 June, therefore, he made a detour across the Bay to pay them a call. He found the Dorchester people in some distress. They had arrived nearly three weeks before after a fairly comfortable but rather long voyage of seventy-one days; but they had been dumped down on a very bleak and inhospitable shore.

When Roger Ludlow had bought and commissioned *Mary and John*, he and John White had instructed its master, Thomas Squibb, to transport the West Country emigrants not just to New England but to a specific place on the Charles River. This was the spot which those friends of White, the Sprague family, who had sailed in *Lyon's Whelp* the previous season, had identified as being suitable. However, Captain Squibb had had a long and, no doubt, difficult north Atlantic passage. Moreover, his had been the first ship to arrive in the Bay that season. *Mary and John*, at 400 tons, had a deep draught, his charts were no doubt sketchy and he had no pilot. He apparently decided, therefore, that to sail into Massachusetts Bay, with all its islands, sandbanks and shoals, would be to endanger his ship. So instead he anchored off Nantasket Point on the ocean shore and, after they had kept the Sabbath on board that last Sunday in May, he decanted his passengers there, presumably on the Monday morning. As a seaman Squibb may well have been right; but his passengers, expecting to be delivered into a sheltered haven on the Charles River where they could settle, found themselves instead, as one of them wrote, 'in a forlorn wilderness destitute of any habitation and most other comforts of life', and were bitterly aggrieved. They declared Squibb was false to his contract and some of them never forgave him.

Left to shift for themselves, they decided that a group of ten able-bodied and armed men under the command of Captain Richard Southcott, one of the Devonians, a kinsman of an Assistant in the company and a veteran of the Low Countries, should set off to prospect for a suitable place to settle; for clearly desolate Nantasket would not do. Fortunately, they found a boat belonging to 'some old planters' and in it they 'felt their way through the islands' in the Bay to Charlestown which consisted of a few Indian wigwams and some English people, including one old planter called Thomas Walfourd who could speak Indian and who fed them an austere meal of boiled bass without even bread to eat with it. Recruiting Walfourd as guide they rowed up the Charles River to where it 'grew narrow and shallow'. There 'with much labour' they landed their goods up a steep bank.

That night they became aware of a large number of Indians whom Walfourd asked not to disturb the English. The next morning, however, 'the natives stand at a distance looking at us but come not near till they had been a while in view; and then one of 'em, holding out a bass towards us, we send a man with a bisket and are very friendly.' Then they built a shelter for their supplies, fully intending, as the advance party, to make this the place of settlement for the whole Dorchester contingent. But they had been there only a few days when they were ordered to rejoin the main group. So they reluctantly left their riverside spot (which was to become Watertown) and returned to their ship's company who, it transpired, anxious to find suitable grazing for their famished cattle, had somehow journeyed to a neck of land within Massachusetts Bay, 'a place called by the Indians Mattapan', which, because of its salt marshes, 'was a fit place to turn their cattle upon'. There, in desperation, they decided to stop.

This was during the first days of June. They had been there upwards of a fortnight struggling to make a wilderness camp for themselves and their livestock when John Winthrop heard about them and made a detour on his way back to Salem. On seeing their sorry plight, he went over to Nantasket where *Mary and John* still lay and 'sent for Captain Squibb ashore'. What the new governor of Massachusetts Bay said to the master of the *Mary and John* is not recorded but Winthrop seemed to think he had 'ended [the] difference between him and the passengers', in token of which Captain Squibb gave the order for a salute of five guns in the governor's honour and it was said that Squibb later paid compensation to Ludlow.

Thus it came about that the *Mary and John* was the first of that great company of ships to arrive in the Bay in the momentous summer of 1630 and that it was a West Country community which first settled themselves on its shores. Thus also was it that our Dorset and Somerset villagers found themselves in the desperate wilderness of Mattapan Neck and not the more protected Charles River which the Spragues had marked out for them.

But stuck there they were; and despite their weakness after the long voyage they determined to make the best of it. For were they not religious men and women whose object was to establish a new Jerusalem in New England? As Roger Clap, who was one of them, later wrote: 'The discourse, not only of the aged but of the youth also, was not: "shall we go to England?" but "how shall we go to Heaven?" ' It was a dedicated mission and they would have said a hearty Amen to Francis Higginson's ultimate judgment on the experience of that Puritan voyage across the north Atlantic:

> Those that love their own chimney corner and fare not far beyond their own towns end shall never have the honour to see these wonderful works of Almighty God.

CHAPTER 4: SOJOURN AT DORCHESTER ON MASSACHUSETTS BAY
1630–35

CAPTAIN SOUTHCOTT WAS NOT PLEASED. NO SOONER HAD HIS EXPLORING party set about the business of preparing a camp for the *Mary and John* community in that fertile place up the Charles River than along came this messenger with the order, no doubt from Mr Ludlow himself, to return to the main ship's company, now at Mattapan. There was nothing for it but to reload their unreliable boat, negotiate the long swan's neck of Shawmut and find, if they could, the bleak, remote bay fringed with salt marshes into which the *Mary and John*'s company had chanced in their desperate search for grazing for their famished cattle.

But find them they did, all 140 men, women and children huddled along the marshy shore, brown and green under the misty-bright sun of Massachusetts Bay. They must have been a forlorn sight, bivouacking in the long grass dressed in their heavy 'drab'-coloured English clothing of canvas and linen, leather and serge, so unsuited to the hot New England summer, and surrounded by the coffers, chests and bundles stuffed with apparel, tools, cookpots, firearms, drums of saltmeats, dried pulses and herbs, hard cheese and ship's biscuit, casks of beer and aqua vitae which they had been instructed to bring with them. They were exhausted and travel weary. The excitement of making landfall after those weeks of confinement at sea was wearing off in the desolation of this wild shore where muddy creeks and unwadable tidewater rivers hemmed them in; only the sound of waves, the

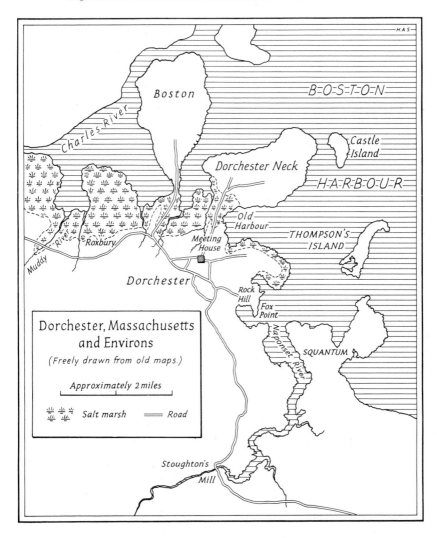

Dorchester, Massachusetts
and Environs
(Freely drawn from old maps.)

Approximately 2 miles

Salt marsh   Road

cry of innumerable sea birds and in the warm night the strange chorus of
tree frogs and cicadas broke the silence. However, pulling themselves
together, they explored a little way from the shore to a beckoning rocky hill
below which were fresh meadows for their cattle. Here they put up their
sailcloth tents and camped. That Sunday Mr Warham summoned them to a
divine service of thanksgiving in the open air.

They remained in a pretty desperate condition, at a low ebb from the
voyage and now exposed to the primitive conditions of camp life in this
unknown country. They were bitten by mosquitoes, fearful of rattlesnakes,
apprehensive of the Indians who watched them silently from a distance, and
concerned to protect their cattle from marauding wolves. Worse, the

unhealthy diet aboard ship took its expected toll; they became sick with that dread deficiency disease, scurvy. Fortunately, they managed to get in touch with the Plymouth plantation further along the coast, and Governor Bradford sent over their physician, Samuel Fuller, who administered remedies and let blood. Despite his efforts the disease became a scourge, for they were debilitated and short of food. The Bay as a whole was short of supplies that summer, the result of bad planning in England; a ship designed to provision Salem had arrived scandalously without its cargo and there were no reserve stocks for the new arrivals who had come too late in the season to sow the corn, and were too ignorant to catch the game, which would have seen them through the winter.

By summer's end the Mattapan community realized that they were in no condition, physical or moral, to make exploratory plans for an ideal place of settlement and that *faute de mieux* they must stay and make the most of the place where they happened to come ashore, namely Mattapan. Having resigned themselves to this, they renamed their settlement after the home town of the man who had inspired their journey across the ocean, John White. The Indian Mattapan became an English Dorchester in New England.

And so, as the summer heat cooled and the crisp frosts of autumn turned the leaves bright reds and yellows, the Dorchester people settled down as best they could to improvise a plan for surviving their first, and unprepared-for, winter. Shelter was the urgent need. Like nearby Boston, Mattapan lacked trees and probably only a few grandees like Rossiter and Ludlow commanded the resources and labour to build timber-frame houses; instead people upgraded their canvas tents to Indian-style wigwams or burrowed into the hillside to make dugouts of earth on timber frames with a hole for a smoky fire. All was higgledy-piggledy and makeshift. In H. R. Shurtleff's words, 'the shores of Boston Bay must have presented a motley and untidy appearance in 1630–31. A few "great houses" sticking up like sore thumbs were surrounded by a disorderly scattering of wigwams, tents and other shacks, pitched without any plan or symmetry'.

These fair-weather shelters kept off showers but were poor protection against winter rains. As Winthrop wrote in his diary: 'the poorer sort of people [who] for want of houses . . . were compelled to live long in tents and lie upon, or too near, the cold moist earth . . . and having no fresh food to cherish them' succumbed to the scurvy. That autumn and winter many fell sick, though unlike Boston and Charlestown there was only one recorded death among the fifty or so heads of families or bachelors who had been passengers on *Mary and John*, and this was not one of 'the poorer sort of people' but Mr Edward Rossiter who died on 23 October leaving his large landholding and company interest to his grown son, the physician and lawyer Brian or Bray. But the autumn was one of misery, affliction and growing disillusion for the settlers for whom this brutal reality contrasted starkly with the expectations engendered by the rhetorical prose of Eburne, White and their fellow enthusiasts for New England planting; and there was worse to come.

All this time there was, for the most part, 'fair, open weather, with gentle frosts in the night'; but on Christmas Eve, remembered though not celebrated by Puritans, winter truly set in, with a nor'wester driving snow and so suddenly cold that fingers were frost-bitten. Two days later the rivers were frozen over and it was so 'very sharp and cold' that it 'made them all betake themselves to the fireside and contrive to keep themselves warm till the winter was over', leaving their cattle to fend for themselves in the open. Fire itself could be a problem. In January, one house burnt down in minutes, and others would suffer the same fate when their wooden chimneys caught fire and could not be put out because all water was frozen.

By this time food was scarce. In Boston even Governor Winthrop had come to the last of the wheat store for his baking oven. Fortunately, the settlers' Indian neighbours helped with presents of their strange maize corn; but as February loomed the outlook was bleak. They survived mostly on fish, although they sometimes had to resort to collecting nuts and combing the frozen shore for clams and mussels. But then, when they must have been near to despair, rescue came. John Winthrop may have been privileged with frame house, servants and oven with its private grain store, but he was not Governor for nothing. As early as the previous July, taking stock of the lack of foodstuffs and fearful of winter, he had commissioned Captain Pierce of *Lion* to sail to Bristol for supplies. That had been over six months ago and even Winthrop must have begun to lose heart; but on 5 February *Lion* suddenly appeared off Nantasket, in good shape, with about 200 tons of goods, all in good condition. One may imagine the excitement and rejoicing. As the vessel made her way through the Bay the governor went out in his shallop to greet her and sailed in her to Boston 'where she rode very well despite a great drift of ice'. Her cargo of provisions was distributed to each of the little settlements dotted about the Bay; the siege condition was relieved and the governor ordered a day of thanksgiving. The cargo included barrels of lemon juice, the cure for scurvy, on a diet of which most of the sick speedily recovered. Not all of them, however; some, defeated by the winter's experience, yearned to return home to England; it was noted that such people were the most likely to succumb to the scurvy.

A few days later, on 10 February, the cold weather relented, the ice melted and, though there were still to be sharp frosts and violent storms, the back of winter was broken. The Dorchester people were not to experience anything so grim again. They discovered that the New England climate was by no means so mild and temperate as that of their own dear Dorset and Somerset. The next two winters would be, if anything, more severe and the summers either hot, dry and liable to drought, or cold and wet, breeding mosquitoes and cornblight; but they quickly became acclimatized to its extremes. They noticed, too, that like their Plymouth neighbours and the old planters of Salem they were becoming less prone to scurvy and other diseases: and once accustomed to New England they declared it healthier, if anything, than their native clime.

As the planters responded to the sun's warmth and the quickening of spring growth, they became conscious of the natural riches around them and set about to make the most of a hunting economy. There were fish from the Bay and from the spring spawning runs upriver. There were birds: flocks of passenger pigeons and doves so dense as to cloud the sun, geese and duck so thick on the marshes that a day's fowling would bring home fifty. There were deer to be stalked; and offshore there were lobsters, crabs and eels to be taken by the score on a single tide, as well as mussels and clams. Winthrop recorded 'great store of eels and lobsters in the bay. Two or three boys have brought in a bushel of great eels at a time and sixty great lobsters.' In the woods there were wild berries, grapes and herbs and the sassafras said to be a remedy against the pox. As they made the acquaintance of their Indian neighbours, they learned to plant their strange corn. All the while they were cutting timber, burning underbrush, planting garden patches and replacing wigwams and dugouts with carpentered huts and houses so that the little settlement began to look more like a village and less like an encampment.

The rocky hill and adjacent flats to which they had struggled from the shore were situated south of Mattapan Neck proper which, being a peninsula and needing minimal fencing, proved best suited for grazing cattle. On the 'plain' where they had erected their wigwams was a pond which fed a brook flowing north. The village site was slightly elevated and dry, with fresh, clear springs. However, the bay where they had landed, later called Old Harbour, proved too shallow for shipping and the brook was not free running enough for fish, not, as they said, an 'alewife' river. So the planters turned their gaze southwards where there was another useful peninsula, Fox Point, and a sizeable river, the Naponset, with a channel, moorings for ships and extensive water-meadows.

For the moment they were each occupied with building a house and clearing an acre or two round it for an allotment. They staked out their plots close together as in the West Country villages whence they came. This was instinctive, though it also conformed to a colonial rationale of defence and a Puritan imperative to gather round a future meeting house. Families who had been fellow passengers on shipboard and neighbours in Dorset or Somerset settled next to one another and worked together to clear their home lots and plant fields. Although most came from neighbourhoods where land had long been enclosed, it is interesting that they cleared the wilderness communally as open fields. One field was as much as they could cope with this first season, but in the next couple of years they would clear four fields, north, south, east and west, and Dorchester would begin to look like an English open-field village. This practical response to necessity was rationalized in the formal land policy of the Massachusetts Bay Company, from which the Dorchester settlers derived their legitimacy.

In theory, land was held of the English Crown through its nominated agent, the Massachusetts Bay Company (although the Dorchester people satisfied Puritan consciences by obtaining some form of land title from the local Indian sachem, one Chickabot). The company in turn granted land in accordance with its own land policy set out in resolutions of the Court of Assistants drawn up in London as early as May 1629. These laid down that land should be allocated as follows: each investment in the company of £50 was to carry a right to 200 acres and a half-acre house plot; an investor who emigrated and paid his own passage was to be entitled to an extra fifty acres for every member of his family; an emigrant, not an investor but paying his own passage, was to be entitled to fifty acres only although at the company's discretion he could be allotted extra land 'according to [his] charge and quality', i.e. his family responsibilities and his social status; and for each indentured servant transported, his master could claim another fifty acres. The settler had the right to choose his own home lot provided it was within the township.

The Court of Assistants first allocated land to its own investors or adventurers. In Dorchester, the two Assistants, Ludlow and Rossiter, were granted farms of 100 acres apiece, large tracts of prime meadow and arable about the Naponset, in Ludlow's case most of the peninsula called

Squantum Neck. Henry Wolcott, Thomas Newberry and Israel Stoughton were granted equivalent holdings. The first and principal settlers chose home lots on Rocky Hill: Ludlow built a substantial house on its south side. Newberry had an extensive home lot about the Rock, forty acres of adjacent upland, forty of marsh, and 100 acres of upland and another 100 of meadow on either side of the Naponset River, a large holding commensurate with the size of his investment, his social standing and his large family. Israel Stoughton was granted not only 150 acres of meadow marching with Newberry's eight or nine miles up the Naponset, but valuable milling and fishing monopolies. The holdings of these grandees were greater than those of ordinary settlers, matched only by similar grants to the other privileged group, the ministers; but it was in accordance with the same guidelines that the ordinary Dorchester settlers negotiated their own choices of home and great lots, meadow and marsh.

The granting of land in this way by the Court of Assistants, meeting in Boston or New Town, quickly became impractical. The scattering, by force of circumstances, of what had been intended as a single unified plantation into half a dozen settlements led to land being allocated to individual townships and soon in Dorchester this function was taken over, first by the church elders and then by the townsmen who continued to grant land consistent with the company's guidelines. The basic house plot was about half an acre, but this became subsumed in a 'home lot' of roughly four acres, large enough for house and smallholding without being so large as to break up the village street neighbourhood. This standard lot could be varied depending on the size of a man's family and his social standing. The position of the home lot was determined, usually in relation to the family's squatter's rights; then came the allocation of the 'great lot', that is, the family's principal holding, usually 16 acres, though sometimes half that and occasionally as much as 20. Finally, there was a separate allotment of 'fresh marsh', meadow for fodder crops and salt marsh for rough summer grazing. These grants tended to be between two and four acres each, often in packets of two or more, scattered about the plantation. There were, of course, exceptions and adjustments to round out a man's holdings: a slip of upland here, a parcel of marsh there, 'the hedgey ground in the bottom' for Mr Newberry, and the habit of swapping lots to make a more convenient holding, and of outright purchases, grew apace. But there were few marked differences in landholding and such as there were reflected family size as much as social position. In Dorchester there appear to have been fewer servants than in Boston, which militated against social distinctions being reflected in property ownership. At first, settlers tended to look for great lots and meadow south and east of the village plain towards Fox Point, Squantum Neck, the fertile water-meadows of the Naponset and south-west towards the Blue Hills and what was to become Dedham. Once the lands 'towards Naponset' had been allocated, the village fathers turned for great lots west towards the brook which marked the boundary with their Roxbury neighbours.

Dorchester's domestic economy centred on the house and its home lot in the neighbourhood of the village street. Here the family cleared a plot for the kitchen garden, experimented with pumpkins and squashes and tended the cabbages, turnips, carrots and parsnips they had brought from England and the herbs so essential for seasoning and preserving. Here they began their first corn-patches, the maize planted in hillocks Indian-fashion with runner beans trained up the stalks. Here they planted the fruit trees they had also brought with them, especially apples for their hardiness and for the cider. Here they erected the outbuildings to shelter cows, oxen and eventually, maybe, a horse, and a pen for sheep; and the women kept hens and geese. Their pigs and goats ranged far afield rooting for themselves, eating anything and fierce enough to keep wolves and the occasional bear away from their prolific litters. The swine especially became animal 'weeds' of the countryside.

Cattle, pigs, goats and sheep needed more grazing than the village street provided and were brought together in communal herds with their own herdsmen. Sheep needed extensive pasture and folding against wolves. In the first years cattle, brought across the Atlantic at great expense and with many losses, were precious. In the spring of 1633 Dorchester could still only boast forty-five milch cows, the ownership of which was some indication of relative affluence, and two years later, in order to increase the stock, the town resolved that four bulls should go 'with the drift of milch cows'. This was Stoughton's responsibility with William Rockwell of Fitzhead, Somerset and Thomas Ford of Simonsbury, Dorset, all three prominent citizens. Each morning about sunrise the cows were brought to assembly points in the village and driven by the herdsmen out to pasture for the day, returning for collection to their home lots at sunset. In Dorchester it was the custom for the cowman to herald his coming and going with blasts on his horn. Cows were milked twice a day and the settlers' wives and daughters made butter and cheese in their makeshift dairies. The beef cattle were herded further afield and in the summer months grazed freely, especially on the common land of Dorchester's Mattapan Neck which was reserved for them because there they could be protected with minimal fencing against wolves. Cattle presented the greatest demand on the domestic economy; they needed between two and ten times as much land as was needed for tillage. In summer the herd grazed freely on the two necks and on salt marshes and after harvest on the stubble of the cornfields; but in winter they had to be kept nearer home and, if possible, in cowsheds during the hard months. And they had to be fed: hence the importance of 'mowing land', the fresh meadow of which each settler had his four to six acres for haymaking, often on Roxbury Brook or Naponset River above tidewater. The English quickly found the native grasses, the broomstraw and rye and the spartinas of the salt marshes, though tall and prolific, less nutritious than those they were used to in the West Country and their cattle grew 'lousy with feeding upon it and are much out of heart and liking'. The provision of good fodder for winter was a worry for the first year or two until English strains such as bluegrass and white clover, sometimes brought over by chance in shipboard fodder and dung, took hold.

Along with haymaking, the corn harvest was the most labour-intensive activity of the farming year. The settlers had a gentle introduction to tillage; they took over old Indian fields which, though partly worn out, they burnt over and cleared. English wheat, barley and rye were for the future. Instead they discovered the virtues of maize, cultivated Indian-fashion by hoe and mattock. To make the four great Dorchester fields meant felling trees and clearing brush. This must have been back breaking, even with the help of oxen; but cleared they were and to an unnecessary English standard before our settlers learned to girdle the trees and let them die. If clearing the fields was a communal effort, so, in a measure, was their planting. Each settler cultivated his own strips in these great fields, unenclosed save for external fences to protect them from cattle and wild animals. The crop to be planted and the dates for the sequence of cultivation – planting, hoeing, harvest and the opening of the stubble to the cattle – were communally determined.

And so the Dorchester community began to settle to a life which, though hard and unaccustomed, developed its own diurnal and seasonal rhythms which were a variant of those they had known in the West Country. In New England spring came later and more suddenly than in Dorset so that, whereas at the beginning of April the ground was still frozen and little could be done, by the end of the month the snow had melted, the streams were running, the marshes were filled and the Naponset River was alive with runs of spawning smelt, alewives, bass, salmon, sturgeon and shad so dense, at times, as to strain the nets and provide a spring harvest for immediate eating, smoking or fish manure. This was the season for planting corn in the fields and vegetables in the garden; and so quickly did spring melt into summer's heat that by June shoots must be hoed and it was time to mow the fresh meadows and to load the hay on rough sledges or lighters for poling back to the home lots for stacking. It was also the season for seafood, lobsters and crabs, clams and oysters. By August it was time to harvest the corn, to pick the fruit, especially apples for cider, and in September to tap the sweet syrup from the maples, and to take the fowling piece to the shore for wildfowl and to the woods for hares, rabbits and deer for venison. Then came the time to slaughter the pigs and to smoke and salt the pork for ham and bacon against the winter. And always there was wood to be cut and brought in prodigious quantities from the family's upland wood lot, to be corded and stacked by the house against the time, early or late in December, when the New England winter would close in and the family withdraw to its fireside to make do and mend implements and clothing, to spin and weave the wool and flax; and outdoors to mend fences, feed the stock and perhaps make a dugout to bury blocks of ice as a store for the summer.

Many activities took place at some distance from the home lot. Wood cutting, and haymaking on some far meadow or marsh, involved long treks by primitive paths and staying away from home; in summer the men, with their sons and servants if they had any, made a habit of camping or even making shacks on some distant meadow, leaving the women to manage the more domestic chores back in the village, and the ministers and elders worried about the men's non-appearance at the meeting house on the Sabbath.

Husbandry was not the only preoccupation. As we noted, Israel Stoughton was granted the exclusive right to build a weir across the Naponset River and a watermill for grinding corn, the first in the colony. To be the town miller was a lucrative franchise. He was also granted the monopoly of netting the alewives as they swarmed upstream, provided he sold them to the plantation for five shillings a thousand. These strategic rights no doubt contributed materially to the fortune which Stoughton was to leave to his son William.

Dorchester people, some of whom came from the little ports of Dorset and Devon, took to fishing in the Bay, especially for cod, a staple food, and mackerel, chiefly for bait. The first fishing stages at Cape Ann and Salem had been manned by Dorset fishermen and, according to a contemporary, Dorchester men were 'the first that set upon the trade of fishing in the Bay'. Seafaring was in the blood and those West Country ships had master mariners among their passengers. John Gallop of Mosterton became a renowned sea captain; Henry Way and John Rocket of the Bridport neighbourhood, Elias Parkman of Sidmouth, John Tilley and William Lovell were all skippers of trading shallops, and chose neighbouring lots with a common landing place at the mouth of the Naponset where they could moor their ships. It was a hazardous occupation. Henry Way, who had lost his son overboard from a spritsail yard on the voyage over, was murdered by Indians on a trading voyage to Narragansett Bay in the winter of 1632; John Tilly was to be cruelly killed by Indians on the Connecticut River in 1636 on a trading voyage in search of beaver.

These seafarers were a noted element in Dorchester's 'trading men' who intended their settlement should become a mercantile port. Among them was a group of Dorset merchant families. There was Bernard Capen and his family, prominent in Dorchester. Thomas Purchase, a Capen kinsman, and his brother-in-law George Way were both Dorchester merchants of standing and partners in a colonizing venture in Maine. Nicholas Upsall, another Dorset merchant, became the first tavern keeper in Dorchester on Massachusetts Bay; John Cogan, of the Chard merchant family and kinsman of Roger Ludlow's wife, had been an Exeter merchant; William Hill of Lyme Regis and Nathaniel Duncan of Exeter, who had married daughters of Ignatius Jourdain the Exeter merchant, both had mercantile interests.

Dorchester proved a disappointment to some of them. The channel to Old Harbour was poor and the landing difficult and, although the Naponset estuary served them better, Dorchester in the end lost out as a port to Boston and Charlestown. John Cogan moved to Boston to open the town's first retail shop. George Way took one look at Dorchester and left for England on the first ship and old Bernard Capen soon died. But most came to terms with their situation, combining farming with trade. Early bartering with the Mattapan and Naponset Indians of butter and cheese for corn and other Indian products led to buying and selling with wampum, the Indian currency, and to a quickening of the latent interest of these Englishmen in the trade in furs, especially beaver. Tilly was not the only Dorchester man to compete with the men of Plymouth and the Dutchmen from Manhattan in opening up trade with the Connecticut River Indians. Within three years of their landing at Mattapan, Dorchester was handling quantities of furs, some from that unknown but beckoning river.

Three years after the arrival of the settlers a visitor to Massachusetts Bay, one William Wood, described Dorchester as 'the greatest town in New England

... well wooded and watered; very good arable grounds and hay ground, fair cornfields and pleasant gardens ... In this plantation is a great many cattle, as kine, goats and swine. This plantation hath a reasonable harbour for ships.' Wood's *New England's Prospect* is as attractive a travel book as any promoter might wish; but what he wrote was confirmed by other chroniclers of this 'frontire towne', who also singled out her fair orchards and gardens, two small rivers and pleasant situation facing the Bay and stretching inland. By 'greatest town' Wood meant the largest in area of any town on the Bay, with limits stretching six miles south from Boston Neck and three miles west to the Roxbury limits. Another chronicler described its shape as a serpent whose head was the Dorchester peninsula, body the village itself, and tail the meadow and marshlands from Squantum upstream on both sides of the Naponset River towards the Great Blue Hills and what will become Dedham. Travelling to the sequestered parts of Dorchester could be tedious. One could go by boat round Fox Point to Naponset; but there was a spidery network of cart- and footways that reached out from the village street north and west with a trestle bridge over the brook to Roxbury and a branch up to Boston, and south to Stoughton's bridge over the Naponset with lanes into the grazing grounds of the necks.

This was a straggling community of houses on the rising ground or 'knapp' south of Old Harbour and adjacent to Rock Hill, which the settlers singled out for their fort with drakes to command harbour and landing. Neighbouring the street was the pond which fed the brook, the burial ground so urgently needed with its bier, and the pound for stray cattle, more important than a gaol, though the stocks were already in use. There was also a wolf trap.

The building round which all activity revolved was the meeting house, situated on the plain at the north end of the village near Old Harbour. It must have been erected before 1632 because in that year the minister, Mr Maverick, 'in drying a little powder . . . fired a small barrel' which singed his clothes and the thatch of the meeting house. It was not only a place of worship. The whole business of the plantation was transacted there. Surrounded by a palisade, it served as an arsenal for military stores and a refuge during Indian alerts. A sentry guarded it at night and every evening people carried in their plate and other valuables. It was a substantial building; an outside staircase and a loft were planned for it, and it was proposed to place a preservation order on all trees within 300 feet of the building. Here, every Sabbath and on lecture days during the week, the whole of Dorchester gathered to listen to the Scriptures expounded, to sermons and, once a month, to celebrate the Lord's Supper, in winter wrapped up against the cold and in summer shaded from the sun's heat. The meeting house was the only gracious experience in a week where life was hard and even those in authority had to compose their letters home, their introspective diaries, their accounts and court papers with writing tablets on their knees for want of a table or desk in the two- or three-roomed cottages which were their New England homes.

Two or three years after their landing, such was the rough but orderly life of Dorchester village. After the first brutal winters these Puritan families became attuned to the rhythms, pains and pleasures of their New England semi-wilderness. As Alice Earle wrote not too sentimentally:

> I see them walking along the little lanes and half-streets
> in which for many years bayberry and sweet-fern lingers
> in dusty fragrant clumps by the road side. I see [them]
> standing under the hot little cedar trees . . . not sober in
> sad color, but cheery in russet and scarlet; and sweetbrier
> and strawberries, bayberry and cedar smell sweetly and
> glow genially in that summer sunlight.

The polity of this little community was governed by a trinity of institutions.

The first was the church. The Dorchester people never lost sight of the fact that their *fons et origo* was that church, gathered in the New Hospital in Plymouth on the eve of *Mary and John*'s departure. Their overriding purpose was to establish in an uncorrupted wilderness the true Protestant Church of England after New Testament fashion. The church was paramount and, to begin with, church order was the order of the community. The first executive government of the plantation was the church, through its officers the two ministers, Warham and Maverick, and the two ruling elders, Rockwell and Gaylord, whose signatures, or two of them, were the authority for all town acts, from allocating home lots to watching and warding, imposing rates for maintaining roads and bridges and appointing citizens 'to view the pales'. The earliest records are lost but it seems likely that the ministers and elders had their decisions ratified by the freemen after Sunday meeting for worship or a weekday lecture as they had been wont to do in the vestry meetings of their West Country parishes. Such a practice was formalized on 8 October 1633 when it was agreed 'by the whole consent and vote of the Plantation' that there should be a general meeting of all the inhabitants on the Monday before the monthly meeting of the Massachusetts Court at eight o'clock in the morning in the meeting house summoned by the beating of a drum, 'there to settle (and set down) such orders as may tend to the general good ... and every man to be bound thereby without gain-saying or resistence.' It was agreed this meeting should select twelve men to conduct the day-to-day business until the next monthly meeting of the town and that the principle of majority votes should prevail. In this, Dorchester was very nearly the first town to institute that famous New England instrument of government, the town meeting (New Town, later Cambridge, preceded them by a year). Thereafter, the new 'select' men took over from the church officers the day-to-day administration of the town's affairs. They held office for only half a year; but most were renewed and the selectmen or townsmen quickly came to be the effective government of the town. Thus did the civic government of the town develop out of the business meeting of the church and under the shelter of the meeting house. The town meeting, unlike the English vestry or court leet, was to develop a robust, populistic character; but it retained a symbiotic relation to the church. Church and town, clerical and civic officers, were close, complementary authorities in a polity which came to be known as the New England Way.

But Dorchester was not independent. Like the other Bay townships it had come into being as the result of an organized emigration and settlement under the authority of the Massachusetts Bay Company; its legitimacy derived from that company's charter which had become by sleight of hand the constitution of the Bay colony. It was the Court of Assistants of the company–colony which authorized its name, set its boundaries, delegated to it such powers as granting lands and taxation, saw to its magistracy and appointed its town constable. In addition to church and civic government there was a third sphere which preoccupied our first generation of Dorchester settlers, namely defence.

The Puritans had no illusions about the paramount need to buckle on the sword as well as study the Bible, as they set about building their uncorrupted city on a hill. There was danger from Indians – memory of events like the Virginia massacre of 1622 was still vivid – and from European rivals Dutch and French, or just lawless pirates and freebooters. From the start these communities of Saints felt the need of support from professional soldiers, especially to provide the defensive works and artillery so fundamental to the warfare they knew. The Leyden Separatists first saw this and engaged Captain Miles Standish for the New Plymouth pilgrimage and each subsequent plantation followed suit by appointing such Low Country veterans as Captains Underhill, Patrick and Gardiner to be their seasoned professionals. Dorchester was fortunate in acquiring the services of Captain John Mason. Mason had arrived on the Bay as early as 1632 when he led a foray, with John Gallop as master of their shallop, against a nest of local pirates. He also had the principal hand in designing Boston's fortifications.

From the beginning, the militia was a central institution of plantation life. It was assumed as a matter of course that the means of defence should be the traditional English trainband: citizen soldiers, compulsorily mustered under amateur officers and trained by professional mustermasters hired for the purpose, usually Low Country veterans. The trainbands were organized at county level into regiments each commanded by a county grandee and consisting of six companies officered by a captain, a lieutenant, an ensign, two sergeants and three corporals. The companies were formed of three squadrons each and these were made up of files from adjacent villages and hamlets. Their officers were scions of the local gentry who exercised the same kind of authority in the militia as their families did as justices in local government, under the command of the lord lieutenant and his deputies. There were local training days for drill in weaponry and hand-to-hand fighting, and every summer a general muster of all regiments in the county. The traditional weapon was the pike, though 'trailing a pike' was by no means universal and musters saw a miscellany of weapons including the billhooks of husbandmen and cotters. For firepower, the bow had all but disappeared, giving place to the matchlock musket. The infantry company under the early Stuarts consisted of pikemen and musketeers; though muskets were cumbersome and indeed dangerous to deploy, the proportion of them increased as their fire power and range improved.

One of the county units was usually a regiment of horse, the militia's elite, a tradition going back dimly to knight service. Recruited from the gentry and superior yeomanry, they provided their own horses, accoutrements and weapons. A gentleman's estate determined the number he was expected to contribute in terms of equipped horsemen. Originally cuirassiers, armed with long sword and pistols, corselet and helmet, whose function was to attack the enemy's horse, they were already being supplemented by arquebusiers, mounted infantry armed with a heavy bore gun but lightly armoured for fast movement. They were to be succeeded by the caribiniers, the light cavalry of Prince Rupert and Oliver Cromwell and predecessors of the dragoons.

Within a year of their arrival, the Court of Assistants were already laying down the basis of a militia system for the whole colony on the English model. Dorchester, like the other towns, had its own company of trainbands consisting of all able-bodied men between sixteen and sixty, trained by its own professional mustermaster, Captain Mason, and officered on much the same lines as the militia companies they were used to in Somerset and Dorset by recruits from the local equivalent of gentry and yeomanry. The company captain was Israel Stoughton who had some military experience and was overseer of fort and ordnance. He would command a force against the Pequots and return to England to serve in the New Model Army. Officers were elected from among the freemen in their company, subject only to confirmation by the colony court. This innovation scandalized the old Low Country professionals and, for a time, was rescinded; but it became accepted practice in those pioneer communities of attenuated hierarchy. In time these town trainbands, each with its own colours, were grouped into three regiments. Dorchester, being the oldest town, was the senior company in the Suffolk County Regiment. The regimental officers, like those in the English shires, were grandees; Governor Winthrop himself was Colonel and the deputy governor, Thomas Dudley, Lieutenant Colonel, of the Suffolk Regiment.

There were training days once a month, for Dorchester on a Friday, with stiff fines for absence, though persons of consequence such as magistrate Ludlow, deacons Rockwell and Gaylord and sea captain Parkman were exempt. In military training as well as organization the settlers transplanted their English practices. They made few concessions to the exigencies of wilderness warfare. Although they did accept that the twelve-foot pike was hopelessly inappropriate to local circumstances they continued to rely on the whole paraphernalia of musketry. Each private soldier carried a heavy matchlock musket with a four-foot barrel and its forked rest, a bandolier of cartridges and powder horn, and wore a cotton-padded corselet as protection against arrows, the only concession to local conditions. Drill was in accordance with the copy books they had brought with them. Musketeers carried their length of slow-burning match in their hand, kept a few bullets in their mouth and a priming iron in case the bullet did not fit the barrel. They fired by ranks, wheeling off to reload. The Indian neighbours who observed them would have found their drilling ludicrous, had they not been in awe of their firepower.

These duties were not necessarily as unpopular as they had been in the West Country. Where Indians were hostile, military training was seen to be relevant. For some, training days were a frustrating distraction from building and planting, but for others, a tonic diversion making for *bonhomie* and a literal *esprit de corps* which was an antidote to daily farm chores and soul-searching hours in the meeting house. It was also a useful secular occasion when private citizen soldiers could air informally matters which they might be inhibited from raising at town or church meeting, such as the level of the minister's salary for the coming year. The establishment recognized this. Ministers might disapprove of the rum or hard cider drunk on training days, but they thought it politic merely to open the exercises with a prayer. The elite quality of the militia was enhanced by the institution of a troop of horse on the English model, recruited from volunteers of standing, able to provide horses and accoutrements, and equivalent to London's Honourable Artillery Company, composed of 'divers gentlemen and others, out of their care for the public weal and safety by the advancement of the military art and exercise of arms'. They were given the privilege of choosing their officers, drawing up their own by-laws and levying fines, and received a grant of 1000 acres of land to provide an 'artillery garden', or exercise range, on the London model.

The militia was a powerful third force, a counterpoise to the New England Way. More than a century later, a fourth generation Bostonian of note, John Adams, was to describe training day, along with meeting house, town meeting and school, as one of the four pillars of New England.

Some thirty families and twenty bachelors, 140 men, women and children in all, had landed at Mattapan from the *Mary and John* in 1630. During the next five years an average of twenty ships a year arrived from England, each carrying up to 200 passengers; and by 1635 the population of Massachusetts Bay had swelled dramatically to upwards of 8000 while the number of heads of families and individuals who had been granted lands by the town of Dorchester had risen to just over 130. Although the origins of most of the later arrivals are not known, many were from the West Country, like the eighty passengers on the Weymouth ship of 1633 which brought those Dorchester merchant families; there was the ship which brought the Newberrys and Humphreys the following year, and the Weymouth ship of March 1635 which brought the Hull colony. Of those 130 heads of families and individuals of 1635, fifty-seven, or 43.5 per cent, are known to have been of West Country origin, a high proportion considering the number whose origins are unknown. Moreover, the West Country element provided the inner core of the community. Of eighty-four Dorchester citizens elected freemen, forty were from the West Country; four out of five of the constables were West Countrymen – three from Dorset, one from Somerset – as were a majority of the selectmen; and the landholdings of West Countrymen were more substantial than the average. Dorchester continued to be a predominantly West Country town, and John White's people remained a kind of oligarchy. They also clung to their own personal friendships and neighbourliness. West Country people seemed to cluster to the north end of the village and, except for the seafarers, to have lots on the Roxbury bounds rather than Naponset. It was not fortuitous that neighbours from the Brit Valley, like the Hosfords and Denslows, or Dorchester merchants such as the Cogans, Duncans and Ways were granted both home lots and meadow next to one another.

Thus, five years after that first landing, the population of Dorchester, despite deaths from disease and hardship and defections by the faint-hearted back to England, increased more than fourfold. The demand for foodstuffs exerted pressure on the land. Fertile land, even in a plantation as extensive as Dorchester, was not unlimited and successive divisions of lots were beginning to press on the remaining commons. At this time the town resolved that no home lots henceforth granted should carry rights of common and young Roger Clap was instructed to investigate 'what marsh or meadow ground is not yet allotted out'. It may be that the existing land cleared for tillage, often old Indian fields, was becoming exhausted.

The increase in livestock was even greater. Those first few wasting cattle, the sustenance of which had been the chief motive for 'setting down' at Mattapan, had multiplied and with those four breeding bulls had become '450 cows and other cattle of that kind'. This was particularly worrying for a rural economy so dependent on cattle raising which demanded from two to ten times as much land as tillage; and raising cattle for the butcher, to feed the rapid immigrant influx and to ship out salted to the West Indies, had become profitable and more congenial than primitive subsistence farming to those West Country people. As early as 1634 the people of New Town were complaining of 'want of accommodation for their cattle' and no doubt Dorchester people felt the same. John Winthrop recorded that 'all towns in the Bay began to be much straightened' especially 'because of their cattle being so much increased'.

As Winthrop also hinted, there was a general unease in all the Bay towns because of 'their own nearness to one another', an ironic comment from the man who had designed a single colony and had only reluctantly accepted the inevitability of a scattering of half a dozen townships on the Bay.

According to another of his contemporaries, Edward Johnson, 'some took dislike to every little matter; the ploughable plains were too dry and sandy for them and the rocky places, although more fruitful, yet to eat their bread with toil of hand and hoe they deemed it insupportable.'

About that time, however, the inhabitants of Massachusetts Bay heard tell of a possible place to settle 100 miles or more to the west which might answer their need for space and pasture. It was, as Edward Johnson recorded, 'a very fertile plain upon the river of Conectico, low land and well stored with meadow . . . This people, seeing that tillage went but little on, resolved to remove and breed up store of cattle, which were then at 8 and 20 pound a cow or near upon'.

Intelligence of the Connecticut or Great River had been filtering through to the Bay for some time. In 1631 a deputation of Indians had tried to interest Governor Winthrop and Governor Bradford of Plymouth in their river as a counterpoise to their threatening Pequot enemies. Meanwhile the Dutch had set up a trading post on the Connecticut's west bank about sixty miles upstream, forestalling the Plymouth people who sent their own expedition up the river in 1631. After a confrontation with the Dutch which just stopped short of shots being fired, the Plymouth party set up their own trading post a mile above, on a point of the river which was to become Dorchester, then Windsor. More arresting for the Dorchester people was intelligence learned from Governor Winthrop's barque *Blessing of the Bay* back from a trading voyage to the mouth of the Connecticut, and from a seasoned old Indian trader, John Oldham, who returned from an overland trek to the upper Connecticut with reports of lush meadows stretching for miles along the river's bank, with samples of black lead from an Indian mine and, specially intriguing to men of west Dorset, good quality hemp. Above all, there was evidence of valuable furs, especially beaver, which the Indians brought down river from its remote, uncharted headwaters, said to be a great and sacred lake far away in the northern wilderness.

The idea of pulling up stumps and migrating to the Connecticut was much talked of in the Bay towns. It was highly controversial; and powerful voices were raised against it: the Indians were hostile, the Dutch menacing, Plymouth had pre-empted a trading post, the river was a white elephant because the sandbar at its mouth prevented ocean-going ships sailing upstream, the journey overland was treacherous with unknown paths and natural hazards, and droving cattle there would be foolhardy. But, more formidable, the whole establishment of Massachusetts Bay Colony was

96

against it. The Governor and his Assistants had all the prudent instincts of a governing class. The Bay, though growing fast, was still small, weak and exposed. Winthrop had been unhappy about the original dispersal willy-nilly into distinct settlements; in the interests of the future health of the colony the people of Massachusetts Bay should stay together in order to face a potentially hostile world which included Indians, Dutch, possibly French, and the English Crown which could raise awkward questions about the legitimacy not only of an outlying settlement but of the Bay's charter itself. In short, dispersal would weaken Boston and stretch her resources. If there was need for *Lebensraum* let land-hungry settlers move a mile or so up the Merrimac or Naponset to colonize a nearby village within Massachusetts Bay. The clergy were also uneasy. Puritan orthodoxy demanded that the pure milk of the Word be cherished and deviations stamped upon. Although each of the plantation churches was a separate congregation, they were intimately connected; their ministers met once a fortnight to concert matters of order and doctrine and some were apprehensive that dispersal would encourage deviation, a falling away and weakening of spiritual and moral discipline.

So the argument went to and fro in the townships and in the Court of Assistants during 1634 and early 1635. The bell-wether was New Town whose petition to the court for leave to depart was refused once; but in the end, and for reasons beyond this narrative and bound up with the powerful personality and standing of Thomas Hooker, resistance was overcome and permission was granted to emigrant goups first in New Town, then Watertown and Dorchester, to depart for the Connecticut in the summer of 1635.

This second swarming was not lightly undertaken; but the result of much soul searching, and the practical problems were immense. In Dorchester's case the upheaval was phenomenal. Of the 170 or so male inhabitants in 1635, about fifty-six sold out to newcomers and joined the exodus to the Connecticut. The process, which took two seasons, could not have taken place without the would-be migrant's ability to dispose of his property. Fortunately, 1635 proved a good season for new immigrants to the Bay and Dorchester people had little difficulty in selling their land and improvements to incomers, in particular to the *James*'s company from Lancashire under the Rev. Richard Mather, who were to provide an essential blood transfusion to a Dorchester church weakened by the departure of its pastor and most of his flock. Thus occurred perhaps the first example of that classic process so characteristic of America's shifting frontier.

Beyond this, who went and who stayed depended on family circumstances, economic incentive and individual temperament, and on the influence of a few in positions of leadership. Four men stand out as leaders of the enterprise: Roger Ludlow, Thomas Newberry, Henry Wolcott and Captain John Mason. These were the chief notables of Dorchester. Apart from Mason the soldier, all were of the gentry, and substantial Dorchester landholders. Alas, Mr Newberry, of Marshwood Vale, Dorset, like Mr Rossiter before him, died before he could make the journey, leaving his large family to make it without him; but the others were the stalwart figures in the operation.

Their principal was Roger Ludlow and the enterprise owed much to his leadership. He had been deputy to Thomas Dudley as Governor of the Bay; but his overbearing and headstrong conduct had so offended his peers that he was not re-elected to that office or indeed to the magistracy in 1635, and he became disaffected. Whereas in office he had been against the Connecticut enterprise, now he was a principal, and effective, advocate. As an early chronicler, J. G. Palfrey, wrote: 'If motives . . . of jealousy and envy of people in authority in Boston . . . had weight with any of the projectors they are more likely to have influenced Ludlow of Dorchester whose ambitious and uneasy temper was sufficiently evinced before and after his departure.' And another, William Hubbard, writing within living memory, probably had him in mind when he wrote: 'there was an impulsive cause that did more secretly and powerfully drive on the business. Some men do not well like, at least cannot well bear, to be opposed in their judgments and notions, and hence were they not unwilling to remove from under the power, as well as out of the bounds of the Massachusetts. Nature doth not allow two suns in one firmament, and some spirits can as ill bear an equal as others a superior.' He may have been wilful and cantankerous, but the man who had bought and commissioned *Mary and John* and had decided on Dorchester as the place of settlement was just the kind of forceful leader that such an enterprise required.

More difficult to assess is the role of the minister, John Warham. His colleague John Maverick was against the move; but the old man died, much lamented, on 3 March 1636 and Warham, on his own, was thought to have been swayed by the majority of his congregation who were in favour. Warham was a deeply religious man, much respected and indeed revered. His leadership was as essential to the Dorchester exodus as that of Thomas Hooker was for that from New Town.

All these notables, save Captain Mason whose origin is not known, were

West Countrymen. Indeed the Dorchester exodus was largely a West Country affair. Of fifty-four heads of families who opted for Connecticut and who can be identified, forty were West Country folk and twenty-six of these, including Warham, Ludlow and Wolcott, had crossed the Atlantic in the *Mary and John* five years before. They were, indeed, the greater part of that ship's company. Dorchester, so predominantly West Country, stood out in that Massachusetts Bay community which was overwhelmingly East Anglian. Dorchester was different: softer in speech, slower in tempo, and distinct in her rural habits and allegiances and, also, in the temper of her religion. John White's recruits were nothing like as far along the road to Separatism as the keen Independents of Suffolk, Essex and Lincolnshire. Though Puritan, they still professed and were deeply committed to the Church of, and in, England; one suspects they felt no particular neighbourliness to Roxbury, Charlestown or especially to Winthrop's bossy Boston and for them swarming to the Connecticut may have come as a release.

CHAPTER 5: ROGER LUDLOW AND THE TREK TO THE CONNECTICUT 1635–36

O N THE EVENING OF 6 MAY 1635 ROGER LUDLOW MUST HAVE BEEN ANGRY and frustrated. At the court of election that day in New Town he who had been deputy governor of the colony for the past year had failed in his bid to succeed Thomas Dudley as governor; worse, he, the first assistant to arrive on the Bay in 1630 and appointed a justice of the peace at the very first session of the General Court – the same day as Winthrop himself – had been defeated in the election by an outsider who had been in the Bay less than two years; worst of all, Ludlow, by his intemperate behaviour, had so offended his colleagues over the question of electing Assistants that they had not even renewed him as magistrate, and when he had offered his resignation as overseer of the Castle Island fortifications the court had not only accepted it promptly but followed it up by instituting an inquiry into his handling of funds as treasurer of the works and removing him from the Commission for Martial Discipline. He had clearly made an enemy of John Haynes, the new Governor – he was to call him his 'evil genius' – and he could count on little sympathy from John Winthrop, especially after his part, along with his Dorchester neighbour Israel Stoughton, in unseating Winthrop from the governorship the previous year. For Roger Ludlow, though a strong and able leader, was also an arrogant, overbearing and opinionated man who did not endear himself to those who crossed him. One of them, a Captain Stone, who challenged his magisterial authority and was subsequently fined for it, called Ludlow 'a Just Ass', a crude caricature no doubt but one not without some element of truth. More important, as that same Israel Stoughton reported: 'Now he is neither Governor nor Assistant . . . and I question whether he will ever be Magistrate more, for many have taken great offence at him . . . They are both wise and godly men that are offended: and not many much sorry.'

It was time for him to take stock and consider his future. At the age of forty-five, with a family of six, he was no longer young and he had come a long way, both in time and space, from his comfortable West Country upbringing, exercising his manifest talents in pursuit of an adventurous public career.

The Ludlows were a family of rank and estates in Wiltshire, regularly representing their county in Parliament. They were also lawyers, members of the Inner Temple. Roger, the eldest son of Thomas Ludlow, was born and bred on the family estate at Maiden Bradley on the Somerset border. In 1610 at the age of twenty he was sent to Balliol College, Oxford for two years before moving on, in the family tradition, to the Inner Temple to learn the law. But he was no Justice Shallow to return to the delights of country life. He seems to have practised law in London to good effect and his legal and administrative talents drove him to a public career. As we shall see, his knowledge, particularly of constitutional practice, was to serve him in good stead in colonial affairs. The Ludlows also had strong Puritan affinities. One of Roger's cousins was to become prominent in the Long Parliament as an extreme opponent of the Crown and another, the famous Edmund, would be one of Cromwell's lieutenant generals and a judge at Charles I's trial. It seems probable that like many of the intelligentsia of his generation Roger also had a Puritan cast of mind and moved in those mercantile and professional circles in the City of London, with its aristocratic connections, which provided so much of the backing for the colonizing of New England. With such a background and his ambition, energy and restless temper, it was hardly surprising that he became an Assistant and stockholder of the Massachusetts Bay Company.

He also kept his West Country roots. Maiden Bradley is almost literally a stone's throw from that part of Somerset which John White was trawling for recruits to his New England venture. The next village across the Somerset border is Batcombe whose parson was Richard Bernard, that contemporary and friend of John White who was such an effective Puritan preacher and tractarian. It may be that Bernard was one of White's talent spotters and identified this young scion of the neighbouring gentry as ripe for his purpose. Ludlow courted and married a Somerset girl, Mary, daughter of Philobert Cogan of Chard, and thereby became connected with that group of mercantile families of Lyme and Dorchester who went to New England. Mary Ludlow's sister Elizabeth also found her way to the Bay and, as a widow, married John Endicott, the Governor of Salem. (At the same meeting of the Massachusetts court which virtually stripped Ludlow of his offices, brother-in-law Endicott was also censured and 'disabled from office' for a year on account of a headstrong act of his own. With his sword he had cut out the cross of St George from the ensign carried by the Salem trainband because it was a papist symbol, to the embarrassment of the authorities who were anxious not to offend the Crown of England gratuitously.) Roger Ludlow, therefore, had a strong West Country kinship with well-established and Puritan-minded families in Somerset and Dorset. We may plausibly see the hand of John White in his recruitment to the cause.

At any rate, at a meeting of the General Court of the Massachusetts Bay Company held in Thomas Goffe's house at the corner of Philpot Lane in London on 10 February 1630, Roger Ludlow was sworn in as an Assistant and thus joined John Humphrey the deputy governor, John Endicott and Edward Rossiter in representing John White's West Country interest on the court. This was only some five weeks before *Mary and John* set sail and the affluent Ludlow may have already become sufficiently involved in the West Country plans to have been persuaded both to buy the ship for the enterprise and that his election as an assistant recognized White's choice of him to lead the West Country element in the great migration of 1630. Of his West Country colleagues, John Endicott was already in post at Salem, John Humphrey was to defer his departure to New England for another three years and Edward Rossiter was ineffective, so Ludlow was the obvious choice to lead the *Mary and John* expedition.

Now that his position of leadership in the Bay had been so directly and humiliatingly challenged, it was natural that he should return to the idea of migrating to the Connecticut River. It did not take him long to make up his mind. In authority, he had been against the project for those good establishment reasons. As deputy governor he had dismissed that proposal from the emissary of an Indian sachem on the Connecticut River offering to the English rights and privileges if they would establish a settlement there; but now that he saw himself in opposition, he was ready to embrace this new opportunity. It is doubtful whether in going for Connecticut he had any deep religious concern for a new spiritual uprooting such as no doubt had Thomas Hooker (though even for him there may well also have been some extra motivation provided by his personality clash with John Cotton). He may in fact have had an anti-clerical motive: he is known to have become hostile to the theocratic practice in Massachusetts of limiting the freemanship to church members – a limitation he was to abolish in his new colony. What called Ludlow to the Connecticut was the opportunity to exploit the God-given natural resources of the wilderness and to foster a pioneer community more nearly after his own heart and without the stiff-necked authority of Winthrop's Boston.

He lost no time. He promptly recruited a party of twelve Dorchester men to explore the Connecticut River to find a suitable place for a new Dorchester. Then a signal event took place which promptly created a sense of urgency and hurried them on their way. On 16 June there arrived in Boston harbour from England a barque, *Christian*, with those twenty servants of Sir Richard Saltonstall led by one Francis Stiles who had a commission to take up land on the Connecticut under Lord Warwick's patent.

This was a jolting reminder that settling on the Great River might be complicated by prior rights under the Crown. It was crucial that the Ludlow expedition should establish a *de facto* right for Dorchester by taking possession of a suitable site there before the Stiles party should arrive. The latter were therefore delayed on purpose at the Bay for some ten days, by entertainment and dilatoriness in procuring for them a sloop to sail round the coast, in order that Ludlow should have time to reach the Connecticut beforehand by way of the overland trail. This ruse was successful.

And so Ludlow and his party hurriedly set out into the forest which, for all they knew, stretched unbroken the hundred miles or so west to the Connecticut River. For them, as for all the English, that forest was undifferentiated wilderness. They had not yet acquired an eye to see that they were journeying through a sophisticated Indian habitat. Had they but understood it, this comprised a highly organized rural economy which the tribes of southern New England managed as intelligently and as fittingly for their purposes as the English managed the rural economy of their Dorset countryside.

The Indians enjoyed natural resources in abundant variety: forest, savannah and river-meadows for wild produce, crops and game; lakes, rivers and seashores for fish. Theirs was an extensive economy *par excellence*, except that they managed it within well-defined principles of husbandry and territorial limits. Their farming was strictly arable

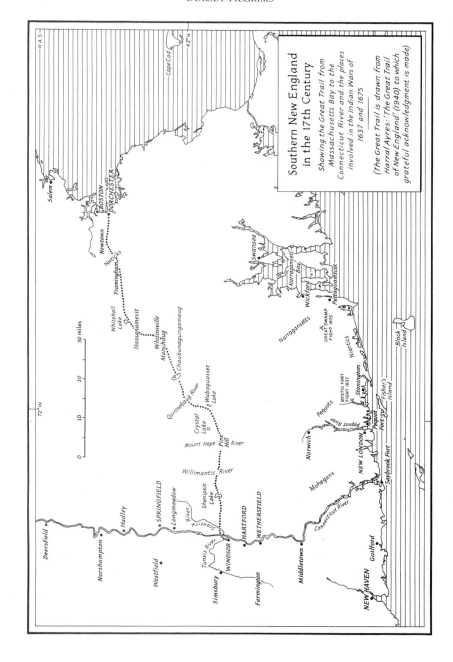

Southern New England
in the 17th Century

Showing the Great Trail from
Massachusetts Bay to the
Connecticut River and the places
involved in the Indian Wars of
1637 and 1675

(The Great Trail is drawn from
Harral Ayres: 'The Great Trail
of New England' (1940) to which
grateful acknowledgment is made)

(domesticated livestock were unknown until the English came), and their grain crop limited to maize which they cultivated with a variety of vegetables, especially beans and squashes. These crops were raised by the squaws in roughly cleared patches of ground round tree stumps, rather than in fields in the European sense, and cultivated with mattock and hoe. When a field eventually wore out, they would fold up their wigwams and move their village to other, more fertile ground.

The Indians were peripatetic, not only in the long term as they shifted their tilling fields, but seasonally as they pursued the other great strength of their economy: harvesting the wild berries and plants of the forest and, above all, hunting game. Forest management was an essential function of their economy. The hardwoods, oaks, chestnut and hickory, and hemlock and pine, were a rich resource in themselves and as a shelter for a variety of game, from bear, moose and deer to jack rabbits which the Indians stalked and hunted. They periodically set fire to the underbrush to make it easier to stalk their quarry and to encourage new growth to feed the game. As a result the forest, far from being a tangled wilderness, was for the most part a range of great trees with a clear undergrowth, a wild native parkland. In due season the Indian males would be on the move in search of game; and at other times the whole village would move to their fishing grounds, especially during the spring spawning runs at river rapids and in summer to the seashore, times of religious celebration. The farming year was in fact an ordered, seasonal rhythm from function to function and from place to place. Their right to the land was not a matter of ownership – either individual or corporate – as in Europe, but of access to its fruits.

If the Indians were peripatetic, they were not nomad. Their tribal units exerted a suzerainty over a recognized territorial area beyond which poaching was discouraged by their tribal neighbours. At first the Ludlow party's trek lay through the territory of the Massachusetts Indians, the eastern boundary of which was Massachusetts Bay itself. This then gave place successively to the territories of the Nipmucks, the Mohegans and the so-called 'river Indians' of the Connecticut River valley.

It was thus that the Ludlow party, trekking through this forested country by way of trails linking the Indian villages, finally emerged towards the end of June at the Great River, at a place some sixty miles from its mouth, on the west bank, called by the local Indians Matianuck. Here, where a tributary river, the Tunxis, joined the Connecticut, Plymouth Colony had established their trading post; and here the party were provisioned and entertained for ten days by the factor in charge, Jonathan Brewster, before leaving to prospect for a settlement. Brewster found them cagey about their intentions. In fact, Ludlow had decided that the only site in the vicinity suitable for their settlement was a great stretch of river-meadow and bluff just above the Plymouth trading post. This was a favourite resort of the river Indians. It was fertile in planting fields and the shoals of the Great River upstream were not only famous for fishing festivals, for salmon spearing and netting shad, but had strategic importance. In low water they were the Indians' first fording place up the Connecticut, the only one for many miles, and the principal trails converged on the river here. No wonder that on its east bank was the fortified headquarters of the local river tribe, the Podunks; no wonder, too, that Ludlow determined to have Matianuck for his new Dorchester. The fact that the right to the land was claimed not only by Saltonstall but by their hosts, Plymouth Colony, was brushed aside.

Meanwhile, word of Ludlow's initiative had gone round the Bay and there arrived almost daily on the river a trickle of pioneers to join the party in staking out claims to land at Matianuck. They were followed during the course of the summer by an organized group of over sixty people, men, women and 'little children', mostly from Dorchester though a few were from New Town and Watertown. Some may have sailed with the bulk supplies round by sea and upriver; but most bravely set out in caravan driving their cows, horses and swine by the Indian trails. The journey took them about a fortnight and, according to Winthrop who reported their arrival at the river in his diary for 15 October, it was 'tedious and difficult' even though they were doubtless helped on their way by friendly Indians. As summer faded into fall, this score or so of Dorchester families once again set about staking out home lots and erecting rude bivouacs just as they had done at Mattapan five years before; but this time not at the edge of a salt-water bay but on a bank above the rich meadows of a majestic river.

Unfortunately, as with their first settlement, the enterprise was hurried and improvised. They had left it too late in the season and winter set in early and severely that year. By 15 November the Connecticut was frozen solid and the encampment, which depended on imported supplies, was short of food; worse, two supply ships had not arrived and could not be expected before the spring thaw. Overnight the situation had become desperate. One may imagine the urgent council of war with Ludlow facing the grim facts in his decisive way. If they were not to starve, there was nothing for it but to evacuate everybody save a few to look after the cattle, and retreat to the Bay. How was this to be done? It was impractical for most of the party, especially women and children, to trek back overland through the ice-bound wilderness. A better bet would be to travel the sixty miles downstream to the river mouth in the hope of meeting one of the supply vessels on its way up. This they did, struggling down the icy wastes of the river, mile after dreary mile, with only such help as the river Indians could give from their winter quarters, and with no sign of Englishmen. But suddenly, when they came within twenty miles of the Sound, they saw a ship, not their supply barque but, unexpectedly, *Rebecca*, a sloop built on the Bay the year before and on a trading voyage up the Connecticut. Alas, she was frozen in the ice; but she did provide shelter and emergency food. Thanks to Divine Providence, there came a slight thaw and a 'small rain' which set the vessel free and drifting down to the estuary. But they were not yet out of trouble. They drifted on to the sandbank across the river mouth and *Rebecca* was fast again. There was nothing for it but to unload her to reduce her weight. This floated her off and, after laboriously reloading, she sailed with her much relieved human cargo for Massachusetts Bay where she anchored five days later, 'which', wrote Winthrop, 'was a great mercy of God, for otherwise they had all perished with famine, as some did.'

Not all followed that escape route. Having organized the departure of the party downstream, Ludlow, with his original company of twelve, next day set out for the Bay overland. It was hard going and it cost the life of one who drowned under the ice. They had limited rations and would have starved to death had they not run across an Indian wigwam. They arrived at the Bay eleven days later, on 26 November. As for the party they had left behind on the river, their food quickly ran out and they were reduced to eating acorns, malt and grains. Most of the cattle died of starvation for lack of fodder, a loss estimated at nearly £200. Curiously, cattle that had arrived late in the summer and had been left to fend for themselves on the east bank survived 'very well all winter without any hay'.

On their return to Dorchester that bleak, snow-bound December the refugees found the situation confused and dismaying. A new influx of immigrants late the previous summer, principally the Mathers and their company, had had to be housed and the settlement was overcrowded. The returning Connecticut party's story of death, hardship and loss of cattle induced a mood of pessimism and defeat. The families of those left behind at Matianuck grieved over their possible fate. The scepticism of doubters was confirmed and many others must have been having second thoughts: none of the town's leading figures had followed Ludlow in his precipitous lunge across to the Connecticut. Thomas Newberry had died in the summer; Henry Wolcott, Thomas Stoughton, even Captain Mason had remained in Dorchester and several people, such as William Hill, George Hull and William Hunnum, all of whom would end up in Connecticut, were still taking out grants of meadowland that winter, which does not suggest an immediate intention of leaving Dorchester. John Maverick was against the whole business.

However, the underlying imperatives pushed them on. There was simply not enough land in Dorchester nor even, with the new immigrants, enough housing. Plans were far advanced for disposing of home lots and chattels to the newcomers; and with the quickening of spring, the Connecticut beckoned once again. Those who had returned from the exploring party could be eloquent about Matianuck's fertile river-meadows and forest uplands, the haven of the Tunxis or Rivulet as they called it, and the Great River, waterway for trade in furs and forest products. There was the caretaker party to be relieved and hillside dugouts to be converted into homesteads. After all, most of them had done it all once before and had learned from bitter experience the importance of starting early enough in the season to grow and catch food and to cut timber for fuel and house-frames in good time for winter. So with spring weather their confidence returned and plans were made for a full-scale emigration. As that early chronicler Benjamin Trumbull put it: 'As soon as the spring advanced, and the travelling would permit, the hardy men began to return from the Massachusetts to their habitations on the river. No sooner were buds, leaves and grass so grown that cattle could live in the woods, and obstructions removed from the river so that vessels could go up with provisions and furniture, than the people began to return in large companies to Connecticut.' On 3 March old Mr Maverick conveniently, if lamentably, died; and John Warham was free to lead his flock westwards into the wilderness.

The hegira from Dorchester to Matianuck took place in the spring and early summer of 1636. The Indian trails were not cart tracks and bulk supplies had to be shipped round by sea. This was easier now that there was a settlement with a landing place and seamen knew more about navigating the Connecticut's estuary and the many shoals and sandbanks on the way upstream to the mouth of the Rivulet. Many settlers, especially women and children, voyaged by water and references to 'the coming up of our next pinnace' and 'up here' indicate an up-and-downstream orientation. But ships were few, holds limited and freights dear. It cost 45 shillings a ton for freight from the Bay to the upper Connecticut that year.

So most people went overland by forest trails. Some of the 'principal gentlemen' made the journey early. The indefatigable Ludlow was already on the river by the end of April, along with William Phelps and Henry Wolcott. Warham arrived by July but left his family behind until a decent home could be prepared for them. The Dorchester migration is less well documented than its sister expedition, led by Thomas Hooker from New Town to Suckiaug, but the two must have been similar. They were orderly affairs, with families, bachelors and servants travelling in groups if not in a single company, carrying what they could by pack-horse and driving their livestock before them. Only a rare and privileged lady like Mrs Hooker, the minister's wife in the other party who was seriously ill, was carried in a litter. Assuming a dry spring, before heat and mosquitoes, and an orderly convoy, well provisioned and with cows for milking, the journey need not prove too arduous or result in special hardship. People and animals could travel unimpeded and cattle graze on the young green shoots. The journey was made easier and more pleasant because it lay mostly along a chain of Indian villages at springs, ponds, lakes and fords which were staging camps of hospitality.

The Dorchester caravan set out on a road already familiar to some of them by way of Roxbury and Muddy River, past New Town, then nine or so miles to the falls of the Charles River and then twenty more through the Natik country to the ancient lake and beaver dam at what is now South Framingham; thence, by way of Magunko Hill, 'a place of great trees', they came to Whitehall Lake, set in a forest of gigantic oaks where the pioneers 'worshipped in Nature's great cathedral' (present-day Hopkinton). Another day would take them over the ford of the river where Nipmucks had their royal seat of Hassanamesit (modern Farnumsville), a 'bating place of note for early travellers'. Westward the country became hilly and wilder. The trail brought them by way of two lakes, Whitinsville and Manchaug, to their welcome half-way mark. This was a sacred Indian reserve called Chaubunagungamaug, or 'Great Pond', a remote, peaceful and beautiful lake, bordered by a forest of Douglas fir where the Nipmucks kept their sacred rites (modern Webster). They looked on it as a sort of Elysian Fields, the abode of the Great Spirit and their departed ancestors. Then, after fording yet another river, the Quinnebaug, they struggled over to Wabaquasset Lake at whose waters the Indians were wont to congregate at the time of the spring planting (modern Woodstock). These Indians were reputed to be especially friendly to the English because they had sent corn to the Bay to relieve them during that first starving winter of 1630. Thence by way of Crystal Lake and the Pochaug River, the travellers found themselves in the attractive oak and chestnut country of Mount Hope Valley at a place which they called Pine Hill because of its isolated pine landmark. Thereafter there remained only one sizeable river to be forded, that of the Willimantic, in country which again was favourite Indian fishing and hunting ground. Finally, there were eighteen or so miles still to travel by way of Shenipsit Lake until that eagerly awaited moment when, after a journey of about three weeks and ninety-two miles, the Dorchester company emerged from green, dappled forest into bright sunlight, and, beyond, the expanse of the great river of the Connecticut. There, on its opposite bank, they could make out the broad stretch of meadowland which was to be their home. It must have been an awe-inspiring sight, a second initiation into the American wilderness; and, Puritans as most of them were, they doubtless thanked God for it at the water's edge. As one chronicler wrote, fulsomely but evocatively:

> Their God gave them courage. With the whipporwill's call at night came the crude blessings of the camp and the bathing of tired feet in refreshing waters. The livestock sought pasture while guards watched. From the campfire arose the aroma of frying fish or of game killed in the forest. They retired on a woodland couch while the wild animals cried in the night and the stars flashed messages from the heavens where their God reigned.

After the end of April when those first swallows of spring, Ludlow, Phelps, and Wolcott, relieved the miserable winter caretakers on the river, there began to arrive from the Bay a swelling company of emigrant families to settle first at Matianuck then, with Thomas Hooker and his party, at the old Dutch fort (to become first New Town, then Hartford) ten miles downstream, and some further down still at Pyquag (to become Wethersfield). By 7 June the Dorchester people were already sufficiently thick on the ground, eager to proclaim their origins and confident of their future to name their settlement once again Dorchester, after their patriarch.

The encampment was still primitive. At first they had to shelter in the dugout shanties on the 'Sandy Bank' which bounded the river-meadows. Most of their heavy supplies were lost in a sloop wrecked on its way from the Bay; but they began to construct their first wooden houses and pace out their home lots on the western brow of 'Great Meadow', and in an inner cluster of homes round a village green at the bend of the Rivulet before it joined the Great River. After the gruelling experience of the previous fall they were conscious of working against time and used every hour of daylight to clear their plots, plant corn and cut timber. Some built their homes in the meadow too near the river, were to be flooded out and would have to start again on higher ground.

By the close of that season, as a result of formidable effort and despite the hazards of moving families and livestock, tools and possessions all that way from the Bay, the new plantation was securely established. Numbers are hard to assess. The earliest chronicler writing over a century later estimated the population of the river plantations at the end of 1636 as about 800 souls in 160 to 170 families, with up to ninety unattached men, either soldiers or other bachelors or servants. For Matianuck, now Dorchester, this would mean fifty or so families of some 235 souls, together with another thirty or so unattached men. The great majority came from Dorchester-on-the-Bay. Of 131 heads of families or individuals who had been granted land at Dorchester (deducting three who had died), fifty-four, with their families, undertook that journey to Matianuck to become original settlers, that is, about 40 per cent of the Dorchester they had left. These fifty-four Dorchester men were the hard core of the new settlement. Moreover, that core belonged disproportionately to the original company from the West Country. Of the fifty-four heads of families, forty, or 74 per cent, had been born and bred in Dorset, Somerset or Devon; and of these about thirty-five, or 65 per cent, had crossed the Atlantic on *Mary and John* or one of John White's associated ships. His recruits were proving a persistently cohesive group, no longer just a ship's company but a pioneer community bound intimately together by a common folk memory and experience of hardships shared over two uprootings.

The settlers were apprehensive about their weak and exposed position on this remote frontier. They were threatened on two fronts: by hostile English and European interests and by the Indians.

They had little more than squatters' rights and there were external principalities and powers with pretensions to territory on the river. The Dutch still held their fort where the Hooker party were settling and no one could tell how seriously they might defend it. By forcing the Stiles party to disembark upstream at Poquonnock, Ludlow had perhaps forestalled them from making good Saltonstall's claim under the Warwick patent – to the indignation of Sir Richard who bitterly protested against the unscrupulous illegality of it all and became disenchanted with the idea of colonizing. More portentous were the building works springing up at the mouth of the Connecticut River: an English fort, no less, sited to command the estuary. It was a comfort to be protected against incursions by foreign intruders like the Dutch, but a worry beause it stood for another, ominous, English claim. The work was in the charge of a professional soldier and Low Country veteran, one Lion Gardiner. He was acting under instruction from the younger Winthrop who, it will be remembered, had returned to New England from London the previous September with a commission from that same syndicate under the Warwick patent to lay out lands at the mouth of the Connecticut as an aristocratic refuge to be called Fort Saybrook after its two principal noble adventurers. Young Winthrop was designated governor. This was exceedingly awkward and would have to be reconciled with the *de facto* rights of the river settlers. For Ludlow this presented a personal problem. He regarded himself as the virtual governor of the Connecticut enterprise and in any case had an uneasy relationship with the Winthrop clan.

It was with such worries on his mind that Ludlow had returned to the Bay from Connecticut through the frozen wilderness the previous November. As a lawyer he was impressed with the need to secure a legal title to the land he and his party had staked out and it was imperative that Massachusetts should underwrite it, especially bearing in mind the rival claims of Plymouth Colony, Saltonstall and the Warwick patentees. He was acutely aware that the Massachusetts court, in granting them leave to depart for the Connecticut, had stipulated that 'they continue still under this government' and that the powerful ex-governor's son was designated governor under the Warwick patent.

The upshot was that during the winter a series of secret conferences took place in Boston between the younger John Winthrop, for the Warwick patentees, and Ludlow and Hooker for the settlers, presided over by Governor John Haynes for the Massachusetts court. It was not an easy negotiation despite the fact that the English grandees needed settlers and Ludlow's settlers needed a secure legal title. Only in the following spring did they reach agreement. This was promulgated by the Court on 3 March. Bearing in mind that the intentions of the patentees were still largely unknown and that 'our loving friends, neighbours, freemen and members' who were removing themselves to Connecticut were too distant to be governed from Massachusetts, the court established a provisional government to act for one year and without prejudice to the interests of the

Warwick patentees. This was to consist of a commission of eight persons all prominent in the new settlement with Roger Ludlow named first Commissioner. The Commission was empowered to administer justice, inflict punishment, make decrees as might best conduce to 'the peaceable and quiet ordering of the affairs of the said plantation', exercise military discipline and, if necessary, make war; in effect, the delegated powers of the court of Massachusetts Bay. The commissioners were the equivalent of assistants and magistrates; they were also empowered to add to their number deputies from the new settlements to make up a court of a similar complexion to that of Massachusetts. There was, however, one significant departure. The deputies were to be elected, as in Massachusetts, by the freemen; but, unlike Massachusetts, you did not have to be a church member to be a freeman. This was a new mutation in representative government to be confirmed two years later in the Fundamental Orders and twelve years after that in the Code of Laws, both of which were drafted by that constitutional lawyer, Roger Ludlow.

The commission met for the first time on 26 April 1636 in the new New Town soon to be named Hartford in honour of minister Samuel Stone's English birthplace. Ludlow, as first commissioner, chaired the meeting. He was in fact the temporary governor of the incipient colony and so acted for that year. But to his great chagrin, in the spring of 1637 there appeared on the river his 'evil genius' John Haynes, the ex-Governor of Massachusetts, who took precedence over him. When that provisional commission became a formal constitution Haynes, not Ludlow, was elected the first Governor. Here was the tragedy of a forceful, able and ambitious leader flawed by an intemperate and impatient personality.

If the colony had reservations about him, his own Dorchester folk still regarded him as their chief citizen. The next February, 1637, his fellow West Countrymen would resolve to change the name of their plantation from Dorchester to Windsor. The reason remains obscure. None of our settlers can be traced to Broadwindsor, Dorset but the village was next to, and historically connected with, Beaminster whence came a number of them and, as moderate and Nonseparatist members of the Church of England, they may thus have wished to assert their continuing allegiance to the Crown; but a plausible explanation is that the name was in honour of Roger Ludlow whose grandmother's family name was Windsor. If so, that his fellow settlers should be prepared to christen their new settlement in honour of his family and to eclipse their old allegiance to John White, the patriarch of Dorchester, was a sign of their appreciation of the power of his leadership.

The minute of that meeting, the first in the Connecticut colonial records, is entitled 'A Corte holden at Newton' and by this sleight of drafting hand the commission appointed by Massachusetts transformed itself into the court of the new colony; and a year later, May Day 1637, it received into membership its first elected deputies, four from each of the three plantations. By this time the court was acting like a fully sovereign legislature to handle a sudden and more immediate menace than territorial claims by alien interests.

Six weeks after its first meeting the court held a second, on 7 June, this time in Dorchester, about to be renamed Windsor. Apart from ordering a survey of the boundaries between the plantations, there were two principal items of business: a watch was formed in every town under the constable, and every able-bodied man was to have in readiness, in addition to a musket, two pounds of powder and twenty lead bullets. Thus the first rudimentary steps were taken to form a trainband for the new colony. This was not a moment too soon, because there were signs that the Indians were becoming actively hostile.

During their trek through the back country, the English had become ever more conscious of the natives and grateful for their help. Equally, now on the Connecticut, they appreciated the friendliness of the Indians who were summering all about them from Poquonnoc upstream down to Pyquag and whose stockaded fort village they could see across the river at Podunk. These were the friendly river Indians whose sachem had sent to the Bay five years before to invite them to settle. On the whole, the Indians had welcomed the arrival of the English to their shores, and the Puritans, for their part, had been conscientious in their dealings with them. However, this was all beginning to change. The tribal equilibrium of New England was becoming destabilized as a result of two principal factors. First, the Indians had little resistance to the diseases which the Europeans brought with them. In the 1620s and early 1630s they succumbed to epidemics of chickenpox and then smallpox, which decimated their numbers and resulted in the abandonment of many of their planting and hunting grounds. (The fact that there were Indian cultivated lands to be had for the asking was an argument in English colonizing literature as early as the 1620s.) In some areas they had ceased to manage the forest edges which had reverted to scrub and there was a general decline in their rural economy and morale. The Indian attitude towards the English whom they were tempted to blame for their declining circumstances became gradually more ambivalent.

The second factor was the upsetting of the political equilibrium. Hitherto, on the whole, despite the aggressiveness of individual tribes, particularly the Narragansetts, the New England polity had been relatively stable. However this situation was changing as a result of the eruption from the Hudson River to the west of a branch of the Mohegans, the aggressively migrating Pequots (Algonquin for 'destroyer'), who, by the 1630s, had become well established between the Narragansetts and the Connecticut River. The Pequots, hungry for territory and with a reputation for brutality, were flexing their muscles and threatening the tribes' territorial equilibrium. According to a contemporary, they had become so 'flushed with Victories over their Fellow-Indians [that] they began to thirst after the blood of any foreigners' (Hubbard). It was the hope that the English would be their allies against these intruders that had led to the delegation from the river Indians to the Bay in 1631. The arrival of the English on the Connecticut at the edge of Pequot country provoked the hostility of the latter who feared English fire power and their clear intention of occupying valuable hunting territory. For the Pequots the English were a mortal threat and their thoughts increasingly turned towards their extermination. The result was a series of bloodthirsty incidents against individual Englishmen which quickly led to open hostilities and war.

The first victim was that same Captain Stone who had called Ludlow a 'just ass'; he had been killed with his crew while exploring the Connecticut River in 1634. His reputation was such that he was thought to have got little more than his due. But towards the end of July 1636 news reached the settlers that John Oldham, whose explorations had first led them to the river, had been killed by Indians off Block Island. Humphrey Gallop of Mosterton, Dorset, passenger on the *Mary and John* and now master of a sloop, spotted Oldham's pinnace with fourteen Indians on her deck, gave chase and, with a crew of only a man and two boys, boarded her, overcame the Indians and found the old trader murdered in his cabin. This goaded Massachusetts into reprisals; and John Endicott, Ludlow's brother-in-law, was despatched with a force of volunteers to Block Island where, laying waste the Indian settlement, he succeeded only in stirring up the Pequots. In October, still nearer home, came the news that another of their West Countrymen, the sea captain and old fishing hand John Tilley of Chilthorne Domer, had been captured, tortured and killed by Pequots after landing to forage on the bank of the Great River (reprobate he may have been, but his executioners admired his bravery under torture). That winter, the settlers became even more apprehensive as they learned that the Pequots were marauding down at the river's mouth and Lieutenant Gardiner and his Saybrook Fort were virtually under seige.

Urgent steps were taken to put the plantations on an offensive footing. In October the General Court had stepped up the readiness of the town trainbands on the lines of Massachusetts with training days monthly, or more often if needed, under recognized officers, with fines for absence or neglect of arms and ammunition. With the spring of 1637, the Pequots were definitely on the warpath. On May Day the court took pre-emptive action by declaring an offensive war against them and decreed that an expeditionary force of ninety men should be recruited from the three plantations with proportionate quotas of arms, ammunition and provisions. This force was promptly despatched downriver and was in action well before the end of the month. Windsor contributed 30 men, six armour, 60 bushels of corn, 50 pieces of pork, 30 pounds of rice and four cheeses. The town also provided the expeditionary force with its commander in the person of Captain John Mason. If Windsor's Ludlow was the *de facto* governor of the infant colony, John Mason was its commander-in-chief.

Mason had already seen to the defences of his town. From the start, he must have been conscious of the need for defensive works to protect it from marauders and worse. The Dutch still had that fort only ten miles downstream and the local Indians were an uncertain quantity. The terrain did not lend itself to a fort such as they had built on the Bay, but the confluence of the Rivulet with the Great River had potential. Some time before the summer of 1637, using the Rivulet's high bluff as its southern base, the settlers designed an extended parallelogram running about 80 rods (443 yards) north along Sandy Bank above the Connecticut, then 50 or 60 rods (280 yards) west, consisting of a wide ditch and an inner earth rampart in which was embedded a palisade of tree trunks (see plan on p.131). This considerable work of earth and timber must have been an immense effort for that small body of settlers. They called it, and it is called to this day for its outline still exists, the Palisado.

Palisado was the Spanish technical term for a semi-fortified town. The concept of 'a garrison town designed to give English minority groups protection from numerically superior but largely unorganized native populations' went back to the bastides which Edward I built to protect his Angevin territories in France. Calais was the last of these; but the pattern persisted in England's newly developing colonies, at Londonderry, Drogheda and elsewhere in Ulster, and at ill-fated Roanoke and Jamestown in Virginia where a palisade protecting church and storehouse was recognizably that of an Ulster 'bawn'. Windsor's moat and palisade, taking advantage of the river bluffs to protect a nucleated village designed round a central square with meeting and storehouses, is an outstanding latter-day example of the means by which the English reinforced their occupation of hostile territory.

The early chroniclers are silent about the architect but circumstantial evidence indicates that it was the work of two men. Roger Ludlow had been the Assistant with overall responsibility for the Castle Island defences of Boston and Captain Mason had been the professional soldier in charge of the works. Although he did not describe himself, like Lion Gardiner of Saybrook, as an 'engineer and architect', Mason had been at the siege of Bois-le-Duc and he understood the art of fortification and the technique of the bastide or garrison town. There is little doubt that between them they designed Windsor's Palisado. As Mason sailed downstream in the sloop with his small force to fight the Pequots he must have taken considerable satisfaction in the knowledge that the Windsor community, at least, was protected within its square half-mile of rampart and ditch against attack from his rear. For the Palisado was large enough to accommodate most of Windsor, whose outlying families took shelter within it and round its village green for the duration of the hostilities to come.

CHAPTER 6: CAPTAIN MASON AND THE MYSTIC FORT FIGHT 1637

O N FRIDAY MAY 26 1637 THE TALL AND PORTLY FIGURE OF CAPTAIN Mason, commander of the Connecticut task force against the Pequots, called a halt and stood in silent contemplation of Mystic Fort on its hill in the cool dawn. He thanked God that after the three-mile march under the moon from that uncomfortable bivouac in the swamp he had achieved his object: surprise. As he later wrote, 'God was pleased to hide us in the hollow of his hand'. The wooden, palisaded fort was silent; its Indian inhabitants were sleeping off the effects of a night of singing and dancing. The Pequots had been celebrating the news, false, as they were to discover, that the English ships in the Long Island Sound had sheered off from attacking them in their wilderness stronghold between the Narragansett country and the Connecticut River. Even the fort's solitary sentry was asleep or, as someone later said, had slipped into the shelter of a wigwam to light a pipe.

It had been a successful *ruse de guerre*. Mason's orders from the magistrates had been to sail his little trainband, seventy-seven strong, from Saybrook Fort to make a direct landing at the mouth of the Pequot River. As a professional, he considered such a landing under the nose of the Indian forts foolhardy. Instead he had proposed a flank attack: to sail along the Sound beyond the Pequot territory to Narragansett Bay where the Indians were more friendly and might be recruited as auxiliaries, and thence back through the wilderness to make a surprise attack on Chief Sassacus's forts.

But those magisterial instructions could not be disregarded by Puritans commited to covenants, contracts between God and man and men and men. However, under God's all-seeing eye there was always a dispensation. Along with Captain Mason and Lieutenant Seeley, the magistrates had appointed to the expedition as chaplain Samuel Stone, the teaching colleague of Thomas Hooker, minister of Hartford church and like him a former fellow of Emmanuel College, Cambridge. Captain Mason, in his own words, 'did therefore earnestly desire Mr. Stone, he being our chaplain, that he would commend our condition to the Lord that night, to direct how and in what manner we should demean ourselves in that respect . . . In the morning very early Mr. Stone came ashore to the Captain's chamber and told him he had done as he had desired and was fully satisfied to sail for Narragansett.'

And so in due course they had landed in Narragansett Bay and sought out the chief sachem of the Narragansett Indians, Canonicus, who, with his nephew Miantonimo, was friendly though sceptical of the power of the English to challenge the much-feared Pequot enemy. The English had two invaluable Indian guides, Wequash and Uncas, who had accompanied the expedition from the Connecticut. Uncas was a renegade Pequot chief, now styling himself Mohegan, who, for his own good reasons, was and remained deeply loyal to the English. On the way he had overcome any doubts that the English might have had about his loyalty by obeying a 'test command' to capture six lurking Pequots and bring them in dead or alive; his braves had killed four and delivered the fifth whom the English had hanged, drawn and quartered; Uncas's Indians had then roasted and eaten the pieces. It was Uncas and Wequash who had guided Captain Mason and his militiamen back through the wilderness. Uncas commanded a force of some sixty of his Mohegans and these were joined, *en route*, by perhaps as many as 200 Narragansett warriors to act as auxiliaries. After a tough two-day march in the heat of late May with cumbersome clothing and accoutrements, they had been brought at last to the nearer of the two Pequot forts, that on the Mystic River.

Mason had with him a fellow officer, Captain John Underhill from Massachusetts Bay, who with eighteen men had joined the force at Saybrook. Together in the quiet of the morning they, with their men, silently yielded themselves and their cause up to God. Then the two professionals quickly reconnoitred the fort. It was a circular structure of just over half an acre surrounded by a palisade of deeply implanted tree trunks with two concealed and fortified entrances. They decided to flank it on both sides, Mason taking the eastern and Underhill the western entrance. They came stealthily within ten yards of the palisade unobserved, then a dog barked, an Indian spotted them and shouted 'Owannux, owannux', meaning 'Englishmen, Englishmen', and their surprise was blown. Thereupon they rushed to the palisade. In a 'ring battalia' and pushing their carbines and muskets through the gaps in the fencing, they fired a resounding volley as the Indians were stirring from sleep. Mason then wheeled his men to attack the eastern entrance, swords in right hand, carbines or muskets in left. The entrance was blocked with bushes and boughs. The captain leapt over these but Lieutenant Seeley, 'being somewhat encumbered' with weapons and equipment, delayed and removed the bushes in order to let his file of sixteen men into the fort, and Mason went on ahead. The fort consisted largely of an encampment of wigwams. Mason broke into one, to find Indians crying out in disarray, some taking refuge under their beds, others breaking out and desperately trying to aim arrows at the intruders. Mason was beset at close quarters and hit by arrows which mercifully stuck in his helmet and quilted coat. He held off the Indians at sword's point, wounding many, until he was relieved by one of his Windsor men, William Hayden, who entered the wigwam and, seeing an Indian drawing his bow at the captain, snapped the bowstring with his sword and so saved his life. Thereupon Mason burst out and set upon some Indians in the alley between the wigwams. He pursued them down to the end where he was met by two of his men, Pattison of Saybrook and Barber of Windsor, coming the other way and together they killed seven or so Indians.

All this took place in the space of a few minutes. Mason then turned round and marched back up the alley. He was out of breath and blinded with sweat; and perhaps at a loss to know what to do next. At this point he saw two of his men standing close to the palisade with their swords pointing to the ground. He shouted to them angrily: 'We shall never kill them after that manner.' They had originally thought the fort should be taken by the sword in order, as Mason wrote, to 'save the plunder'; but he now realized that the space between the wigwams was too constricted for swordplay let alone the cumbersome business of loading and firing matchlock muskets. In any case the English were heavily outnumbered. So on the spur of the moment he decided, We must burn them. Stepping back into the same wigwam he went to its fireplace, siezed a firebrand and with the help of Lieutenant Bull and Nicholas Olmstead of Hartford set alight the thatch with which the wigwams were covered. Meanwhile Underhill had fired the other end of the fort with a train of powder. In no time the fort was blazing.

It burnt down within half an hour.

The effect on the Indians was catastrophic. Many fought to the last with great courage until they were scorched and burnt even to their very bowstrings, and so, in Underhill's words, 'perished valiantly'. Others in their terror at the sudden conflagration fled as from avenging gods, some into the flames. Many men, women and children were burnt to death. Mason gave the order to withdraw outside the fort, surround it and pick off the Pequots as they climbed over the palisades like rats from a burning rick. About forty of the most courageous warriors rallied and subjected the English to a rain of arrows only to be cut to pieces in their turn. One, described by an eye-witness as 'the Indians' Goliath', broke through 'and although one sergeant stroke him on the neck with his cutlash, he got by him and by five soulders more, but the sixth killed him'. Many more surrendered but received no mercy and were killed. Those that escaped were shot down by Uncas's Indians.

Perhaps four hundred were killed, in the space of an hour. Some died instantly, shot, put to the sword or cleft by tomahawk, and hundreds died of wounds; but most burned to death. Only a handful were captured or escaped. Thus the entire Pequot community here was destroyed; in an early chronicler's words, 'parents and children, the sannup and squaw, the old man and the babe, perished in promiscuous ruin'. The sounds and sights of that horrifying hour on a summer morning haunted those who witnessed them. 'Great and doleful', wrote Underhill, 'was the bloody sight to the view of young soldiers that never before had been in war, to see so many souls lie gasping on the ground, so thick, in some places, that you could hardly pass along.'

The holocaust was caused by Mason's decision that the only way to save his outnumbered English force was to fire the fort. It had been a desperate venture from the start. Mobilizing that Connecticut task force had been a deliberate, pre-emptive strike against a life-or-death menace. The Pequots were a serious enough threat to the men of Massachusetts; but the latter could withdraw beyond the Narragansetts to the Bay; whereas the Pequots threatened the very survival of the infant settlements on the Connecticut. However, the catastrophic nature of the denouement took some explaining. Even their Indian allies, though rejoicing at the English success, considered it too ruthless. They cried, 'It is too furious and slays too many men.' The participants and the early chroniclers went out of their way to explain and justify it.

Fortunately for their consciences, they had an overwhelming justification at hand in their covenant with the almighty and righteous God who had brought them and their families through so many trials to establish a gathered community in the wilderness; and the rationale was in the Old Testament of the Geneva Bible. Captain Underhill had to steel himself against his own pity for the innocent as well as his admiration for the enemy's courage by remembering the torture, scalping and burning of the English traders and seamen on the Connecticut River, the killing of settlers as they planted corn and the capture of the English girls. In his own words:

> It may be demanded, Why should you be so furious? . . . Should not Christians have more mercy and compassion? But I would refer you to David's war. When a people is grown to such a height of blood, and sin against God and man . . . there he hath no respect to persons but harrows them and saws them, and puts them to the sword, and the most terrible death that may be. Sometimes the Scripture declareth women and children must perish with their parents . . . We had sufficient light from the word of God for our proceedings.

And so

> every man bereft of pity, fell upon the work without compassion, considering the blood they had shed of our native countrymen, and how barbarously they had dealt with them.

And Mason himself:

> Thus were they now at their wits end who not many hours before exalted themselves . . . threatening the utter ruin and destruction of all the English, exulting and rejoicing with songs and dances; but God was above them who laughed the enemies of his people to scorn, making them as a fiery oven; thus . . . did the Lord judge among the Heathen, filling the place with dead bodies.

It has a Cromwellian ring.

Of the English, only two soldiers were killed and about twenty wounded. There were some narrow escapes. Two Windsor men, John Dyer and Thomas Stiles, both received arrows in the knots of their neckerchiefs;

Lieutenant Seeley was shot in an eyebrow, Mason himself pulling out the arrow, and Lieutenant Bull received an arrow in a piece of hard cheese he was carrying; which, wrote Mason, 'may verify the old saying, a little armour would serve if a man knew where to place it'.

Despite their victory the little force remained exposed. They must make their way back through a hostile and Pequot wilderness from the Mystic to the Pequot River where they had arranged to rendezvous with their ships. The wounded were a growing problem. The force had travelled light and they were short of food and especially, since the weather was hot and dry, of water. Most were thirsty, many faint from loss of blood and swooning with pain. They had brought one pint of strong liquor, which Mason carried, and even when it was empty 'the very smelling to the bottle would presently recover such as fainted away'. They had no doctor. The surgeon, a Mr Pell, 'not accustomed to war, durst not hazard himself where we ventured our lives, but like a fresh water soldier, kept aboard [his ship]'. Four or five of the wounded had to be carried and the men became so weak it took four to carry each one. The rest were so burdened with their weapons and those of their dead or wounded comrades that there remained only about forty free to fight.

Meanwhile, a strong force of Pequots came up from the other fort at the mouth of the Pequot River but were beaten off by the English musketry. When they came upon the appalling, smoking charnel house which was all that remained of their Mystic Fort and of their kinsmen they were stricken and tore their hair in an agony of shock and rage. When they had recovered sufficiently they set off to attack the English on the march. The English rearguard, some twelve or fourteen men, fought them off and, because arrows were no match for musket bullets, the enemy eventually fell back with some casualties. Underhill was impressed by the discipline of the raw trainbands and by their musketry: 'We could not but admire at the providence of God in it that soldiers so unexpert in the use of their arms should give so complete a volley, as though the finger of God had touched both match and flint.' This professional soldier had earlier noted how intelligently these amateur soldiers had taken the initiative in storming the fort without waiting for orders: 'Men that run before they are sent, most commonly have an ill reward'.

The English could now pause at a brook to refresh themselves, having 'by that time taught them a little more manners than to disturb us', as Mason put it with soldierly understatement. The Indians continued to harrass their flanks and to shoot from ambush; but they shot their arrows in such a desultory way that, in Underhill's words, 'they might fight seven years and not kill seven men . . . This fight is more for pastime than to conquer and subdue enemies'. When the English killed a Pequot their Indian auxiliaries '(as the dog watcheth the shot of the fowler to fetch the prey), fetched them their heads'.

At this point some of the Narragansetts declared they would go no further, and turned back east; but they were chased by Pequots and had to appeal to Captain Mason to rescue them. He was furious: 'How dare you crave aid of us when you are leaving us in this distressed condition, not knowing which way to march out of the country. But yet you shall see it is not the nature of Englishmen to deal like heathens, to requite evil for evil, but we will succour you', and he detailed Underhill with thirty men to cover the Narragansetts' retreat back to the main body killing about a hundred Pequots on the way.

Although they were marching close to the shore they could see no signs of their ships which were to sail to the mouth of the Pequot River to pick them up. But within two miles of that river the enemy suddenly left them and when they reached the top of a bluff overlooking Pequot harbour they saw the reason: there below was their little fleet at anchor. The ships had been delayed by a strong offshore wind. The expedition marched proudly down to the harbour with colours flying (though without their drum which had been left at the bivouac the night before). 'To our great rejoicing', in Mason's words, '[we] came to the water-side [and] there sat down in quiet'.

They were worn out and anxious to get their wounded on board. However, who should come ashore from what they recognized as their own sloop but one Captain Daniel Patrick with a company of soldiers from Massachusetts Bay, fresh and eager for the fray and, so they said, to rescue Mason's force from pursuit – though, as Mason wrote, 'there did not appear any the least sign of such a thing'. Patrick made difficulties about the use of the sloop to convey the wounded to the pink at anchor, and over the use of a barque. In the end it was agreed that if Patrick would stay with the barque in Pequot harbour and look after the return home of the Narragansetts, Underhill would sail in the pink with the wounded to Saybrook Fort and return the pink to Pequot to ship the Narragansetts home. So Underhill and the wounded departed for Saybrook. However, Captain Patrick would not stay aboard but came ashore with his force to join Mason and his depleted little unit of twenty to make their way with the Indians overland to Saybrook. He was clearly not popular. As Mason wrote: 'We did not desire or delight in his company and so we plainly told him; however, he would and did march along with us'. Mason and his Connecticut men were damned if this Johnny-come-lately from the Bay should share in the final stages of their victorious operation!

The march along the low, wooded hills of the shore from the Pequot to the Connecticut took them through the country of the western Niantics. The English overran one of their villages but were too spent to do more than chase them into a swamp. By this time it was between two and three o'clock on the Saturday afternoon and they were anxious to get to Saybrook before the Sabbath so they pressed on. At sunset they broke through the forest and scrub to see ahead salt marshes and, beyond, the wide, blue estuary of the Great River shimmering and noisily running against the tide in the afterlight. It was a wonderful moment. They signalled their presence over to tiny, distant Saybrook Fort on its point across the estuary. In return Lieutenant Gardiner gave the order for a salute of guns. As Captain Mason wrote, 'We were nobly entertained'.

It was too late to make the river crossing that night and it was Sunday when Lieutenant Gardiner sent over to ferry the little expeditionary force to the fort on its salt marsh and sand spit. The rudimentary, wooden strong house with its stockade and saker guns commanding the estuary and the Sound was a welcome haven, and the victorious men of Connecticut settled down to rest their limbs, nurse their injuries and enjoy their triumph in the hospitality of the commander and his garrison. 'We were', wrote Mason, 'entertained with great triumph and rejoicing and praising God for his goodness to us in succeeding our weak endeavours, in crowning us with success and restoring of us with so little loss.' Within the limits of the larder and cellar, the soldiery were no doubt treated to a celebratory supper in what Lion Gardiner elsewhere described grandiosely as 'the Great Hall' of the fort.

That Sunday evening was a reunion for the four commanding officers, Lieutenant (General) Gardiner and Captains Mason, Underhill and Patrick, and the conversation no doubt took a reminiscing turn. In their late thirties, they were all professional soldiers seasoned in the campaigns against the Spaniards in the Netherlands who had then decided to chance their arms in the service of Puritan emigrants in New England. They had not been the first of their kind. Captain Miles Standish had served in the Netherlands under Sir Francis Vere who had trained so many young Englishmen ambitious for a military career in the Protestant cause; there he had made contact with the English Separatists at Leyden, had been hired for the *Mayflower* expedition of 1620 and had become military captain of Plymouth Colony. A decade later young John Underhill had followed in his footsteps. Underhill's father was an officer in the Dutch service and his son was 'bred to arms' as a cadet in the Prince of Orange's guard. In 1628 he had married a Dutch girl, Helena de Hooch, and two years later, whether or not under Puritan influence, had taken ship with the Winthrop fleet to New England. In Boston he and Daniel Patrick, their unpopular fellow officer, had been joint captains of the Boston militia and two winters previously Underhill had been back in England buying military stores for the colony.

John Mason, like Standish, had served in the English army in the Netherlands, under Sir Horace Vere, brother of Sir Francis, and had been under him at the siege of Bois-le-Duc, called the Maid of Brabant because she had never been taken. In the trenches encircling that fortified town in the early summer of 1629 were to be found many young English gentlemen wearing the orange and blue scarf who were to become household names on both sides in the English Civil War: Thomas Fairfax and Philip Skippon, organizers of the New Model Army; Jacob Astley and Thomas Glenham, Royalist generals; Lords Doncaster, Fielding and Craven; Sir Thomas Culpepper; Sir John Borlase; a Luttrell, a Bridgeman, a Basset, a Throgmorton, a Fleetwood, a Lambert, a Cromwell. Among them was John Mason. His special comrade-in-arms appears to have been the Yorkshireman Thomas Fairfax, a gentleman volunteer freshly down from Cambridge. He and Mason were to keep in touch and in a few years Fairfax was to try to recruit Mason for a senior commission in the Parliamentary cause. It was at the siege of Bois-le-Duc that these young men learnt the rudiments of professional soldiering: the complicated orders and drills for pikemen and musketeers, marksmanship, gunnery and siege engineering. Mason may well have recalled that each night before the relief guard marched off to the trenches they were paraded before the colonel-in-command for prayers and a psalm; but, apart from this, although there was a preacher for each regiment, church service was not compulsory, a fact worthy of remark, for the Saybrook company had nevertheless learnt to endure New England Puritan discipline.

Lion Gardiner, the commander of Saybrook Fort and the host that memorable evening, was the most recently arrived of them all. Two years before he had still been serving under the Prince of Orange. Like his fellow officer Mason, he was an engineer and described himself formally as 'Engineer and Master of works of Fortification in the lagers of the Prince of Orange in the Low Countries'. He, too, married a Dutch girl, Mary

Wilemson of Woerdon. He became acquainted with members of the English church in Rotterdam whose minister Hugh Peters had been chaplain to an English commander in the Dutch service. Peters, a staunch Cambridge Puritan, had been lecturer at St Sepulchre's, London, and associated with the fund to buy up impropriations to support Puritan preachers and a member of the Massachusetts Bay Company. A refugee in Holland from Laudian persecution, he and John Davenport turned their thoughts towards migrating to New England. Peters was connected with the associates of the Earl of Warwick in their patent for the Saybrook settlement and it was he who had recruited Gardiner for this enterprise. Gardiner was paid £100 a year for four years to serve the company of patentees 'in the drawing, ordering and making of a city, towns or forts of defence'.

Gardiner and his wife arrived in Boston on 28 November 1635 and at the mouth of the Connecticut in the following spring. Here he found a Lieutenant Gibbons, a sergeant and some carpenters at work constructing some temporary housing on the site chosen by young Winthrop for a fort. Gardiner's contract envisaged him as a military engineer and architect and he had been promised 300 able-bodied men from England. Instead, there came only George Fenwick, one of the patentees, and his servant, together with three other temporary visitors from the Bay, one of whom was Hugh Peters, fresh from Holland.

Gardiner thus commanded a tiny and, as it turned out, beleaguered garrison. That summer the murder of John Oldam, coming after a number of other Indian atrocities, goaded Massachusetts to send an expedition to the Pequot country to punish the culprits and demand compensation. This was the last thing Gardiner wanted, isolated on his sand spit at the mouth of the Connecticut with the whole of the Pequot country between him and Massachusetts Bay. He had already pleaded with the Bay people not to stir up the Indians for a year or two until Saybrook was established, 'for', he wrote, 'I had but twenty four in all, men, women and boys and girls and not food for them for two months unless we saved our corn field which could not possibly be if they came to war for it is two miles from our home'. His plea went unheeded. Instead, the hamfisted and headstrong John Endicott had been despatched with his seaborne force to Pequot harbour to teach the Pequots a lesson, the effect of which was to incense the Indians still further. When the expedition turned up at Saybrook its commander told them in no uncertain terms that their commission was ill-conceived and worse; for, he said, 'you come hither to raise these wasps about my ears, and then you will take wing and flee away'.

Thereafter the Pequot wasps were indeed swarming about the garrison. They ambushed foraging parties in the long meadow grass, burned haystacks and barns on Cornfield Point and killed cattle. That winter the fort was virtually under siege. Foraging parties had to be protected by armed pickets; in February Gardiner himself and a logging party were attacked and were lucky to escape: two were killed and several injured, including Gardiner who was hit in the thigh. Two of his men threw down their weapons and ran. Gardiner was reluctantly dissuaded from hanging one of them for cowardice, for they were under military discipline and as he said 'the articles did hang up for them to read'. In the spring thaw the Pequots struck closer to home. On the morning of 23 April a group of Wethersfield settlers on their way to a day's work in the fields were set upon; six men and three women were killed as well as twenty precious cows. The Indians also captured two young girls in the vain hope that they would teach their captors how to make gunpowder. At Saybrook, Gardiner saw the flotilla of Indian canoes coming downriver in war order, their crews defiantly wearing captured English shirts. Gardiner's only weapons were his two saker guns; these he loaded and fired and they shot off the bows of the canoe carrying the two girl prisoners; later a friendly Dutch boat in a tricky negotiation redeemed the girls, thanks to one of the sachem's squaws. Fortunately for the beleaguered Gardiner, Captain Underhill turned up again from the Bay with reinforcements, eighteen 'lusty men', according to Gardiner, commissioned to stay for at least two months.

On 1 May the General Court declared war on the Pequots and within weeks Mason and his task force sailed downstream in their pink, pinnace and sloop to Fort Saybrook, a staging post on their way to attack the Pequots in their home territory. When they reached Saybrook Lieutenant Gardiner was not impressed by them. These were indeed raw recruits. The last thing the able-bodied men of the river settlements wanted was to go to war against these savages just as they were repairing the ravages of the past two winters and starting to build homes, sow crops and herd their cattle. The town constables must have had not unfamiliar difficulty in finding volunteers. At any rate they presented a motley impression. 'When Captain Underhill and I had seen their commission, we both said they were not fitted for such a design, and we said to Major Mason we wondered he would venture himself, being no better fitted; and he said the magistrates could not or would not send better; then we said that none of our men should go with them, neither should they go unless we that were bred soldiers from our youth could see some likelihood to do better than the Bay men with their strong commission last year.' So he suggested that Underhill's contingent from the Bay should be incorporated into the little force thereby releasing the least promising score or so of the Connecticut volunteers who were sent back upstream to their homes, ignominiously but no doubt to their relief.

And so it came about that the task force had been mustered and commissioned under Captains Mason and Underhill for their do-or-die expedition against the Pequots. Gardiner had provided them with the fort's surgeon, Mr Pell, and such necessaries as he could spare, and bade them Godspeed. One suspects that he remained sceptical; and two weeks later no one could have been more relieved than he when the flotilla appeared at the mouth of the Connecticut, having hugged the Sound from Pequot harbour, and even more when, on that Saturday evening in May, there also appeared the little infantry force, flags flying, a quarter of a mile away on the opposite bank, waiting to be ferried across the Great River.

For Mason, at any rate, the hand of an Old Testament God was to be seen in the event:

> Thus was God seen in the mount, crushing his proud enemies and the enemies of his people; they who were ere while a terror to all that were found about them, who resolved to destroy all the English and to root their very name out of this country, should by such weak means, even seventy seven (there being no more at the Fort), bring the mischief they plotted upon their own heads in a moment: burning them up in the fire of his wrath and dunging the ground with their flesh; it was the Lord's doings, and it is marvellous in our eyes.

Meanwhile, the enemy, in their grief and despair, found a scapegoat for their defeat in their chief sachem, Sassacus, whom they came near to assassinating. However, after a debate, they concluded that their defeat was after all caused by the English firearms which so outshot their arrows, and that it was so complete that they had no alternative but to disperse. And so, under Sassacus and with their women and children, they set off westwards towards the Hudson River whence their tribe had come. Those Pequots that remained in the region of the Mystic and Pequot rivers would be mopped up by a new force which was shortly to appear from Massachusetts Bay under Captain Israel Stoughton. Many were captured; the braves among them were loaded on to a sloop, shipped out of the harbour mouth and pitched into the Sound. Mason grimly nicknamed the sloop 'Charon's ferry'.

Its master was that West Countryman, Captain John Gallop, who had boarded John Oldham's boat off Block Island the summer before and had overcome his Indian murderers. Gallop was in no mood for mercy.

The Pequots were finally defeated in a famous swamp fight near Quinnipeag, later called New Haven, in which Captain Mason also took part, after which Sassacus was assassinated and the tribe completely dispersed. This catastrophic denouement resulted directly from the destruction of Mystic Fort by those seventy-seven English amateur soldiers, most of them from the little one-year-old Puritan settlements on the Connecticut River.

After their triumphant reception at Saybrook Fort, the members of the task force were only too anxious to return home to their families and homesteads in Wethersfield, Hartford and Windsor; and so, probably the next morning, Monday 29 May, they bade farewell to the garrison and its commander and set sail upriver in their little flotilla. They arrived home probably on Friday 3 June. One can visualize their home-coming, first putting in at Wethersfield, then at Hartford, and finally, up the Great River still, watching out for the wooded entrance on the left bank of what they called the Rivulet. They warped or poled up that last stretch of river to the ferry landing of their own little settlement, which they must get used to calling Windsor.

It is not hard to imagine the satisfaction of the returning soldiers as they disembarked and stumbled up the river bank. They had only been away three weeks and three days but it had been a baptism of fire, a strange, exhausting but, thanks be to God, triumphant experience for this motley company of Puritan companions-in-arms, already inured to the husbandry of the wilderness and now seasoned in Indian warfare. Nor is it difficult to picture the joy and thankfulness with which the men were greeted by their families and neighbours, by their minister John Warham, their ruling elders John Witchfield, John Branker and William Hosford, their magistrates Roger Ludlow and William Phelps, and their constable Henry Wolcott. For them, the three weeks' absence of half their menfolk had been an anxious void. They had been badly needed in the fields for the spring planting, and in the Palisado which Roger Ludlow had been responsible for manning with the few able-bodied men who remained. As he said, the fatigue of manning the watches was so great that the men 'could scarce stand upon their legs'. In the words of an early chronicler of these events, 'every family and every worshipping assembly spake the language of praise and thanksgiving.'

Of the returning warriors we know the names of some sixteen. Two were

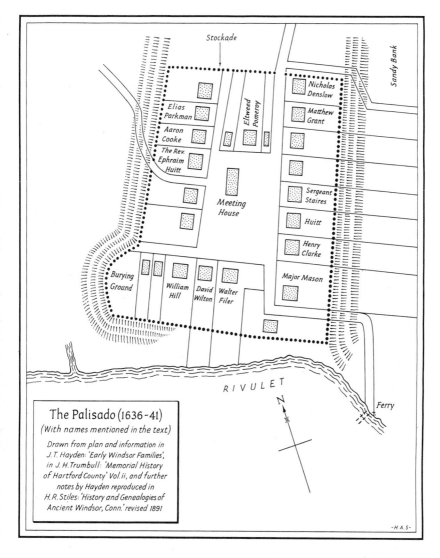

The Palisado (1636 - 41)
(With names mentioned in the text)

Drawn from plan and information in
J.T. Hayden: 'Early Windsor Families',
in J. H. Trumbull: 'Memorial History
of Hartford County' Vol. ii, and further
notes by Hayden reproduced in
H. R. Stiles: 'History and Genealogies of
Ancient Windsor, Conn.' revised 1891

sergeants, Benedict Alford and Thomas Staires, the former from Somerset,
both probably in their late twenties. Staires was to depart again almost
immediately with Mason and Ludlow for that final action against the
Pequots at Quinnipeag. Of the private soldiers, five were young men or boys
who had come as servants with the Stiles party in 1635, including Thomas
Stiles of that family. Of the rest, William Thrall, of Sandridge, Hertfordshire
was older, a quarryman and stonemason, Thomas Parsons would become
the Rivulet ferryman; there was young James, seventeen-year-old son of
Bigot Eccleston, of Craven in Yorkshire, and Thomas Gridley, a transient of
whom little is known save a court conviction for drunkenness. Two of them

had come by way of Dorchester, Massachusetts with the original *Mary and John* company: Nathaniel Gillett, the son of the vicar of Chaffcombe, Somerset, and William Hayden, the man who had saved Mason's life by cutting the Pequot's bowstring, who also hailed from Somerset. They all lived within a stone's throw of one another; and as they dispersed to their homes to remove their corselets and quilted coats, to lay aside their swords, muskets, powder flasks and shot pouches, and no doubt to claim their private's pay of 1s 3d a day, they were thankful to be back in their neighbourhood community, primitive though it still was.

Captain Mason was the man of the hour. The General Court would shortly elect him a magistrate, commission him commander-in-chief of the final operation against the Pequots and the colony's chief negotiator with all the Indian tribes, and award him 500 acres to distribute among his own soldiers as a tribute to his and their services in the Pequot campaign. Above all, the next spring, on 8 March 1638, the court would appoint him Sergeant-Major General, that is, commander-in-chief of all the Connecticut forces with responsibility for training the militia, at a stipend of £40. This commission was for twelve months, but he would hold it for thirty years. He was also at various times to be deputy governor of the colony and responsible for relations with the Indians. Although he would leave Windsor in due course to command Saybrook Fort and later establish yet another settlement, to be called Norwich, he remains the outstanding military figure in Windsor and in Connecticut as a whole.

At a special ceremony in Hartford, the minister, Thomas Hooker, sometime fellow of Emmanuel College, Cambridge, presented Mason, or 'the Major' as he would henceforth be universally called, with his military staff of office. As Connecticut's early historian, Benjamin Trumbull, commented: 'This he doubtless performed with that propriety and dignity which was peculiar to himself and best adapted to the occasion'. The place might only be a roughly cleared settlement in a wilderness on the edge of the world; but the occasion merited all the symbolism and style that Puritan dignity could bring to it.

CHAPTER 7: THE PLANTING OF WINDSOR 1635–41

IN THE FALL OF 1637, WITH THE PEQUOT MENACE AT AN END, THE WINDSOR planters could resume the interrupted work of settlement. The families who had huddled in and about the Palisado could venture further afield to replace their dugouts with homesteads and to clear the meadow grounds for tillage. Come the spring thaw there was great activity on the bank above the Connecticut meadows.

Roger Ludlow and his companions had chosen well two summers before when they determined on that salient bounded by the Tunxis and the Great River. It included nearly 1000 acres of rich meadowland: deep, silt soils and, unlike Massachusetts Bay, hardly a stone to impede cultivation. 'Great Meadow', stretching some two miles upstream, 'Sequestered Meadow' further upstream still, and 'Plymouth Meadow' south across the Tunxis, constituted a fertile territory for their cattle and crops such as they had dreamed of but failed to find on the Bay. Great Meadow was about 600 acres in size, half a mile broad at its southern base and tapering to a few hundred yards at its northern end. It was flanked to the west by a low bluff which the settlers called Sandy Bank and on which they were building their homesteads. To the north was a stone outcrop called Rocky Hill from which they were to quarry good red sandstone. At its southern end Sandy Bank became a broad, three-sided bluff, a quarter of a mile at its longest point, bounded by Great Meadow, the Rivulet and a tributary creek. This quadrilateral with its village green was the natural centre of settlement. Because of its elevation, with banks and ditches, Captain Mason shaped it easily into the Palisado. The two rivers were highways and sloops could sail up the Connecticut and pole the quarter of a mile or so up the Rivulet to the Palisado landing. Away to the west, whence flowed the Rivulet, stretched mile on mile of deciduous forest into the distant hills; only the near upland fringes were explored for use as wood lots; otherwise the forest was uncharted except for Indian trails.

For this beautiful wooded, rolling country, with its broad river and vistas of blue hills, was the territory of the 'river Indians'. These interrelated tribes had undergone great hardships in recent years. It was with the east-river Indians that Uncas, that dissident Pequot of royal blood, had taken refuge and it was Podunk and Scantic braves whom he had recruited for Mason's expedition. More devastating even than the Pequot enemies was a natural disaster, a plague, probably the smallpox, which ravaged the river Indians. The Matianucks had suffered severely, losing their chief sachem Nattawantut so that by this time there were probably hardly more than 300 Indians on the whole west bank. War and pestilence, therefore, had reduced the local Indians to such a sorry condition that the Windsor settlers found them by no means menacing. The sight and scents of their cooking fires became part of the village scene; and the settlers came to take for granted the importunities and kindnesses of the squaws on their doorsteps with offerings of corncobs, squashes and game. For a generation their Indian neighbours remained an easily contained problem of parochial government, an affair of local magistrates' courts, of theft, drunkenness, the illicit sale of muskets and only occasionally of mayhem. Across the river, opposite Great Meadow, the Podunks in their stockaded fort under their sachem Tontonimo were more numerous and were able, it was said, to mobilize 200 bowmen. Nonetheless, they remained friendly to the English under the guidance of Uncas and were to take their side in the intermittent skirmishing and diplomacy characteristic of Anglo-Indian relations at that time.

One reason for these relatively harmonious relations may have been the scrupulous way, according to their lights, in which these God-fearing Puritans took care to purchase a legal title to their lands. In this they took their cue from the Plymouth Colony on whose behalf Jonathan Brewster had negotiated the sale of the Matianuck homelands on which the Dorchester settlers were squatting. The Windsor people bought these rights from their Plymouth neighbours in 1637. This made a substantial beginning; but like

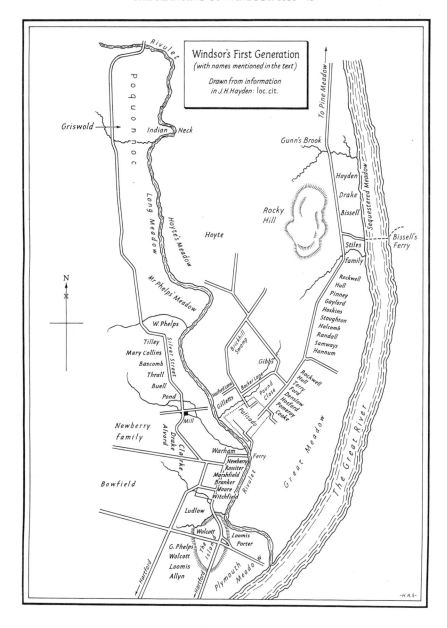

Windsor's First Generation
(with names mentioned in the text)

*Drawn from information
in J.H.Hayden: loc. cit.*

good English country landowners they were concerned to round out their estate. William Phelps, Ludlow's partner on the 1635 commission for Connecticut, had already in that year acquired from its sachem, one Sheat, rich, pleasant meadowland towards Poquonnoc at the bend of the Rivulet north-west of the Palisado, which came to be called Indian Neck; in 1637 a syndicate of four acquired for the town a large tract stretching north and west towards the hills of Massaco; another sachem, Nassahegan, who held sway over the whole wilderness north and west of Poquonnoc towards the Massaco hills, sold off his extensive rights piecemeal and his son sold Samuel Marshall the island in the Rivulet opposite Indian Neck. A similar process of accretion took place with the lands on the east bank of the Connecticut. The agent here was John Bissell who bought from a Namerick Indian a wide stretch of territory which, except for 200 acres, he transferred to the town. In such ways did the infant settlement of Windsor acquire from the local Indians the land titles to a vast territory.

It is notorious, however, that such land titles were ambiguous. English and Indians both seem to have acted in good faith; but it is hardly surprising that their understanding of the nature of the contract differed. For the Indians the rights they were transferring were those of a peripatetic people to hunt and fish and cultivate their corn patches in a wide and ill-defined range of territory; for the English, the principal right they thought they were acquiring was the freehold ownership of a specifically defined tract of land on which to build a homestead and farm, that cherished possession for which, in part, they had braved the Atlantic. This incongruity is seen in the wording of the conveyances recording these transactions, so obviously drafted by Englishmen with a smattering of legal training, but with an Indian's mark and purporting to be his own wishes. Thus:

> Know all men by these presents that I, Nassahegan of Paquanick, sachem, have freely given and granted and do hereby alienate and assign unto John Mason of Windsor, all my right and interest in all my land lying between Paquantock and Massacoe ... there to be enjoyed fully and freely without any future disturbance by the said John Mason or his assigns. Witness my hand this 13th of March Anno Domini, 1641.

The crucial agreement whereby Plymouth Colony conveyed to Windsor the title to the Indian lands at Matianuck was signed, sealed and delivered at Windsor on 15 May 1637, at the onset of the Pequot offensive, between Mr Prince for Plymouth and Roger Ludlow and William Phelps, the two commissioners, for Windsor. It was the final act of a long and difficult negotiation. When Ludlow and his exploring party squatted on Plymouth land at Matianuck in the summer of 1635 the Plymouth people protested; but it was only the next winter, when Ludlow returned to the Bay, that the question of Plymouth Colony's rights was tackled as part of the secret negotiation with the Warwick patentees. On 24 February 1636 the Dorchester principals and the representatives of Plymouth Colony came together and 'labored to drive a bargain'. Those labours were only concluded over a year later.

Meanwhile the Windsor planters were already staking out claims to their lands. The first land distribution in Windsor, which ran its course between 1636 and 1641, amounted in all to 16,600 acres. The earliest records for Windsor are not extant but it seems probable that the first distributions were made by a few key people such as Ludlow and Phelps, the two Windsor commissioners; Henry Wolcott the constable; John Warham the minister, and the three ruling elders of the church, John Branker, William Hosford and John Witchfield. They would probably have decided which home lots, meadow and upland should be granted to each of the eighty or so families and individual householders. The town surveyor, Matthew Grant, surveyed the land, and the town clerk, Bray Rossiter, recorded them. They were then reported to the court at Hartford. They are still extant in the colony records.

The disposition of home lots was determined largely by the *faits accomplis* of the Sandy Bank squatters. This bank, stretching nearly two miles north from the Rivulet, was the natural site for the first settlers who claimed their own immediate strips of the rich meadowland lying between the bank and the Connecticut. The first Windsor settlement, therefore, consisted of a line of about forty-five homesteads which Matthew Grant set about surveying and recording during those first two seasons of 1635 and 1636. Situated along the brow of the hill, they were easily aligned by the surveyor to a uniform frontage which became a rudimentary village street. These home lots were normally between four and five acres. The street frontage varied similarly from 10 or 12 rods (55 to 66 yards) to 20 or so rods (110 yards), with a few significant exceptions such as that of Thomas Stoughton with his 150-yard frontage.

This was to be a different kind of village street from those they had known in their native Dorset and Somerset. The first homesteads may have been small and primitive cabins but their home lots were no mere cottage gardens. They were smallholdings with corn and vegetable patches, cow pastures and, in time, orchards. With an average street frontage of 95 yards, their freeholder's relationship with their neighbours was spacious and expansive; and once established, the contrast with the more cramped circumstances so many had grown up to in the west of England must have been a lasting satisfaction. South of the street was that quadrilateral of thirty acres or so which made up the Palisado. At its centre was the village green with about seven home lots allocated for the most part to Windsor notables such as John Mason. And so the town fathers and their surveyor used natural features and squatter preferences to shape the beginnings of a rationally planned township based on street, square, river, meadow and upland.

At the beginning, they confined themselves to the area north of and adjacent to the Rivulet; but, especially after May 1637, when the Plymouth people waived their rights (save for the trading post itself which they kept for the time being), the Windsor people turned their attention to the Little and Plymouth meadows, prime land, equal to the meadows on the north side. Some of this low-lying land was liable to flooding, as settlers like Ludlow and William Phelps discovered in the disastrous spring flood of 1638. More fortunate were those who settled on what came to be called 'the Island' because in such times it remained high and dry. This, with the bank flanking Little Meadow, was the area preferred by more prominent settlers like the Ludlows, Wolcotts, and Rossiters, those West Country gentry who had put such initiative and investment into the Dorchester enterprise. Here, too, were to be found the 'clerisy': the minister John Warham, deacon John Moore, elder John Witchfield, schoolmaster John Branker and those parson's sons, the Gillett brothers, as well as other substantial citizens a year or two later like the Loomises and the Porters. Adjacent to this nucleus and to a brook which became the millstream were the lots of the seven Newberry children, and beyond a further cluster of more modest homesteads running down to the Rivulet. This, together with a similar hamlet on the other side of the Rivulet (to be called Pound Close), thickened out the village topography and added a more rounded settlement pattern to the north–south line stretching from Rocky Hill at the north, down across the Rivulet to the Island and Plymouth Meadow to the south.

Windsor was designed as a compact village community. Some home lots were larger than the norm – 10 to 13 acres was common in Plymouth Meadow – and a few were much larger. Roger Ludlow held 122 acres in the heart of the southern hamlet between Little and Plymouth meadows at the fork of two brooks which provided him with his own landing from the river. William Phelps, after his house had been 'drowned deep' in the 1639 flood, removed to those extensive meadows he had negotiated from the Indians up the Rivulet half-way to Poquonnoc; further up still, Edward Griswold had a 30-acre homelot; Thomas Stoughton had 52 acres on Main Street: and the Stiles family, cold-shouldered by the Dorchester people, settled on adjacent home lots of some 45 acres at the north end of the plantation together with the 360 acres of Saltonstall Park on the east side of the river. But these were exceptions. In general, however well-to-do the family, the size of home lots was designed to be comparable. The pattern of settlement, like that of Dorchester, was an oligarchy with a strong egalitarian base.

But no planter survived on his home lot, however fertile. For a living he depended on access to meadow and upland for corn and hay, to marsh for pasture and to woodland for fuel and feed for swine. And so his grant from the plantation included meadow, upland and marsh. The grant of meadow normally took the form of large strips in whichever of the meadows was most accessible to his home lot, and more roughly defined acres of upland behind the village plots in Northwest Field, Browfield, Brickhill or Pipe-Stave swamps. Of these, the most important was the meadow, that rich silt which had first beckoned them from the Bay. This was allocated on the old English principle of open-field strips, though much larger than those of an English village. Beyond the accessible meadow, marsh and upland, most of the unimproved land continued to be held 'in common' by the plantation, except for the east bank of the river where upland and forest stretched for miles into the wilderness. The Windsor people had some sort of title to the latter from the Podunks, and on this basis the first settlers were granted long strips of land in the form of a river frontage defined as so many rods, extending three miles inland. This was long-term investment, save for riperian meadows which were used for mowing and pasture (except by John Bissell who, as ferryman, had a vested interest in developing the east bank territory and would be the first to build there, at his ferry landing).

Home lots were homogeneous; but the size of a man's total allotment depended on his investment in the original enterprise (his contribution to the expenses of removal, the purchase of land from the Indians, the cost of its survey and so forth), together with the value of his 'estate', i.e. his social status, and the size of his family obligations. Grants to family heads ranged widely from 20 or 30 acres at the lower end of the scale to upwards of 300 acres in the first quarter. A few grandees were allotted land a whole order of magnitude greater than that of the generality. Ten families had more than 400 acres each; a few were truly affluent like the Newberrys, Bissells, Stiles, Fords and Wolcotts with between 600 and nearly 800 acres each. The top 10 per cent received over 37 per cent of the total and the top 25 per cent

57½ per cent, in contrast to the bottom quarter of nineteen families with less than 5 per cent, an average of only 42 acres each. From the beginning, despite the relative uniformity of home lots, property owning was a fairly stratified affair.

The town's minister was also treated with special favour. In Windsor, as in Dorchester, John Warham was well provided for. In land wealth he was among the first 10 per cent and this was prime land: a home lot with adjoining meadow of 16 acres next the Rivulet in the centre of settlement; 24 acres in Great Meadow; two acres of meadow over the river; and further meadow, upland and wood across the river 60 rods (320 yards) wide and stretching two miles inland (i.e. 360 acres). In addition he was granted 82 acres sandwiched between the Newberry lots on both sides of the Mill Brook. Alongside all this he enjoyed the right to tolls from the town's grist mill. In this unique way the town fathers ensured the wellbeing of their respected minister of God's Word.

Determining the size and location of land grants was not the only, though no doubt the most onerous, of the town fathers' duties. They had also to survey the highways and define the incipient by-paths which the feet of settlers and their beasts, and the weight of sleds and ox carts were pressing out on the way to and from meadow and wood lots. The Palisado had tracks round its perimeter; and from its north entrance there was laid out Main Street two miles long and one chain (22 yards) wide. At its northern end Main Street gave access to the stone quarry of Rocky Hill before crossing Gun's Brook and petering out on its way up to Pine Meadow. Out of the Palisado's west side gate there was laid out a secondary highway north-west towards Indian Neck and connecting with other back lanes. Similarly, a highway went south from Mr Warham's to Roger Ludlow's and thence past Plymouth Meadow over the Island on its way some ten miles downstream to Hartford. At its upper end a branch went north-west past the Newberrys to Warham's mill and thence across the millstream out towards William Phelps and Poquonnoc; and here, also, a spidery network of back lanes linked home lots in meandering village fashion (see plan on p.135).

But for a settlement bounded by two rivers, roads were not enough. From the beginning, the Rivulet was a barrier and a ferry across it essential. The Rivulet ferry, approached by a lane at the south-east corner of the Palisado, was in operation from earliest days and the appointment of a ferryman and details of his franchise were to be a regular feature of the town records. Limits were set on the number of passengers: thirty-five in the large canoe, six in the small, and precedence given on the Lord's Day to magistrates and elders. It was tantalizing to have to use a ferry over so small a river with high banks, and a bridge was an early priority. Unfortunately the bridge was shortly carried away by a spring freshet and not replaced during the time of this chronicle; so the Rivulet ferry continued to be the vital passage between north and south Windsor, part of the diurnal routine of the village. Its ferryman was usually a humble sort of fellow, like John Bartlett who lodged in a cellar beneath his boathouse because his own home lot was too far away at Poquonnoc.

Not so his fellow who kept the other ferry, that across the Great River. This, at the upper end of the settlement and reached by lane from the Main Street opposite Rocky Hill, was strategically essential not only for Windsor but for the whole colony's communication with the outside world. One branch of the Great Trail from the Bay terminated at Windsor ferry above Scantic River and the road upstream to William Pynchon's settlement at Springfield started here. This ferry was so important that the franchise to operate it was under the control of the General Court. The first recorded ferryman was John Bissell to whom the colony granted a licence in 1648 and in whose family it was to remain throughout our period. As we have seen, Bissell had a large grant up near Rocky Hill and this, together with his ferry privilege and his large holdings east of the river, made him an important figure at the upper end of the settlement.

Apart from ferries and grist mill, other public facilities had to wait until the Windsor families had cleared home lots, planted fields and built proper houses to replace the hovels, dug into Sandy Bank and roofed with turf, which had been their bivouacs for too long. Building houses was no easy task for those who were not skilled craftsmen. Fortunately Windsor could muster a number of settlers trained in building trades, including the surveyor himself, Matthew Grant, Francis Stiles who had brought six apprentices with him, and William Buell, who was to fit out the meeting house. Eltweed Pomeroy was a blacksmith, as was his son and Grant's son Tahan. Indeed, most of these craftsmen brought up their sons to these trades. William Thrall was a mason whose Rocky Hill quarry provided stone for cellars, chimneys, well-linings and gravestones; and Thomas Bascomb, of Bridport, Dorset, was also a brick- and stonemason. With such skilled cadres to call on, this first Windsor generation built sturdily in the tradition of the English house they were used to and which the tradesmen among them had been apprenticed to build.

Roger Ludlow, as the would-be squire, ordered a house of stone to be built on Plymouth Meadow; unfortunately for him, it had to be abandoned in the flood of 1638; and Matthew Allyn may have acquired the Plymouth trading post which was reputedly built from prefabricated parts imported from England. Otherwise, Windsor homes were built on the spot of local wood except for stone chimneys and essential ironwork such as bolts, nails and locks which in early days were imported.

Their cottages were constructed in true English fashion, of timber frames erected with a minimum of foundation on the bare earth and with a sharply pitched roof. Though other woods were plentiful and some more easily worked with adzes and broad axe, the beams and joists were of oak, as in England. Oak was traditional and so hard-wearing that a number of such houses, with their broad, uneven floor beams, are still standing, notably the original part of Walter Filer's house, built as early as 1640 within the Palisado. But the New England climate had already forced the settlers to make some adjustments. George Phelps's house on Plymouth Meadow was burnt to the ground on Sunday 11 October 1640 while the good Windsor people were at meeting listening to a sermon by their new minister, Ephraim Huitt. The risk of fire in those dry hot summers led them from bitter experience to build chimneys of the local red sandstone or of brick (though still bonded by clay mixed with hay as in England), and to abandon West Country thatch in favour of the less combustible wooden shingles. The clunch infilling of the West Country proved inadequate against the harshness of the winter and was supplemented by the clapboard or weatherboard more characteristic of Essex and now of New England.

These first cottages were modest affairs of two rooms, parlour and hall or kitchen, divided and heated by a central chimney, and a loft reached by a circular stair encased beside the chimney, with low ceilings and small windows which sometimes lacked proper glazing. Sometimes by raising the roof line, lofts were converted into upstairs rooms, the 'chamber over the parlour' or 'over the hall' or a 'cockloft' over a porch. Then a lean-to might be added at the rear, roofed with that extension from the main roof which was to give such houses the appearance of a salt box and provide a kitchen separate from the hall.

If you entered the front door of Mr Huitt the minister's house, you found, to the left of the central chimney, the parlour; this was a low-ceilinged but fair-sized room on the right wall of which was a large, open fireplace. It was furnished as a 'keeping room' with a long oak table and bench, six stools and chairs with velvet seat covers, carpets and cushions; it also served as the master bedroom with the principal, ornate bedstead and hangings. Ranged against the walls were a chest, three trunks and a box remaining from the

142

Atlantic voyage containing bolts of cloth, table and bed linen including fourteen pairs of sheets, towels, napkins and wearing apparel on some scale. There were also two desks and a valuable library of books, as befitted a man of the cloth. Displayed on the trestle table and on shelves were pewter salts and bowls, a silver dish and 'thirteen spoons given to children, having their names on them'. Passing through into the hall you found another long table, with a bench and four chairs and some pewter; otherwise this was a work room with three spinning wheels and linen yarn, four muskets and fowling pieces, swords and bandoliers and some kitchen ware. In the Huitt house the hall was not itself the kitchen but led into it. Here was the great kitchen fireplace flanked by an oven and furnished with bellows, irons, crooks, tongs, spits and pothangers. Ranged on shelves were brass and iron pots and pans of various kinds, skimmers and ladles and, cluttering the floor, tubs, pails, churns, butter barrels and implements such as saws, axes and pitchforks. Outside the kitchen door across the yard was a barn storing wheat, peas, oats, rye, hay and flax. Coming indoors again and up the cottage staircase by the chimney you found two loft rooms on the upper floor. The chamber over the parlour was a family bedroom containing three beds with bolsters, pillows, rugs and blankets and more storage chests, in one of which there were nine dozen trenchers. The chamber over the hall, called in the inventory the 'corn chamber', was just that: like the barn it was used for storing grain.

Because he was the minister, Ephraim Huitt's home was more substantial than most. Towards the other end of the scale was the modest dwelling of Thomas Barber, veteran of the Pequot fort fight. His parlour was furnished with a bed, two tables, a cupboard, some chests and old trunks filled with bed and table linen, a saddle and bridle, a halberd, cutlass and belt, two guns and a book or two. The kitchen had little more than its array of brass and iron kettles, skillets, pots, and a table. The hall, apart from its two beds and bedding, was not only cluttered up with bolts of cloth, timber, corn, wheat, peas, hay and flax, scythes and a cart and tackle, but also sheltered horses, cows, bullocks and sheep. In addition there was a lean-to which housed more timber, a barrel of cider and another cow; and there was a shop containing carpenter's tools and yet more timber. Such were the modest domestic possessions of this one-time apprentice of Francis Stiles who made his living as a carpenter and small farmer.

Within a few years the Windsor landscape became dotted every hundred yards or so with upwards of eighty such dwellings, a few already aspiring to be full two-storey houses. Functional but of satisfying proportions, their shingled roofs and clapboard walls weathered into soft grey tones, and they were flanked by outhouses and barns and roughly landscaped with orchard trees from England and shelter trees and shrubs from the wilderness around them.

The planters' energies were so absorbed by building homes and clearing lots that they had little time for community enterprises. Perhaps constructing the Palisado had taken too much out of them. At any rate even that first priority, a meeting house for worship and instruction, was some years getting off the ground. Meanwhile the settlers who formed Windsor church must make do as best they could, listening to sermons and lectures in the open if the season were clement or, if not, crowded into one of their neighbour's larger Palisado homes. This was also true of town meetings. It was over a decade later, in the early 1650s, that Nicholas Denslow's house and orchard in the Palisado were sold to the town for a 'town house' and its barn used for the payment of taxes in kind; and it was also only at this time that a smithy and a barber's shop were built on the Palisado green, Tahan Grant being the smith. One public facility could not wait. The burial ground was established as early as 1636 in the south-west corner of the Palisado on the river bluff where it remains to this day.

By the end of 1641, Windsor's first land distribution was virtually complete. Thereafter the town clerk's new entries were for a trickle of latecomers or for purchases either from the town or from existing landholders. The total lands thus distributed consisted of grants to ninety-four heads of families or single individuals. Of these, sixty-three (67 per cent) are known to have come to Windsor from Dorchester, most in the great migration of 1635 and 1636. Of the rest, we know that five came from elsewhere in Massachusetts Bay and eleven (12 per cent) travelled upriver to Windsor directly from England. This leaves some thirteen (14 per cent) whose origins cannot now be traced but who may also have drifted south from the Bay. One or two of the latter would make their mark, but the evanescent circumstances of most suggest they may have been servants. Windsor remained dominated by Dorchester people, who formed perhaps as much as 70 per cent of the founding population.

The minority who arrived upriver direct from England consisted of two groups. The first was the Stiles family who have already been mentioned, Saltonstall's advance party for a settlement of gentry (known in Windsor folklore as the 'Lords and Ladies'). The other group came in 1638 in the company of the Rev. Ephraim Huitt, John Warham's new teaching colleague of Windsor church, successor to John Maverick who, it will be remembered, had died just as the Dorchester congregation were on the point of departure. Like Warham, Huitt had been harrassed by Archbishop Laud and had been impelled to leave his living near Kenilworth, Warwickshire and to emigrate. His advent gave new strength to Windsor church and his inaugural sermon on 18 August 1639 galvanized the congregation. He was a practical pioneer as well as a spiritual teacher. He set on foot the building of a meeting house and of that bridge which was swept away in the flood, and enjoyed supervising the construction of the latter. (So preoccupied was he with this one afternoon that his two Hartford colleagues, Masters Hooker and Stone, who had come to call, tiptoed away saying to each other 'Ephraim is joined to his idols; let him alone'.) Sadly, he was to die within five years and his tomb was the first of its kind in the burial ground where it remains. During his short pastorate he exerted a considerable influence on Windsor's affairs. He and his family brought with them a party consisting of Warwickshire neighbours like Edward Griswold; Joseph Loomis and John Porter from Essex; Daniel Clarke and, probably, John Bissell the ferryman.

Despite the arrival of these Midlanders, the families from Dorset and Somerset remained the central core of the settlement. Of those ninety-four heads of family, fifty-two (56 per cent) are known to have come from the West Country and there may well have been others whose origins cannot now be traced. Thirty-two were passengers on the *Mary and John* and a further eleven on one of the other voyages from Weymouth or Plymouth which John White masterminded between 1629 and 1634. Of the West Country people in Windsor, some 82 per cent were seasoned by their common Atlantic uprooting a decade before. Even after all the vicissitudes of the voyage, the sojourn at Dorchester, the wilderness trek and the grim first winters on the Great River, the West Country congregation who had dedicated themselves at the New Hospital in Plymouth that day in 1630 continued to dominate the Windsor scene.

The coherence of this West Country community is revealed by the way they arranged to settle next one another in the same neighbourhoods in Windsor, as they had done in Dorchester. We have noted how the gentry and clerisy 'set down' on home lots next each other in Little and Plymouth meadows and the Island. With few exceptions these were the notables of the *Mary and John* and her related ships. On Little Meadow there were John Warham the minister (of Crewkerne, Somerset), Roger Ludlow the magistrate (of Maiden Bradley, Wiltshire), Brian Rossiter the town clerk (of Combe St Nicholas, Somerset), John Branker the elder and schoolmaster (of

Ilminster, Somerset) and John Moore the deacon. On the Island, beyond this row of neighbours, with lots in Plymouth Meadow, were Henry Wolcott, magistrate and the town's first constable, and his sons, and William Phelps, also magistrate, and his brother George, all of Somerset. Prominent in this neighbourhood were the Newberry family. It will be remembered that Thomas Newberry, of Marshwood Vale, Dorset, one of the principal investors in Dorchester, Massachusetts, had died on the eve of the trek to Connecticut. He left a widow, seven children and an estate valued at over £1500. His extensive rights in the Connecticut venture were distributed among his children who had a combined family holding of nearly 800 acres. Fortunately his widow, Jane, promptly married John Warham whose wife had recently died, and the Newberry children were taken under his wing and into his new home on Little Meadow. Each Newberry child had his or her own holding next to one another and to Warham's own lands. Finally there was Matthew Allyn who probably bought the Plymouth trading post; he was a man of means and, though not from Dorchester, he hailed from Braunton, Devon and was thus an acceptable neighbour.

Here in this hamlet south of the Rivulet were to be found the homes of all the gentry and most of the notables and principal officers of the town, all West Countrymen: two magistrates and Assistants of the colony court, the minister, the town clerk, the schoolmaster who was also a ruling elder, the deacon, the constable. And the process of intermarrying among the children of suitable neighbours had begun. Henry Wolcott the younger had recently married the girl virtually next door, Sarah Newberry; Daniel Clarke who came with Huitt and would become prominent in the colony would shortly marry another Newberry daughter and buy a home lot next the Warhams.

Equally striking are the neighbourly relations of those who elected to settle next each other along Sandy Bank. With very few exceptions, the first thirty or so families with homes on Main Street were old Dorchester people. Of the twenty-four with home lots nearest the Palisado, sixteen came from the West Country, ten from Dorset and six from Somerset. Of the Dorset people, all but two families (the Terrys of Dorchester and the Hannums of Caundle Purse) hailed from one small Dorset neighbourhood: the secluded little valley of the River Brit, six miles or so upstream from Bridport. The Randalls and the Denslows from Allington, Thomas Ford and Aaron Cook from nearby Simonsbury and the Pomeroys, Hosfords, Hoskins and Samways from Beaminster. Twelve years before, the Hosfords and Randalls had sailed in the same ship along with the Parkmans from Sidmouth whose home lot was nearby in the Palisado, and the Pomeroys, Hoskins, Denslows, Thomas Ford and Aaron Cook as well as the Terrys and the Hannums had sailed in the *Mary and John.* The propinquity was deliberate. William Hosford and Nicholas Denslow, both from the Brit Valley, had owned contiguous meadows in Dorchester and were again next-door neighbours, both in home and meadow lots, in Windsor. The fact that these homesteads were the first in sequence north of the Palisado suggests that these were among the first to settle on Sandy Bank, probably that first summer of 1635.

Further up the street the Somerset people show a similar neighbourliness. Of the six Somerset families, two were from Broadway, two from Chilthorne Domer, one from nearby Crewkerne and only one, the Rockwells, from further afield, from Fitzhead and that not so very far; and all save Thomas Dibble were passengers in *Mary and John.*

This Main Street community included men of substance and position. Three were members of the General Court: Thomas Ford, one of the richest men in town, William Gaylord, deacon, and George Hull. William Hosford was a ruling elder; William Rockwell an original deacon of Warham's church in Plymouth and would have been prominent in Windsor had he not died in 1640; his widow, Susan Capen of the Dorchester merchant family, married their neighbour down the street in the Palisado, Matthew Grant, the town surveyor; and Stephen Terry was a parson's son and nephew of John White. These families were also intermarrying. Humphrey Pinney's homestead was sandwiched between those of the Hulls, father and son: he married George Hull's daughter Mary whom he first got to know on shipboard in the *Mary and John.* William Hosford's elder daughter Esther was in process of marrying Richard Samways whose homestead was just along Main Street; they had both been born and brought up in Beaminster, Dorset. Aaron Cook had recently married Thomas Ford's daughter Mary; they, too, had been brought up in Dorset, in the Ford home in Simonsbury and Dorchester.

Main Street and Plymouth Meadow, with their notable and substantial planters, were in marked contrast to those subsidiary neighbourhoods, Backer Row and Mill Road. Here in the back lanes lived more modest people, especially in Mill Road where only two or three families could boast grants from the plantation of anything approaching 100 acres, and several, like the widow Collins, only a few acres. This was the poor end of town; it came snobbishly to be called 'Silver Street' because its inhabitants were reduced to eating alewives, those tiny fish used for manure which was all they could afford and which left their telltale silver scales in the lane. Only one inhabitant of Silver Street, Thomas Bascombe, brickmaker and mason of Bridport, Dorset, came from the West Country.

CHAPTER 8: MATTHEW GRANT AND WINDSOR'S FIRST GENERATION 1641–62

A KEY MEMBER OF THE WINDSOR TEAM WHICH NEGOTIATED THE conveyance of the Matianuck lands from Plymouth Colony in 1637 was the man whom we have met briefly as the town surveyor. Matthew Grant, then thirty-six, was to play a pivotal role in the settlement of Windsor. He was one of the original settlers of Dorchester, Massachusetts where he became a freeman as early as May 1631 along with a number of *Mary and John* people, and he, his wife Priscilla and an infant daughter may have been passengers on that ship and from the West Country. When Priscilla died he married William Rockwell's widow Susan, also of *Mary and John*, who had been a Capen of Dorchester, Dorset. In Dorchester-on-the-Bay he was nominated to 'view the pales' and surveyed the great lots there. He was on Connecticut River with Ludlow's advance party in the summer of 1635 and was one of the twelve who returned overland so dramatically to the Bay that December. In Windsor his grant from the plantation was comparatively modest and he continued to work at his trade as a carpenter; but he quickly became a person of note. He had been trained as a surveyor and in Windsor he began to make his mark in that profession. He surveyed the Great Meadow as early as September 1635 and when the pioneers returned to the Connecticut River a second time in the spring of 1636 he was quickly at work as the official surveyor measuring home lots, meadow and upland. He was to continue in this key role for the next forty years. As he wrote in old age in 1675: 'I have been employed in measuring of land and setting out of lots to men, which has been done by me from our first beginning here, come next September is 40 years.' In due course Matthew Grant, surveyor, will by a logical progression become town clerk and make an even greater contribution to the foundation, as well as the history, of Windsor in its first generation.

For the time being life in Windsor was a matter of surviving from harvest to harvest. The people soon settled into the habits of subsistence farming they had practised in Dorchester, except that the fertile meadows of the Connecticut were far more rewarding for their husbandry. In these, Windsor's 'planting fields', lots were carefully apportioned in fairly uniform units: in Plymouth Meadow an average of 5.4 acres for each of its eleven original householders, in Great Meadow 8.3 acres for each of the forty-nine. These were contiguous strips in a vast open field cultivated according to a communal plan. Thus the 400 or so acres assigned to individual settlers in Great Meadow (about two-thirds of the whole) were farmed on a single-crop pattern. The decisions as to what crop should be planted and when, and who should be responsible for the fencing needed to protect the young grain from predatory cattle and swine, were made in March; the dates of harvest and the subsequent day when the cattle were allowed to feed on the stubble were decided early in September, usually on the militia's summer training day. The latter date, which applied to Great and Plymouth meadows and those over the river, came traditionally to be 25 September, one of the cardinal dates of the farming year.

In those early years there was little argument about the crop. It was normally maize, drilled and hoed in rows five or six feet apart as the Indians had shown them. In May the shoots were protected by hummocks of earth manured by alewives caught as they so conveniently spawned up the river or by even less salubrious cods' heads. In June when, as the Indians had it, the leaves on the white oaks were no bigger than mouse ears, the patches between were weeded and planted with squashes, pumpkins and beans trained to run up the growing corn stalks. It was a well-tried system and the only improvement made by the English was to cross-plough the field at six-foot intervals to facilitate planting and weeding. Maize was the most prolific crop, the staple for cattle and, on the cob or ground into meal, for cooking pots and skillets. Most of this first generation whose inventories are extant held stores of Indian corn in their lofts and barns.

However, the planters soon improved the local husbandry by introducing English grains, especially spring wheat. As early as 1644 Ephraim Huitt's inventory lists a stock of English wheat and thirteen of the next twenty extant inventories include a stock of it. Also evident, though in much smaller quantity, were oats (as fodder for horses) and rye; and although there was no barley in store, there were good supplies of malt for the beer which, together with cider, were the universal beverages. Henry Wolcott owned a hopyard. Judging by the amount in store, the pea crop was almost as important as wheat.

English crops needed more than mattock and hoe, and ploughs were soon imported. Made of wood with iron shares and coulters, they were repaired by local blacksmiths like Tahan Grant and Eltweed Pomeroy. Of twenty-eight settlers dying with itemized inventories before the end of 1662, thirteen had their own ploughs, usually with tackle and sometimes harrows. These were pulled by oxen. All plough owners and others too had at least one yoke and often young doctored steers being trained as draft animals. Out of those twenty-eight, fourteen people owned upwards of 30 oxen and 20 steers.

These teams were also needed to clear the upland. This sometimes broke ploughs and demanded the traction of two or even three yoke. Upland was a general term for higher ground away from the river, often uncleared and merging into the ubiquitous woodland. The nearest upland was Northwest Field, Bow Field and land on the highway towards Hartford. These were granted in larger lots than the more valuable meadow. The Island people owned an average of 25 acres each of such land towards Hartford, the people on the Main Street upwards of 20 in Northwest Field, and there were even larger grants further afield, chiefly towards Poquonnock and Pine Meadow. In the early years, the settlers probably lived largely on the proceeds of their home and meadow lots, using their upland to graze livestock and for wood: but before long they might need the extra arable and this would demand all the ox power they could muster.

Horses, whether of Flemish or English stock, were no match for oxen as draft animals; they suffered more than other livestock from the Atlantic voyage, dying from disease and the buffeting of shipboard, and they were expensive to keep. They were used chiefly for riding. Of our twenty-eight owners of inventories, twelve owned horses (eight stallions and eight mares) together with seven colts, most with saddles, bridles and pillions; and in one case a side-saddle, cloth and cloak bag for the womenfolk. Horses, which cost between £9 and £18, were valuable beasts and with very few exceptions belonged to more affluent settlers.

Crops were vital for subsistence but the chief concern of Windsor people

151

was their cattle, for dairying and rearing for market. Most Windsor folk had been brought up in the parts of Somerset, Dorset and Devon where the rural economy was based on mixed farming with a strong emphasis on dairying and livestock. They had brought their own cattle with them in *Mary and John*; it was their owners' urgent need for grazing that had forced their improvised stay at Mattapan and had attracted them to the Connecticut. The original stock from which the New England herds were bred probably came in those West Country ships. The familiar red Devon proved better able to survive the New England winter in the open than its rival Dutch strain.

Most families had their own milch cows and often a calf or two along with goats and hens kept on their home lots in open weather and in the shelter of a barn for the worst of the winter. Milking and making butter and cheese, together with looking after the poultry, were domestic jobs for wives and growing children as they had been in the West Country. Many families reared store cattle to be butchered for their own table, for neighbours, for what soon came to be Hartford market and then for markets further afield. Despite the disastrous experience of those first winters when so many cattle were lost, the Windsor herds bred apace. Of the twenty-eight inventories for those first twenty-five years, 22 persons left cattle totalling some 92 cows, 26 heifers, 17 bullocks and calves. Since these belonged only to that small minority who happen to have died, the Windsor herds must have grown into several hundred beasts.

The management of the herds was a matter of conscious breeding control. From time to time the General Court or the town appointed individuals to regulate the killing of calves in order to determine which should be 'reared for bulls', and to ensure that enough beeves should mature to provide a supply of hides. (The tanning of hides for leather was an important adjunct to cattle raising. The first tanner was Thomas Thornton who employed several workmen. In 1647 he sold his business in the Palisado to John Strong of Chard, Somerset, who came of a tanning family. His son, Return Strong, would inherit his father's tanyard and carry on the leather business, becoming a man of some property.)

The cattle were herded to and from their pastures morning and evening by the town cowherd with his horn. After 25 September they grazed on the stubble to fatten for the winter, then during the winter months sheltered under cover or near the homestead, feeding on hay harvested from those parts of the meadows which the town had left for pasture. Nearly one-third of Great Meadow, 200 acres, remained common land and was left fallow for mowing; and strips in the common field might be laid down to pasture in crop rotation. Cattle had a voracious appetite for fodder and needed all the available grassland because the local wild rye, broomstraw, reeds and sedges, though prolific, were rank and not very nourishing compared with English clover and bluegrass. Only in the 1650s did hay from these 'English grasses' become significant as fodder and even then it was exceptional. (In 1657 when the town wanted to smarten up its burial ground, the fathers decided 'to sow it with English grass that it [might] be decent and comely' like a lawn.)

Apart from beef cattle, swine were important animals. The English archbacked hogs adapted well to the New England wilderness; they were tough, used to rooting for themselves in the woods and fierce enough to fend off marauding wolves and rattlesnakes. Although their habit of breaking down fences to forage among the growing crops made them a notorious menace and their owners liable for heavy fines to retrieve them from the hog pound down by the Rivulet, these swine were a cardinal feature of the domestic economy. Every family had its hogs and sows to be killed in the late fall and salted down for pork and hams. By contrast sheep were difficult to establish, subject to disease and easy meat for wolves. Only Thomas Buckland with his flock of seventeen sheep and lambs, his 'weaver's gear' and stock of woollen yarn, appears to have persevered with the making of woollen cloth.

This presented Windsor people with a problem. By the early 1640s the stock of clothing they had brought with them ten years before, however long lasting their linen, woollens and canvas, was beginning to wear out and efforts were made to encourage home spinning and weaving. An attempt at making cloth from cotton imported from the West Indies was an expensive failure though the cotton was used to pad out the corselets the militia wore against Indian arrows. More promising were linen and canvas. John Winthrop perceived this in 1638. He wrote from Boston: 'You must turn your corn into flax and hemp, by which course you may soon outstrip us, for that is a merchantable commodity and one acre with you will yield more than 4 with us'. And three years later, the General Court, noting in good mercantilist style that 'whereas it is observed . . . that much ground within these liberties may be improved in hemp and flax, and that we might in time have supply of linen cloth amongst ourselves', resolved that each family should plant a spoonful of English hemp seed 'in some fruitful soil' and provide at least half a pound of hemp or flax. This was followed by further instructions in the next two years for the making of ropes and canvas for rigging ships. Windsor people from west Dorset, and especially the Brit

Valley with its flax and hemp for the looms of Beaminster and the rope-walks of Bridport, would have needed no prompting. Unfortunately, the quality of yarn which resulted from these measures was so inferior that 'many weavers [were] discouraged from going on with their trade', and so the court appointed two 'experienced men' to regulate the price and quality of the yarn. It is significant that one of the two people appointed by Windsor to do this was Eltweed Pomeroy from Beaminster. It is unclear how successful this promotion was, but judging by the inventories flax and hemp were spun and woven inside those early homesteads. There were four homes with more than one spinning wheel each, two with looms 'and gear', others with cards and combs, eighteen homes with stocks of hemp, flax or wool, mostly in yarn, and all but two with hemp and flax. Of these eighteen, nine were West Country families.

Another activity to which Windsor's West Country people paid early attention was planting orchards. In New England, as once in Somerset, cider was their staple drink morning, noon and night. They must have brought apple trees with them or sent for them very early because orchards were sufficiently established to be separately itemized in inventories as early as 1649 when William Hill of Lyme Regis died leaving an apple orchard and a nursery of eleven grafted young trees valued at £15. The twenty-eight inventories before 1662 feature ten orchards, all, save Hill's, in home yards. Seven of the ten owners came from the West Country.

So much for the growth of Windsor's cottage economy; but what of those extractive commodities which had figured so largely in the imaginative accounts of exploring traders like John Oldham? The fur trade was a disappointment. No sooner had Roger Ludlow and George Hull acquired their monopoly of the beaver trade with the Indians in 1636 than William Pynchon, by settling twenty odd miles upstream at Agawam (renamed Springfield), denied them access to the ever-receding source of supply; and the fur trade never became an important factor in the Windsor economy. Similarly with minerals. The Indians had hinted at the mining of 'black lead' (graphite) but the mine was too far away to serve much purpose in Windsor. More important were the forest products. The indigenous oak, elm, hickory and walnut provided timber for houses, fencing and barrels, sumac dyes for tanning and yellow pine and candlewood provided resins for the pitch, tar and turpentine used in ship and house building. Distilling pitch and tar and extracting turpentine was a process pioneered by two Windsor men, Michael Humphrey and John Griffin. They had trouble with the Indians who 'burned up their tar and turpentine and [destroyed] their tools and instruments to the value of a hundred pounds or more' and with their Windsor neighbours who complained 'about the burning of tar in or near unto the Town to their offence and prejudice'. But Griffin was eventually granted 200 acres by a grateful court for establishing the process. Michael Humphrey belonged to a mercantile family of Lyme Regis, Dorset and was probably kin to that John Humphrey of Chaldon, Dorset who was deputy governor of the Massachusetts Bay Company. He arrived in Windsor in 1643 and was to become a considerable man of business and overseas merchant.

For its first few years Windsor was sustained by the influx of new planters bringing with them substantial resources, not only master, mistress, children and servant power, but household goods and valuables, farm animals and implements and sometimes large sums of money and credits with English merchants. Thomas Newberry, for example, brought over wholesale quantities of woollen cloths, of which at his death he left 70 yards, linen (41 yards), canvas (81 yards) and kid (40 yards) as well as over 40 cattle, a dozen muskets, stores of ammunition, furniture and farm implements on a large scale; altogether his personal property amounted to £1520, a considerable fortune for those times and a valuable investment for his children in Windsor. He was exceptional; but the personal estate of the first Windsor settlers was substantial and, together with the proceeds from the sale of their Dorchester land and improvements, provided essential capital backing for the enterprise in its founding years. The influx of settlers, notably the Huitt contingent of 1638, so inflated the demand for good land that there developed a positive land boom. As Matthew Griswold, one of the Huitt party, recalled, 'land at Windsor, near the town and ready for improvement, was at a high price'. Griswold had settled at Saybrook. When he wanted to buy into Windsor to be near his brother Edward and his new father-in-law Henry Wolcott, the latter advised against it, telling him that he 'had bid high enough' for some land of John Bissell's.

The old man was right. The expectation of continuing waves of planters to sustain the buoyant late 1630s was not borne out by events. 1639 proved to be the last of the boom years of Puritan migration to New England. Towards the end of 1640 a fishing boat brought intelligence that the Scots had invaded England and a new Parliament had been summoned. Such was 'the hope of a thorough reformation' that Puritans suddenly stopped taking ship to New England and some Puritan New Englanders, in Winthrop's words, 'began to think of returning back into England'. Others, weary of the extremes of the New England climate and 'despairing of any more supply from thence and not knowing how to live there if they should return, bent their minds wholly to removal to the south parts, supposing they should find better means of subsistance there'. They made plans to settle in the West Indies or with the Dutch on Long Island. Land was put on the market and 'sold out at poor rates'. There was a sudden drop in morale and land values.

This was reflected in Windsor. Several people 'of note' expected from England, such as Mr John St Nicholas, a gentleman neighbour of the Huitts in Warwickshire, failed to materialize, and a few Windsor people removed themselves 'to the seaside', that is, to new settlements to the west on Long Island Sound. A cardinal event was the removal of Roger Ludlow in 1639 to Fairfield whose potential he had noted when active against the Pequots two years before. This was not the end of his Connecticut career; his most signal service was to draft the Code of Laws of 1650; but he ceased to be a figure in Windsor and the departure of this founding father, however awkward his personality, must have been a considerable shock to the morale of the Windsor community.

1640 saw the arrival of 'great store of provisions both out of England and Ireland' and without new immigrants to absorb them. This, together with a bumper harvest, produced a glut and a collapse of prices. As a result, in Winthrop's words, 'he who last year or but three months before was worth £1000 could not now, if he should sell his whole estate, raise £200'; and the following year the price of cows slumped from £20 to £5 and of corn from 4s to 2s 6d a bushel. There was a consequent drain on specie abroad and the payment of debts was authorized in corn and wheat at regulated 'country rates'. The slump equally affected the Connecticut River plantations, which had to face the prospect of surviving in isolation, cut off from new injections of capital and labour and yet with the realization that they could not be self-sufficient but must continue to import essentials from England. In February 1641 the court, 'not knowing how this Commonwealth can long be supported unless some staple commodity be raised amongst ourselves', offered generous grants of land and other inducements to anyone prepared to raise English grain, promoted the growing of hemp and flax, sent that ship to Barbados for raw cotton, and investigated the feasibility of building a ship of their own on the Connecticut River.

The early 1640s were hard years for Windsor people; but gradually they adjusted to more limited horizons and in time discovered that their husbandry provided surpluses which could be turned into good money, credit and essential goods from Massachusetts Bay, Rhode Island, Long Island, the West Indies and even from England. As early as 1644 a surplus of wheat from the river towns produced a glut in the markets of Plymouth and Boston and after complaints from those colonies the general court resolved that wheat, meal, biscuit and malt should only be shipped downriver by two designated Hartford merchants to regulate the trade. Soon a variety of other products found their way to those markets, such as beaver, milch cows, horses and hogs; and beef cattle were driven overland. Later farm produce in the form of biscuit, barrels of salt beef and pork and hogsheads of cider, together with oxen and horses, staves and barrels, tar and turpentine, were shipped further afield, to Barbados and the Leeward Islands. In the 1650s rudimentary but promising trading connections were being fostered.

Such mercantile activities were undertaken by a small number of the more substantial Windsor settlers. For some this was only a part-time extension of day-to-day farming or smallholding. Half a dozen or so became known for dealing in land, like John Bissell, who combined his ferry and keeping a tavern for stranded travellers with land dealing over the Great River, and Matthew Grant for whom this was a natural extension of his surveying. Edward Griswold with his holdings at Poquonnoc, the Allyns, the Wolcotts and young Benjamin Newberry all dealt in real estate. Others handled goods, for instance George Hull whose beaver franchise may not have been profitable but whose inventory in 1659 included over 40 yards of cloth and over 40 pounds of white soap, part of his stock-in-trade; and even the Rev. Ephraim Huitt had 2000 feet of planking ready to be shipped out when he died. A few had the resources and enterprise to become fully fledged merchants with connections abroad. John Porter senior was a prosperous merchant who employed his son James as his agent in London, where he was to become agent for Connecticut. Michael Humphrey likewise dealt with his brother Samuel in St Malo, though apparently not very successfully as he was sued for debt by Samuel's partner there. Above all, there was the younger Henry Wolcott whose extensive import business in general merchandise far transcended his horticultural interests. He would be worth £4000 when he died in 1680.

None of these Windsor merchants appear to have ventured into shipping, which seems to have remained the province of the independent shipmaster. The only Windsor shipmaster on record is Elias Parkman, once of Sidmouth, Devon, who practised his calling as master of a shallop in the coasting trade between Connecticut River and the Bay. His homestead was in the Palisado within a stone's throw of the Rivulet with its clutter of river craft where he had his landing staithe. For a while Walter Filer, at his home in the Palisado, acted as a customs officer to clear the manifests of shallops and pinnaces loading in the Rivulet on behalf of Mr Fenwick of Saybrook Fort, who had the right to toll on merchandise shipped downriver. However, the Rivulet provided only limited facilities and in time Windsor fell behind Hartford as a port. In 1646, Parkman removed to Saybrook, the Connecticut River's port of entry, in partnership with Jonathan Brewster, once the factor of the Plymouth trading post.

Of the score or more individuals mentioned in this chapter, many have been known to us at least by name since their origins in the West Country and some by reputation from Dorchester days. They were now emerging as the principal 'planters' and 'undertakers' – to use their terms – of this first Windsor generation. Most were not just entrepreneurs but men of affairs in a civic sense. They were Windsor's notables, serving their term as officials in town and colony. Only one of the entrepreneurs and only two of the ten most substantial heads of families fulfilled no public office. A close-knit oligarchy, they shouldered the responsibility of governing and managing Windsor in the colony for their generation.

The most important were those who served on the General Court of the colony. Connecticut's court, unlike that of Massachusetts from which it derived, was a single chamber made up of assistants, who were magistrates and from whose number the governor and his deputy were elected annually by the freemen, and deputies, representing the towns, at first four from each, elected annually by their 'inhabitants'. Of these, the Assistants exercised the greater influence both in the court and as the colony's justices of the peace. As justices they presided over the colony's 'Particular' (later, county) Court which heard civil and criminal actions with a jury after the manner of an English quarter sessions. The magistrates were as near as the colony came to the English squirearchy, entitled Esquire or Mister, and in the meeting house, in Stiles's words, 'honoured with a seat in the "great pew" which was wainscotted and expressly designed as a place of special dignity'. With a quorum of six and with rarely more than nine serving at a time and re-elected for long periods, they were a small, powerful group. During the whole of this first generation until 1661, on the eve of the new royal charter which revised the constitution, there were only six magistrates chosen from Windsor.

Of these, the two most distinguished left town early on, though remaining powerful influences in the colony. Roger Ludlow continued as a magistrate and was from time to time deputy governor and commissioner to the United Colonies; John Mason, who took up his command at Saybrook Fort in 1647, also remained a magistrate and was for a time deputy governor. Apart from Ludlow and Mason, the Windsor magistrates consisted of William Phelps, a founding commissioner in 1635, Henry Wolcott, the first constable, Matthew Allyn, a commissioner to the United Colonies, and Henry Clarke. All served long terms, Phelps over twenty years, and were men of substance and authority.

These six men were all of a generation. But in 1662 the freemen elected the first two Windsor magistrates of the second generation. One was the younger Henry Wolcott. As a successful merchant and scion of the oligarchy it was natural that he should follow in his father's footsteps, having first served as a deputy. The other was a rather different case. Daniel Clarke probably came in the *Christian* in 1638 with Ephraim Huitt who chose him as his executor. He bought a home lot on the Mill Road behind the Rossiters and married into the Newberry clan. He is supposed to have been an attorney and he was clearly an expert draftsman because the General Court recruited him in 1657 to draft diplomatic letters and he soon became secretary and recorder of the court. The only member of the Huitt party to become a magistrate, he appears to have been something of an outsider who bought and married into the oligarchy. He had a long and important career as a competent man of affairs. Daniel Clarke and Henry Wolcott were, significantly, the two Windsor notables to be named as Assistants in the royal charter of 1662.

The Windsor magistrates were a powerful group bound by intimate ties of English background, landed and personal property. Apart from Captain Mason and Henry Clarke who lived in the Palisado, they lived cheek by jowl on or adjacent to the Island, though William Phelps abandoned it after the flood. All owned land and personal estate well within the top quartile of property owners; all were members of the church in full communion at a time when only a minority chose or were admitted to it and their families were intermarrying. Five of the eight came from the West Country, four as passengers in *Mary and John*.

There were more deputies to the General Court from Windsor than magistrates because four were elected at a time; but only twenty individuals served as deputy in that quarter-century; these, too, were a cohesive group and six subsequently became magistrates. They served an average of four and a half terms each, but several served considerably longer and these were the most influential: Deacon Gaylord was a deputy for twenty-one years,

William Phelps for eleven, George Hull for ten, John Bissell, Edward Griswold and David Wilton for five each; and with very few exceptions they were men of means, with land and personal property among the most affluent in Windsor. Here, too, the second generation began to make an appearance, in Benjamin Newberry and George Hull's son Josiah, and there was intermarrying. Of the twenty, at least twelve came from the West Country, including eight *Mary and John* passengers.

More immediate to Windsor than the General Court were the five or seven townsmen, later 'selectmen', established by the General Court in 1639 as the town government. Elected annually at a town meeting of all the 'inhabitants', they met every month under a moderator as a court of first instance to try civil actions (mainly for debt and trespass) and to exercise the other functions of town government such as managing the common lands, maintaining the ferry, roads and bridges, policing livestock, registering land grants, wills and inventories. Here, too, one recognizes the same cohesive family groups. Only twenty-one people served as townsmen during the twenty years between 1642 and 1662. Twelve of these went on to become deputies and five became magistrates; many doubled as townsmen and deputies and only five were not at some time members of the General Court. Most of those who became deputies also served for the longest terms as townsmen and here the same family names predominate: Wolcott, Newberry, Gaylord, Griswold (seven terms each), Moore (six), Bissell, Phelps and Ford (four each). Of the twenty-one townsmen, fifteen came from the West Country, eleven on the *Mary and John*.

This by no means concludes the roll call of office holders in this small, self-governing community. We have noticed the Englishmen's habit, brought from their English villages and town wards, of appointing ad hoc someone or a committee of two or three to regulate an aspect of the town's affairs. The more important of these were laid on the town by the General Court. There was the rating commission appointed every other year to assess the property of the town for the purpose of setting the rate for colony taxation. This 'review of the state of the Town' was an invidious job entrusted to reliable men and chaired by a commissioner of the standing of a Henry Wolcott or a Matthew Allyn. There were the 'bound viewers' appointed annually to meet with those from Hartford to review the boundaries between the two plantations, an annual excursion after the English custom of beating the parish bounds during which a good deal of liquor was drunk. Some were more parochial. There was a committee of way wardens to survey the highways and another 'to view the pales' or

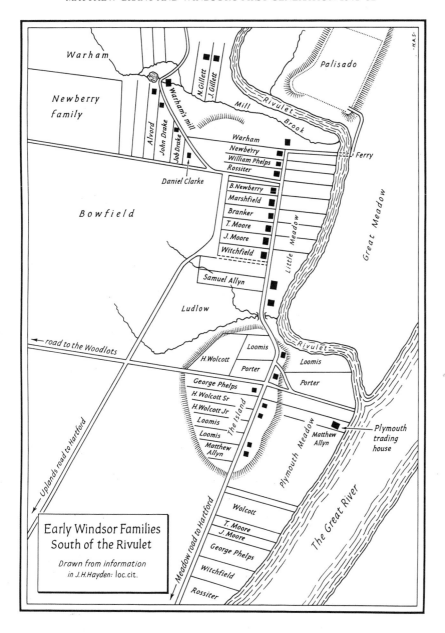

Early Windsor Families
South of the Rivulet

Drawn from information
in J.H.Hayden: loc.cit.

fences 'about the cornfields' and ensure they were in good repair. There were haywards, one for the area north of the Rivulet, the other for the south side, charged, among other things, with impounding stray hogs. There was the committee (Elder Gaylord and John Strong) to determine what cows should be put to the bulls for breeding and the other (John Bissell and John Porter) to ensure that enough calves were reared for the supply of hides.

There were cow-, swine- and goatherds and a shepherd, a chimney viewer or fire marshall to prevent houses catching fire, a clerk of weights and measures, who for a time was Samuel Grant the town clerk's son, two sealers of leather, two who regulated the quality of yarn (William Gaylord and Eltweed Pomeroy) and the customs officer who cleared the ships' cargoes. Some of these men were notables, but many were homely villagers who performed their duties without benefit of penmanship.

It will be understood, therefore, that the Windsor planters were used to a good deal of government. The General Court, like the court of the trading company from which it derived, was still a largely undifferentiated court-cum-legislature-cum-executive. It drew up and administered the Code of Laws acting on appeal from the Particular Court; it conducted diplomatic relations with the other New England colonies and the Indians and in due course launched Governor Winthrop on his expedition to England to obtain a royal charter; it organized the defence against the Indians and the Dutch, training and equipping the militia; it controlled all unallocated land under its jurisdiction, regulated external trade and traffic on the Connecticut River, and exercised detailed supervision over most economic activity.

The Windsor people were in no doubt that the writ of the General Court ran through their town. As colonists they were especially conscious of a mercantilist imperative to regulate their affairs. In the early 1640s the court put through a spate of legislation to promote the colonial economy: measures to encourage the growing of English wheat, hemp and flax, to monitor cattle breeding and the supply of hides, to control grain exports and regulate overseas trade through named merchants, to license monopolies in the fur trade, in the quarrying and mining of minerals and the extraction of tar and turpentine; it encouraged home spinning and weaving, promoted shipbuilding and offered bounties in the form of land grants to attract artisans. The court controlled prices, especially of staples such as corn, wheat and pork used for paying debts, and laid down strict hourly wage rates for artisans, hiring rates for ox teams, standards for such commodities as yarn, leather, pipe-staves and meat packing and appointed official sealers of weights and measures. It undertook to survey and construct highways, notably that between Hartford and Windsor, which had to be resited to assuage the wrath of Hartford people whose northern uplands were being trampled by foot and cart tracks; and it controlled that single ferry across the Great River, at Windsor.

In addition, court and town felt a duty to exercise a considerable degree of social control. As early as 1644 the court recognized the needs of travellers by setting up an 'ordinary' in each town whose innkeeper must be approved by the magistrates. Drunkenness was a problem and from time to time the authorities acted to control excessive tippling especially on vessels moored in the river where people were fined for 'unseasonable and immoderate drinking at the pinnace'. No one was allowed to sell wine or strong waters without a licence. In the ordinaries, only half a pint of wine might be drunk at a time; half an hour was allowed to drink it but not after nine o'clock at night. No one under twenty years, or anyone at all who was not an addict, was allowed to smoke or chew tobacco without the equivalent of a doctor's certificate and then only at dinner time in the privacy of the home. Cards, dice and other games of chance were proscribed on penalty of a substantial fine.

The court recognized a special responsibility towards the poor and needy, making provision for poor widows and for orphans who were usually bound apprentice to suitable citizens to learn a trade. As early as 1637 it instructed Francis Stiles to teach his servants the trade of carpenter.

Schooling was also of deep concern. The townsmen had the duty to ensure that parents taught their children and apprentices to read, to know the laws and 'some short orthodox catechism, without book'. If a parent failed to bring up his child properly, the townsmen, with magistrates' approval, could take the child away to be apprenticed to someone more appropriate, or alternatively a 'stubborn or rebellious child' could be committed to the house of correction. Further, the court laid down that once a town had become a community of fifty families, as Windsor had been from the start, it was obliged to appoint a schoolmaster to teach the children of such as chose to pay the fees to read and write; but it was only in 1657 that old Mr Branker, master of arts of New College, Oxford and once of Ilminster, Somerset, was voted £5 out of the town rate 'towards his maintenance of a school', though he had probably been teaching classes in his own home for some years. After he died in the early 1660s, the town finally built a schoolhouse and much later still established a grammar school. Meanwhile, as early as 1644, the town was enjoined to make an annual collection for the support of Harvard College.

Such watchfulness on the part of the townsmen over the upbringing of children was characteristic of this close-knit Puritan community where the concept of personal privacy scarcely existed. As the Code of Laws explicitly, and ominously, put it: 'the Select Men of every Town, in the several precincts and quarters where they dwell, shall have a vigilant eye on their brethren and neighbours'. There were also strict rules for the discipline of apprentices and indentured servants arising out of great concern lest young people and bachelors of any age should get out of hand. As in England, strangers were not allowed to lodge in the town, let alone become inhabitants, without permission and proper credentials; the townsmen must approve a family taking in a lodger and the constable or the watch could pick you up for walking abroad without good reason after curfew at nine o'clock, an offence called 'night walking'.

Where such prying into personal and family life was officially encouraged in the interests of public morality, it is hardly surprising that the greatest number of criminal charges brought against Windsor citizens in the Particular Court during this period were for family misbehaviour including violence, and for sexual offences, much more than for murder or theft. Sexual offences included two cases of adultery and four of fornication and 'unclean practices' or 'wanton dalliance and self pollution'. The penalty for adultery was death by hanging; but this was usually commuted to a public whipping after the Wednesday lecture, also the normal punishment for fornication. Most serious of all were the cases of sodomy and bestiality, the penalty for which, according to their Old Testament code, was hanging. One such case was deemed so vile (though to us it reads pathetically) that the death penalty was carried out despite the social standing of the accused. John Newberry, aged eighteen, a member of one of the most prominent families in the town, was convicted of buggery on 2 December 1647 and hanged a fortnight later. He was never referred to again.

There were two cases of witchcraft in Windsor during this period. In May 1647 Alse Young was tried as a witch, the first such trial in Connecticut, found guilty and hanged. The second, Lydia Gilbert, was found guilty by a jury on 28 November 1654 of 'conspiring with the devil to cause the death of Henry Stiles' and sentenced to death. These were tragic and scandalous cases. Fortunately, not all accused of such offences by malevolent tattle-tales or officious constables were found guilty. Thomas Marshfield's widow sued Mary Parsons for slander in 1649 for having called her a witch and won her case; Parsons had to pay damages and was given a whipping. Cases of slander and defamation such as this were common, along with cases of debt, trespass and fraud. William Phelps was a member of a hung jury in a nice case of fraud which concerned whether or not a horse could have been seen to be lame when it was bought. Windsor people were as litigious as any in that litigious age and were suing their neighbours in civil actions, and being sued in return, with great frequency. Otherwise, the Particular Court was occupied with petty crime, occasional mayhem and drunkenness, with penalties ranging from hard labour and a coarse diet in Hartford's house of correction to a public whipping 'at the cart's arse' and/or a spell in the pillory or the humble stocks during and after the Wednesday lecture.

The largest number of court decisions, after those concerned with familial or sexual matters, come under the general heading of the derogation of authority. This was regarded most seriously. Even Roger Ludlow when he was deputy governor was fined for being absent from the General Court and David Wilton, another Windsor worthy, was fined for being late for jury duty. You could be imprisoned for being absent from your turn with the watch and fined for absence from church. Only the General Court could absolve you, and normally only on grounds of ill health, from militia training. What seem to us now some of the most severe penalties were meted out for offences against religion and the church. Profanity, 'filthy and profane speeches and carriages' could earn a public whipping and prison for a month, especially if, as in one case, the accused added for good measure that 'he hoped to meet some of the members of the church in hell ere long and he did not question that he should'. 'Disorderly carriage in the Meeting House' earned a prison sentence; and contempt for God's word or the minister's made you liable for a £5 fine and the pillory on a lecture day with a placard round your neck reading 'An open and obstinate contemner of God's Holy Word'. For no one must be allowed, or was indeed likely, to forget that blasphemy, as defined in the Book of Leviticus, was a capital crime in this community where church and state were twin authorities, inextricably related in mutual support and authority.

The execution of the law and the maintenance of order in Windsor were the complementary functions of two most important town officers, the constable and the town clerk. The first, the town's law enforcement officer, is a recognizable version of the English constable. Elected by the town inhabitants, his authority derived from the colony, his appointment being confirmed by the Particular Court. He was the colony's agent, responsible for promulgating and enforcing colony laws. He executed the decisions of the magistrates and court verdicts and maintained order by exercising police powers, on his own and with the help of the watch. He was also charged with collecting the taxes or 'rates' which each fall the General Court imposed on the town. This was on the basis of the rate commission's assessment of each adult male's real and personal estate together with an element of poll tax; the amount of tax was then calculated at a rate in the pound, usually one penny. The constable, as the collector, on a set day received his fellow citizens' rate contributions, usually in the form of Indian corn or wheat. This he stored in the town barn in the Palisado until it was time to deliver it, after deducting the town's own outgoings, to the colony treasurer in Hartford.

The constable was thus a key figure in the town. Originally there was only one, the first being the elder Henry Wolcott (who was also actually called 'collector'), followed by the elder John Porter, both men of weight. However, because the constable was responsible for arresting, prosecuting and punishing his fellow townsmen and for extracting their taxes, it was scarcely a popular office and two came to be appointed at a time. It is not surprising that only one man in our period was ever persuaded to take on the job for more than one term. The twenty-five for whom we have a continuous record in this period were men of less weight than the townsmen and certainly than Wolcott and Porter; but with few exceptions they came from the same nexus of families, younger than the townsmen, and eight or nine of them second generation: a Hull, an Eglestone, a Drake, two Loomises, a Bissell and a Gaylord. It must have been a testing beginning in community office-holding.

The office of town clerk or register, also with English origins, was established by the General Court on 10 October 1639 for each of the three river towns. The immediate purpose was to ensure a proper legal record of all the land transactions which were the predominant activity of that boom year; the new officer was to 'keep a ledger book with an index and alphabet' and provide a fair copy for the colony's official land register. He was also to record wills and take inventories of all deceased persons' real and personal estates. He was later instructed to keep a record of all births, marriages and deaths in the town. The town clerk's authority rested on these very specific beginnings. Unlike the constable's, the office was not annual but more or less permanent, albeit without salary, only expenses, and his authority was thereby all the greater. There were to be only two town clerks of Windsor during the whole forty years spanned by this account.

The first town clerk of Windsor was Brian or 'Bray' Rossiter, son of the squire of Combe St Nicholas, Somerset. Bray was a person of education and standing and he also acted as the town's physician. The first volume of Windsor's land records, dating from 1640 in that very ledger with its index or 'alphabet', is in Rossiter's hand; and he continued to act as town clerk until 1652 when he left Windsor for Guilford. He appears to have served the town well; but it was his successor who made the influence of the town

A portrait of Robert Rich, second Earl of Warwick, by Daniel Mytens.

Meeting House Hill, Roxbury in Massachusetts, in a painting by John R. Penniman.

An engraving of Fort Saybrook.

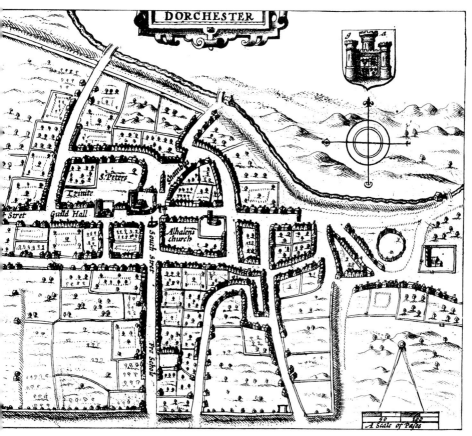

Plan of the town of Dorchester, a detail from the Dorset map by John Speed.

Prospect of Dorchester from the amphitheatre.

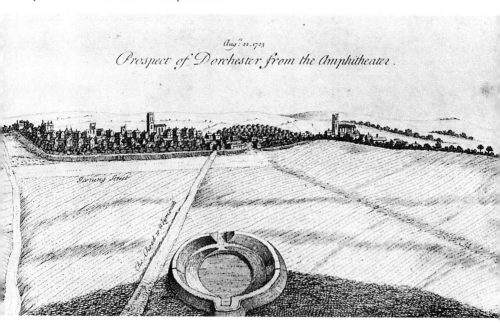

Aug. 22. 1723
Prospect of Dorchester from the Amphitheater.

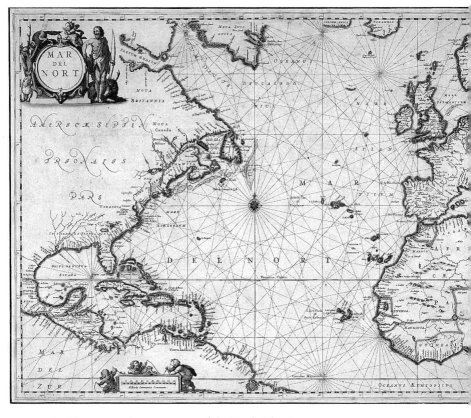

A mid-seventeenth-century map of the North Atlantic.

King Philip of Pokonoket, engraving from *Long Island Antiquities*.

A painting of Chief Ninigret by an unknown artist, said to have been commissioned by John Winthrop.

A portrait of John Winthrop the Younger

The Wolcott Homestead, South Windsor, from *Wolcott Genealogy: the Family of Henry Wolcott, one of the first Settlers of Windsor, Connecticut.*

NEVVES FROM AMERICA;

OR,

A NEW AND EXPERI-

MENTALL DISCOVERIE OF

New England;

CONTAINING,

A TRVE RELATION OF THEIR
War-like proceedings these two yeares last
past, with a Figure of the Indian Fort,
or Palizado.

Also a discovery of these
places, that as yet have
very few or no Inhabi-
tants which would yeeld
speciall accommodation
to such as will Plant
there,

$\left.\right\}$ *Viz.* $\left\{\right.$

Queenapoick.
Agu-wom.
Hudsons River.
Long Island.
Nahanticut.
Martins Vinyard.
Pequet.
Naransett Bay.
Elizabeth Islands.
Puscat away.
Casko with about a hun-
dred Islands neere to
Casko.

By Captaine IOHN UNDERHILL, a Commander
in the Warres there.

LONDON,
Printed by *J.D.* for *Peter Cole*, and are to be sold at the signe
of the Glove in Corne-hill neere the
Royall Exchange. 1638.

The title page of *News from America* by John Underhill, 1638.

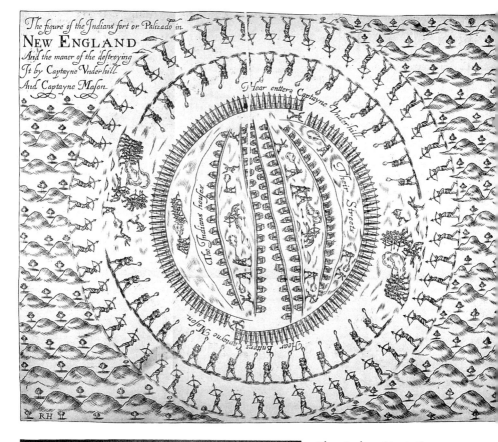

The attack on Mystic Fort: an engraving from *News from America*.

A portrait of Captain John Underhill by an unknown artist.

clerk truly felt for this first Windsor generation. He was our friend Matthew Grant, the town's surveyor. A natural successor to Rossiter, he was appointed on 20 August 1652 at the age of fifty. He was to handle the town's business for a quarter of a century.

The work, like most administration, was a miscellany of petty transactions interspersed with larger and more difficult issues. The town clerk had the duty of calling town meetings and of convening the bi-monthly meetings of the townsmen; and then of executing their decisions. These concerned motley topics, many recurring predictably like the appointment of the Rivulet ferryman or a miller for Warham's mill, regulating the herding of cattle, opening the meadows or collecting fines for swine damage. In 1661, at the close of the period looked at in this chapter, Matthew Grant dealt, among other matters, with the following: he paid bounties to Captain Aaron Cooke for wolves killed; he arranged for and paid a drummer to announce the time of Sunday meeting and for cleaning the meeting house; he recompensed Henry Wolcott for the liquor drunk by his bound viewers; he paid the 'bonesetter'; he bought a new canoe for Parsons the ferryman; he arranged for repairing the stocks; he put in train the construction of two new hog pounds and the renewal of the town's stock of gunpowder. A great deal of time and money was spent that year on improving the meeting house. A contract was let to Grant's own son Samuel for shingling the roof and renewing the guttering on both sides of the lanthorn, though after a full debate it was decided not to alter the line of the roof; and another contract was let to that other carpenter, William Buell, to divide the great pew into two parts, one to be reserved for the magistrates. Grant was away for four days across the Great River with one of his sons surveying the town line at Podunk.

He carried out the resolution of a special town meeting to license a consortium of Windsor people to string a weir across the Rivulet below the ferry and to enjoy a monopoly of all the fish caught there. More delicate was the job of chasing up those who had not paid for their seats in the meeting house and of going discreetly from house to house to obtain subscriptions towards minister Warham's annual stipend. There was also a good deal of paperwork to be done including the transcription of eighteen court orders. He went to some time, trouble and expense drawing up the town's own account of disbursements to be deducted from the 'country rate' and in negotiating with the colony treasurer in Hartford where he had to spend two days and nights. On top of all this he had the continuing duty as registrar of reporting to Hartford all land transactions, births, marriages, deaths, wills and inventories in Windsor during the past year.

It is possible thus to reconstruct the business affairs of Windsor's town clerk because Matthew Grant proved such a scrupulous recorder. From 1652 the decisions, the 'town acts', were recorded in his crabbed but legible hand and in a laconic but sufficiently informative style. But this was by no means his whole contribution to the Windsor archive. He had an unusual sense of the importance of recording information, derived no doubt from his heightened consciousness of the epic and, he would have felt, divinely inspired character of the enterprise, and stimulated by the record of births, marriages and deaths which he had to transmit to Hartford every year. At any rate, he began to make a habit of accumulating lists of names and vital statistics. In 1674, towards the end of his life, he transcribed them into a volume of forty-eight pages which was kept in the family, lost, and then found only by chance in the ruins of a family homestead around 1800.

Traditionally called 'Matthew Grant's Old Church Record', it is much more besides. There are comprehensive lists of church members, including those in communion from the original church in Dorchester, those in communion in 1677 and those later taking the 'half-way covenant'; dates of communions celebrated and even the cost of wine and church levies; in addition to the complete record of all births, marriages and deaths there is his own chronological list of deaths in Windsor and an alphabetical list of all Windsor heads of families with numbers of children and population totals. There is an account of the famous flood of 1639, some documents relating to the controversy about the half-way covenant and an early page of town acts. In short, this is a volume of historical documents, deliberately put together by someone who was concerned not just with operational matters but with a record for posterity.

He also kept what has traditionally been described as a diary but which in fact is a kind of commonplace book into which he copied lists of his own family's births and marriages, a dictionary of terms, rules for surveying, the Windsor church covenant, notes of sermons, particularly sermons preached by Thomas Hooker, and devotional passages like Ainsworth's Version of the Canticles. This was in addition to his careful accounts of the town's business. All must have been written down at the family table or on his knee, and in the evenings by rush- or candlelight. It is evidence of a persistent and dedicated character.

With all these demands on his time it is hardly surprising that Matthew Grant did not undertake any other public office, save that of townsman, not even in the trainband. He lived a busy but seemingly modest life in his

Palisado homestead with its small orchard. His second wife brought five Rockwell children with her and he had four of his own. Of the latter, his daughter Priscilla married Michael Humphrey's son; of the boys, Samuel married John Porter's daughter and John the daughter of Josiah Hull, son of George of Crewkerne, and both were useful citizens. Tahan, however, was a problem and must in the end have been a disgrace to his father. In 1663 when he had only been married a year, he was tried by jury at the particular court 'for his notorious, lewd and lascivious practices with Sarah Lindley' and sentenced to be whipped twelve stripes on his naked body in Hartford and again in Windsor and struck off the roll of freemen. Perhaps because the defendant was the son of Windsor's town clerk and therefore conspicuous, the court was, unusually, presided over by deputy governor John Mason and six other magistrates. In the upshot, out of consideration for his father and at his request, the court substituted a fine for the second whipping, on the excuse that it was to have taken place on the Sabbath. Tahan was given a second chance, resumed his trade as a smith and seven years later was appointed constable; he died a substantial citizen with a large family. However, his father left him only £5 in his will, the same amount he left his daughter, so perhaps Tahan was never fully restored to family favour.

One hopes this episode did not cloud Matthew Grant's long career of service to the town which was crowned with the warmest respect. He acted as an executor or witness of the wills of forty-one of his fellow citizens, a far greater number than anyone else; the only people to approach him were Henry Wolcott and Benjamin Newberry. This virtual lifetime's stint as surveyor and town clerk reflects the trust which his fellow citizens placed in his probity and fairness. As he proudly wrote: 'I can say with a clear conscience I have been careful to do nothing upon one man's desire'.

Shortly before he retired, the General Court granted him 100 acres of land across the Great River as a token of the colony's esteem. He assigned this present to his two sons Samuel and John; and after his wife's death in 1666 it was with John, his youngest son, and Mary his daughter-in-law that he spent his last years in his old Palisado home. When he died aged eighty in 1681 he had little to leave save this old family homestead, some acres in Great Meadow, some pasture and a wood lot, his clothing, two swords and some books. But like his more famous descendant Ulysses S. Grant, he was in his own way a great man.

CHAPTER 9: JOHN WARHAM AND WINDSOR CHURCH 1635–70

A T ITS MEETING ON 26 AUGUST 1639, AFTER THE WEEKLY LECTURE IN Governor Haynes's house in Hartford, the General Court solemnly resolved 'that there be a public day of thanksgiving in these plantations upon the 18th of the next month'. This resolution, conveyed by the magistrates and deputies to the elders of the three churches, marked the institution of an official Day of Thanksgiving each fall 'to the Lord for his great mercies'.

This came at an appropriate moment in the affairs of the colony and of Windsor. The terrifying Pequot threat had been faced and conquered. Although the bill of £620 is staggering for such infant settlements, it had already been paid, in money, wampum or beaver (Windsor's share was £158 2s 0d), and a new annual rate of £100 had been set (Windsor's share £28 6s 8d). The river plantations were now established as a colony. The General Court had adopted Roger Ludlow's Fundamental Orders as its provisional constitution the previous January and at its next meeting, on 10 October, it would follow this up with ordinances concerning its relations with the towns and their government. In Windsor the land distribution was going successfully. Those fertile meadows were attracting so many settlers that land was at a premium and those who must had to buy at boom prices. The advent of the Huitt party only a week before had been a cardinal event; and the impact of Ephraim Huitt's inaugural sermon the day after their landing was still ringing in the ears and minds of the congregation of Windsor church.

If these matters were cause for thanksgiving they were not unalloyed with other matters sent to try the souls of Windsor people. The past years had been hard. Their makeshift farming had not yet made them self-sufficient. They had lost cattle and the corn yield was not enough to feed them through the year. The general court had to procure grain at considerable cost: from William Pinchon in upstream Springfield, from the Indians in a deal which John Mason negotiated, and from Narragansett Bay by Elias Parkman, once again master of a ship. The climate had not been kind. That spring, melting snows had caused the Great River and the Rivulet to overflow their banks. The ensuing flood, which began on 5 March and only subsided over a fortnight later, was the most disastrous the Indians could remember. It 'drowned many houses very deep' and swept away trees, fences, pales, cut timber and haystacks. Two boys were drowned in their canoe trying to save floating pales. The season's crops and much valuable cattle were destroyed. This grim experience was followed by a tragic number of deaths, chiefly of wives and children, including a son of Matthew Grant, and the mortality would continue to be severe. During the coming winter a further nine children would die including the offspring of such prominent people as Brian Rossiter, the newly appointed town clerk, Captain Mason, Elder Hosford, Stephen Terry, Eltweed Pomeroy and John Dewey, whose son was drowned in the Rivulet.

In their rough and dangerous life, Windsor people were sustained by the belief in their elect destiny under Almighty God who had brought them to this New World and to whom their solemn and public thanks were given that 18th day of September. In their conviction that a divine providence supported them they searched for signs of God's grace. At its next meeting, the General Court would set up a committee, with Ludlow and Mason for Windsor, to seek out acts which revealed God's special dispensation towards their enterprise, to scrutinize the spiritual experiences of individual persons and to certify and record them as genuine 'passages of God's providence'. This resolution of the court shows that amid the secular business of planting a spiritual purpose remained paramount.

This account has so far been chiefly concerned with the urgent secular matters of settlement. But we have been conscious of that pervasive force, Puritan Christianity, which all along determined the actions of our principal characters. The dedicated resolve of that church community gathered at the

New Hospital in Plymouth had impelled them through hardship and adventure on their long odyssey to the Connecticut River and continued to sustain them in the spirit of the colony motto: *Sustinet Qui Transtulit* ('He who transported us sustains us'). Religion infused the affairs of Windsor through this first generation, the religion of a purified Church of England, free from superstitious liturgy and modelled on the primitive church of the early Fathers. When on 18 August 1639 Ephraim Huitt preached his inaugural sermon as teacher of Windsor church he chose as his text I Corinthians 12.31: 'And yet show I unto you a more excellent way'. It was to practise a more excellent way that they had crossed the Atlantic. This was the ultimate end to which all secular activity was directed and for which church and state were fused into one. Windsor's founding fathers still belonged to that corporate body, gathered in Plymouth, which continued to inform their tradition and habits of worship.

Because of the circumstances of their founding that day in Plymouth, the appointment there of the Oxford-educated and ordained Warham and Maverick as their ministers, their identification as a ship's company and then as a community of settlers, there was little question of their legitimacy as a congregation in a purified Church of England. After Maverick's death, so long as Warham remained their minister there was no need for a new gathering, a new covenant, such as gave a more radical emphasis to other Massachusetts churches, including Dorchester on Richard Mather's arrival. John Warham's Church of Christ in Windsor remained conscious of its continuity with the past, however radical its congregational church order.

The ship's companies of the *Mary and John* and of John White's other ships had been members of Dorchester church as a matter of course and this remained largely the case for those who transplanted to the Connecticut. But as time went by and the population grew, with children, servants and later arrivals from differing backgrounds, the proportion of full communicants diminished until they were only a minority: church membership was jealously guarded; to be a full member one must convince the elders of having received 'saving grace', a genuinely spiritual conversion to Christ, and this was too formidable an examination for many. Though the theology was scholarly and grounded on the Bible, doctrine was simple and rigid. There was no tolerance of dissent and there was a constant watch for heresy. When word of Quakers and Ranters reached Connecticut the general court imposed severe penalties against harbouring them, and only ruling elders were permitted to read their tracts.

The settlers' habits were punctuated and shaped by the church calendar.

Attendance at church was compulsory for all the town's inhabitants whether or not they were full church members, with fines for absence. There were two services on Sunday, one in the morning, the other after dinner. Worship consisted largely of prayers, psalms and the sermon, the length of which was regulated by an hour-glass to guard against short shrift. Attendance at the rather infrequent celebration of the Lord's Supper was also compulsory, though non-members were, of course, excluded from the sacrament. In addition, there was a mid-week 'lecture day' for which the whole settlement must again down tools and leave the fields to be instructed in the Scriptures; and there were those special days of Humiliation or Thanksgiving. With all the able-bodied men in the meeting house, the settlement was thus exposed, especially in the early days, to attack from the Indians and a guard of musketeers was mounted to protect the congregation and a drummer or trumpeter called the people to worship.

This activity took place in the meeting house which Ephraim Huitt had set himself to build with such enthusiasm. He not only designed it and supervised its construction but raised the money for it, £200, a large sum, most of which he borrowed from his Hartford friend George Wyllys to be repaid out of the proceeds of the toll from the corn mill which, like his colleague Warham, he had been granted by the town. The meeting house, which was finished in September 1641, was at the upper end of the Palisado green. At first there were only four rows of pews and four special and separate box pews for the notables, one each for ruling elders and deacons, the 'great pew' with its wainscoting for the magistrates and a fourth pew for the wives. Most of the good people of Windsor may well have had to stand throughout worship and lecture. But by 1660 there was seating for well over 200, including nine long and thirteen short pews with doors. The box pews and short benches were raised a little from the floor for better sight and hearing. There is no mention of a fireplace or chimney though the roof was surmounted by a lanthorn turret like that of a medieval hall for ventilation and additional light. There was a clock and pegs for men to hang their hats. The interior must have been a simple affair of unpainted woodwork with rushes on a plank floor, lit by glazed casement windows. Externally the walls were clapboarded; the steep roof was shingled and from the lanthorn to its ridge there was a platform from which the trumpeter or drummer summoned the congregation. Later a 'housel' was built at the north end of the Palisado green to shelter a dozen or so horses 'when they ride to meeting'. Judging by the number of entries in the town accounts the meeting house demanded a good deal of maintenance in the way of renewing clapboarding, gutters, shingles, sills and window glass. Bigot Eglestone, who lived next door, had the cleaning contract. Similarly David Wilton, who lived three doors away, looked after the burial ground and in return was allowed to use it to pasture his cows. John Hillier was the gravedigger.

The meeting house was the centre of community life. Church government was a small, self-perpetuating junta of ministers, elders and deacons. The two ministers in Church of England orders shared the twin functions of pastor and teacher, a division of labour unknown to the church in England and an improvement on the single-handed rector or vicar. The pastor's role was the care of souls, that of the teacher the exposition of doctrine and the Scriptures. John Warham remained, as he had been from the beginning, the pastor and spiritual leader of the whole enterprise. He was unlucky in his partners in God, the teachers: as we saw, John Maverick died in Dorchester and Ephraim Huitt died after only five years in Windsor. Thereafter Warham was on his own.

In another sense, he was not on his own. He was supported, in this congregational style of church government, by the ruling elders and the deacons, supposedly modelled on the early church. Only the pastor and the teacher, as ordained clergymen in the Church of England (and graduates respectively of St Mary Hall, Oxford and St John's College, Cambridge), were empowered to administer the sacraments. The role of the ruling elders was to assist in church government, watch over church members and bring forward cases of discipline, visit and pray with the sick and, in the absence of the pastor or teacher, to pray with the congregation and expound the Scriptures.

The ruling elders were persons of spiritual commitment, character, education and intelligence and were usually addressed respectfully as Mister. After Huitt's death, when Warham was first on his own, they helped out by occasionally preaching the sermon. There were three. John Witchfield had come from Exeter in 1630 and had been a member of Warham's church since Dorchester days; he would go on living in the Palisado, a much-respected figure, until he died at an advanced age in 1677; the second was the schoolmaster John Branker, of the clerisy if not the minor gentry from Ilminster, Somerset; his widow was to marry John Warham. The third was William Hosford.

William Hosford is worth pausing over. He came from Beaminster in the Brit Valley of Dorset where his family had been substantial yeomen and husbandmen since Henry VIII's time. One of his kinsmen was a prosperous merchant tailor and burgess of Dorchester whose daughters married into the gentry. William had sailed from Weymouth for Dorchester, Massachusetts with his family in the summer of 1633 in the same ship as those merchants of Dorchester and Lyme, the Cogans, Hills, Ways and Purchases and his Bridport neighbours the Randalls. He and his family had moved to Windsor as original settlers in 1636. By this time he must have been in his fifties. He was a lettered man, probably educated at Netherbury Grammar School; and he was clearly a person of mark. He was a deputy at that first meeting of the General Court at Hartford on 1 May 1637 which declared war on the Pequots. More to the point, he was a convinced Puritan recognized for his spiritual gifts. He was one of the first ruling elders of Windsor church and for fifteen years one of John Warham's close confidants. In 1652 he himself received a call to the ministry of a church. In that year William Pynchon, the founder of Springfield upriver, himself at odds with the Massachusetts clergy, determined to return to old England taking his minister with him. Elder Hosford accepted an invitation to fill the vacancy at a stipend of £50 a year and moved up to Springfield. The venture was not a success. The fact that he was not a university man nor ordained was no impediment where ministers were scarce; but although a spiritually proven elder, he seems to have been a disappointing preacher – in Windsor he was not invited to preach again after his one sermon – and without university schooling he may not have been up to those weekly lectures. At any rate he decided, like Pynchon and Moxon, to return to England.

The early 1650s were a time when the idea of repatriation was in the air: the Protectorate was firmly established and the religious climate congenial to Independents. Elder Hosford went back to England for good in 1655. At that time New England ministers were having quite a vogue; as one of them, Nathaniel Mather, son of Warham's successor at Dorchester, Massachusetts, wrote to a Boston friend: 'Tis a notion of mighty and great and high respect to have been a New-Englishman, 'tis enough to gain a man . . . yea almost any preferment'. William Hosford benefited from this. One surmises that he first went back to Dorchester. John White was dead by then but his colleague William Benn was there and possibly through his influence Hosford in 1657 obtained the living of Calverleigh, near Tiverton, Devon whither his wife followed him. He was inevitably ejected at the Restoration and he died sometime after 1665 at a considerable age. Perhaps old age, homesickness, a sense of having had enough pioneering or even disillusion with the enterprise combined with the rigours of the Connecticut frontier had all proved too much for this elderly man.

The deacons also had a more specifically secular function, handling money matters to do with the minister's stipend, the meeting house fabric and church expenditure in general. The first deacons, William Rockwell and William Gaylord, both of Somerset, had been appointed that March day in 1630 in the New Hospital at Plymouth and so symbolized in their persons the continuity of Warham's church in Windsor with the church that had been left behind. Rockwell, alas, died in 1640 but his old colleague and friend Gaylord continued as deacon of Windsor church for another thirty-three years. He was joined in 1651 by John Moore, a younger man who was to become a powerful church figure in the 1660s and 70s. He, too, had been a passenger on *Mary and John*.

All these six church officers were of West Country origin; four sailed on the *Mary and John*, and all had been members of Dorchester church. The West Country element was nearly as predominant in the church as a whole. Of Windsor's founding settlers, most had belonged to the Dorchester church and most of these had been *Mary and John* passengers, had been in the congregation at the New Hospital dedication or had voyaged later in related ships. Although the death toll was high in this first Windsor generation, most of the victims were small children. Only a dozen or so were original heads of families so that the church worthies remained dominantly West Country. In addition, during these years the church admitted at least sixteen men (the record is incomplete) to full membership and, of these, at least half were West Country born. Thus did the Church of Christ in Windsor continue to carry the original inspiration of the Rev. John White of Dorchester into a second generation.

Despite the influence of elders and deacons there was no questioning the authority of the church's minister, John Warham, as the spiritually ordained shepherd of his flock and a man of learning. Ministers were by convention precluded from secular office but they commanded a respect and exercised an influence in secular affairs all the greater for its being indirect and for life. The minister was first in precedence after the governor. He was the only salaried person in the plantation: John Warham's stipend, determined annually, fluctuated between £90 and £100 a year which made him affluent in town and colony. As we have seen, he was also well endowed with land and other perks. In Warham's case there were special reasons why the minister should be supported with dignity and means. For most of his pastorate he officiated alone without the support of a fellow minister as teacher. More important, along with John Maverick, he had been chosen by John White.

FAMILY CONNECTIONS
ALLYN : NEWBERRY : WARHAM : WOLCOTT

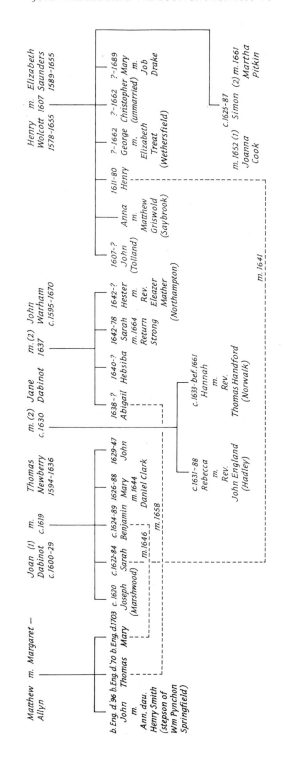

As we saw in Chapter Two, John Warham was born about 1592 of gentle Dorset stock. He was sent to Oxford where he graduated from St Mary Hall, returned to the West Country where he practised as a Puritan lecturer in the 1620s, was silenced or suspended by William Laud, and then became curate of St Sidwell's, Exeter. It was from St Sidwell's that, at the age of about thirty-eight, with a wife and two daughters, he accepted the call to be the spiritual leader of White's ambitious venture. He was appointed by the *Mary and John* congregation in the New Hospital, ministered and preached daily on the Atlantic voyage, established the church in Dorchester, led his flock to the Connecticut and re-established it as a church in Windsor. He became so closely identified with it that it became known as 'Warham's Church'. At his death in 1670 at an advanced age of about seventy-eight, he had served as its minister from its foundation for forty years, thirty-four of them in Windsor.

Those thirty-four years span the entire period of Windsor's settlement and first generation of growth. Shortly after migrating to Connecticut his wife died; but as we have seen he then married Thomas Newberry's widow, Jane, who brought with her a considerable portion and her young family of Newberrys, three stepsons, two stepdaughters and two daughters. The minister was thus surrounded by a large and growing family; the stepdaughters, as we noted, were to marry Henry Wolcott junior and Daniel Clarke. In addition Jane gave him four daughters of his own, three of whom married respectively Thomas, son of Matthew Allyn, Return, son of John Strong, and Eleazer, son of Richard Mather, Warham's successor at Dorchester. Later in life he married yet again, this time the widow of one of his elders and fellow Oxford man, John Branker. All his wives came from the same part of Somerset or just across the Dorset border. John Warham was thus not just the minister–patriarch but the father of a well-connected Windsor clan and his home, prominent at the top end of Little Meadow, was very much the manse.

It seems clear from White's choice of Warham and the loyalty and affection of his flock that he was a person of some charisma. Though sufficiently Puritan in his convictions to be proscribed by Laud, he was no extremist. As a master of arts, his ministry was that of an educated man. He owned a considerable library, valued at his death at £84 4s 0d, nearly a year's stipend. According to Cotton Mather, he was the first minister in New England to write out his sermons instead of preaching *ex tempore*, a practice for which he was criticized by more radical Puritans. Cotton Mather, who approved and admired 'the notable energy of his Ministry', commented caustically: 'He was a more vigorous preacher than the most of them who have been applauded for never looking in a book in their lives'. He was no Separatist and was liberal in his beliefs concerning faith and church order. When in that summer of 1630 Samuel Fuller came over from Plymouth to Mattapan to give succour to the *Mary and John* company he engaged Warham in a discussion about the nature of the true church as understood by the Plymouth Separatists. Fuller seems to have become exasperated by Warham for he reported to Governor Bradford that he 'had conference . . . till I was weary. Mr. Warham holds that the visible Church may consist of a mixed people, godly and openly ungodly, upon which point we all had our conference, to which I trust the Lord will give a blessing'.

Warham still believed in a church which embraced both saints and sinners. Such broad sympathies were more characteristic of the reformed church of the Elizabethan settlement than of Separatist New England. When, in the late 1650s, the demands of a second generation made the half-way covenant a question of controversy on the Great River, Warham again took the liberal side and, practising what he preached, began to admit to partial membership of Windsor church parents who could not show evidence of a spiritual conversion but who wished to have their children baptised into the church, as they themselves had been in their parish church in England.

Yet after ministering his half-way covenant for some years he began to have serious scruples about the spiritual justification for it and in 1665 he would suspend the practice until he could satisfy himself that he was not sinning in so indulging it. His nature was, in fact, flawed by self-doubt. Such was his sense of his own sin that often when he administered the Lord's Supper he did not feel justified in administering it to himself 'through the fearful dejections of his mind which persuaded him that those blessed souls did not belong unto him'. He suffered from a dreadful melancholy. In Mather's words again: 'Tho' Warham was as pious a man as most that were out of Heaven, yet Satan often threw him into those deadly pangs of melancholy, that made him despair of ever getting thither . . . The dreadful darkness which overwhelmed this child of light in his life did not wholly leave him till his death.' Yet there were those who said that this cloud was dispelled before his death. Let us hope so, for this gentle and devout man was a true patriarch, father of his flock and held in reverent affection. According to Mather, 'the whole Colony of Connecticut considered him as a principal pillar and father'.

On the evening of this, the first Wednesday of November 1658, Master Warham was sitting at his fireside meditating on the day and taking stock of his soul. The General Court had made this a public Day of Thanksgiving; and as minister he spent much of it over the Rivulet ferry in the meeting house, leading his flock in prayer and thanksgiving for God's mercy in bringing them all safely to the end of the season. He could not help thinking of the contrast with two months before when the court had decreed a Day of Humiliation and he had led his congregation in earnest prayer, in the court's words, 'to implore the favour of God towards his people in regard of the intemperate season, thin harvest, sore visitation by sickness in several Plantations and the sad prolonged differences that yet remained unreconciled in Churches'. The harvest had indeed been poor and the townsmen were still concerned about the supplies of grain, salt meat and winter fodder. But the controversy which had so bitterly rent Hartford church over baptism, in which he himself was distressed to have had to play an intercessionary role, had so far, thank God, not spread to Windsor. The Farmington Indians who had been so threatening had gone into winter quarters; and the sickness so prevalent up and down the river appeared to have spared Windsor; indeed he had only taken one burial service that whole year and that was for old Joseph Loomis who lived to a ripe age. The previous year there had been nine deaths, including the wife of his own deacon and friend, William Gaylord. He had known many worse years, especially those grim times of 1647 and 1648 when he had committed to burial over sixty, many of them small children.

On an anniversary like this he could not help brooding about those so close to him who had gone, leaving him a little lonely, an ageing man of sixty-six, 'growing ancient' as the court would describe him. There was John Maverick, his first partner in God's work in New England, who never saw the Promised Land of Connecticut; nor did Thomas Newberry whose widow Jane became his own wife only to leave him for a better world eight years later; there was William Rockwell, his first deacon from that never-to-be-forgotten day at the New Hospital in Plymouth, who died in 1640, and old Henry Wolcott, also from those days, who died three years ago. Above all there was Ephraim Huitt, dear and energetic colleague who had done so much in establishing the church in Windsor and who had been gone those fourteen years leaving him to soldier on for Christ alone. Today he had made a point of walking over to the burial ground to see his old colleague's tomb, and that of those other Somerset neighbours Henry and Elizabeth Wolcott, carved so simply, yet with dignity, in sandstone from Rocky Hill by their son-in-law Matthew Griswold. Even Roger Ludlow,. never a favourite of his, and John Mason had long since left Windsor, as had others, like George Hull and William Hill, for the seaside on the Sound and there was now talk of founding another settlement at Massaco up the Rivulet, yet a further drain on Windsor church.

He must put such gloomy musings aside. He could not objectively find any reason but to praise the Lord for the wellbeing of his own condition and that of the church congregation under his charge. There was no gainsaying that, despite adverse passages like those which had led to this year's solemn Day of Humiliation, Windsor was becoming prosperous. Looking back to those first few primitive years, it had been a feat of wonder-working providence that church and plantation should have grown so healthily. What he remembered as a settlement of fifty or so households had become, over the two decades, one of 160; what had been a small village plantation now boasted over 700 souls, despite too many infant deaths and migration to other settlements; and a colony valuation per household of about £100 represented a fair degree of worldly prosperity.

Although church membership had not kept pace with population, he took satisfaction that new applications come forward each year. Windsor church, as yet without schism, adhered to the Puritan quest. As its minister he was well supported by his ruling elders and deacons. Of the elders, his old friends John Witchfield and John Branker were still with him, but William Hosford had gone up the river to try his hand at being minister of the church at Springfield after Moxon went back to England. This venture had not succeeded and he, too, had returned, to the West Country from which he came, a sad loss to Windsor church. However, through God's mercy his wife Jane, who had followed him to Devon, left to Windsor church the valuable Hoyte's Meadow, the income from which was to be used for the church and its minister. As for the deacons, there was still William Gaylord, his old friend since the New Hospital; the other deacon for the last seven years had been John Moore whom he remembered of the *Mary and John* company. His principal worry about Windsor church was the state of the meeting house fabric which, after fifteen years, was badly in need of repair. He took some satisfaction in that meeting house: it was a fitting and true place of worship for a reformed church; yet there came vividly and unbidden to his mind the picture of that beautiful two centuries' old church with its masonry and its many-lighted windows in dear Crewkerne where he had grown up.

He must not let his mind be distracted in this way. He must be thankful to the Lord for his own personal wellbeing. He had to remind himself that he lived in comfortable circumstances. His considerable acreage of choice land in Great and Little Meadows and elsewhere and his extensive tracts across the Great River provided a more than ample endowment for his own and his children's future; and the income from the tolls of his mill was a considerable supplement to his annual stipend as minister. He had to admit that he lived most comfortably in the family home. It was spacious now that extra rooms had been added; and the view, from its curtained windows, of his sixteen acres of meadow and orchard stretching down to the Mill Brook was pleasant on this fall afternoon as the light faded. He did not want for the pleasant things of life: good furniture, velvet hangings, cushions, fine table and bed linen, a gold piece, a silver cup and spoons as well as pewter plates, and copper and brass shining in the firelight. Above all, he had his books, several hundred of them, handsomely bound and shelved and giving a warm, cultivated air to the parlour. They were his solace as well as working tools for his preaching. This evening the parlour was looking particularly cheerful after his daughters had decorated it with corn cobs, pumpkins, squashes and berries, and scented it with sweet-smelling herbs from the garden and a bowl of apples sent over by his son-in-law Henry Wolcott in honour of this Day of Thanksgiving.

His children were the special object of his meditation. His four daughters were an immense consolation and support to him especially now that they were growing up into young women and competent mistresses in the household. His eldest, Abigail, at twenty, had just left home and he missed her. Less than a month before she had been married to young Thomas, son of his friend and neighbour Matthew Allyn; it was a suitable match. Of his Newberry stepchildren, Joseph had long since returned to the family home in Marshwood, Dorset; young John, executed so tragically at the age of eighteen, was never spoken of, though he prayed for the poor boy. But Benjamin, now thirty-four and married to another of Matthew Allyn's children, was clearly a coming man, just elected captain of the Windsor trainband. Sarah's husband, Henry Wolcott, and Mary's, Daniel Clarke, were both promising men. Daniel Clarke was a deputy and recorder of the court (no doubt it was he who had drafted the call to this Day of Thanksgiving); and he and Benjamin were both townsmen. He understood that Daniel, Thomas Allyn and Henry Wolcott's brother Simon had just volunteered to join this new troop of horse which John Mason was organizing: it seemed to be the fashionable thing to do. More important was the fact that Benjamin and his sister Mary Clarke had been recently admitted to full membership of Windsor church.

Again, as he looked into the fire, John Warham's mind wandered off into worldly satisfactions. But even the contemplation of Benjamin and Mary joining the church was somehow too self-centred a matter and he must return to a more proper meditation: Thanksgiving Day. He had so much to be thankful for; but what of his church? The crisis in Hartford was of the gravest concern. He was, after all, an ordained clergyman in the Church of England still and enjoined to baptise into the church all children of God-fearing parents. Who was he to consign such infants to perdition? It was against natural law. And so, yes, for a year now he had baptised the children of such parents as were prepared to take at least a 'half-way covenant' to the church without undergoing the rigours of full membership; and he would justify it. He had always seen the Christian religion as an expansive, generous commitment and he could not, like his colleague Stone down the river in Hartford, stand unyielding on such harsh Calvinist ground. Was it because Stone was an Emmanuel man whereas he came from the milder, more accommodating climate of Oxford? He could not tell; but he had committed himself to embrace his half-way convenanting flock and they clearly appreciated him for it.

And yet . . . and yet, was he being weak? Was there truly a justification in Scripture for what he had undertaken? As he gazed into the dying embers of his fire that November night, a mood of melancholy came over him and he began to doubt whether he, who was such a sinner, had the spiritual strength or justification to presume to administer the sacrament of baptism to the infants of such half-believers. He would have to think hard on it.

CHAPTER 10: A TROOP OF HORSE 1658

THE TIME WAS THE MORNING OF THURSDAY 11 MARCH 1658; THE PLACE, the town of Hartford on Connecticut River; the occasion, the quarterly meeting of the colony's governing body, the General Court. The courtroom, guarded by armed musketeers in ceremonial corselets, was thronged with the thirty or so magistrates and deputies who comprised the court, together with attendant petitioners and witnesses. They had travelled hither by boat or on horseback in the semi-frozen or muddy conditions of early spring from Windsor, Wethersfield, Middletown and Saybrook on the Great River, from their tiny offshoots at Fairfield and Stratford on the Sound, and from up-country Farmington. Except for immediate neighbours, most had not seen one another since the October court because weather made a winter court impractical. In any case, the past season had been exceptionally difficult owing to sickness and Indian trouble. Even the court the previous May, when new officers were elected, had been poorly attended because of a new threat to the plantations and exposed homesteads from the Indians, whose internecine tribal conflicts implicated the English as allies of the Mohegan chief, Uncas. The Indians had pursued their skirmishes into their own homes where they slaughtered one another in the presence of the families 'to their great alarm and astonishment'; and the memory of 'a most horrid murder' of the English in outlying Farmington the previous spring was still vivid. As for Uncas, he was recently so hard pressed that the colony had to send a contingent of troops to reinforce the defence of his fort at Niantick against the Narragansetts.

The court was called to order by the new Governor, John Winthrop, eldest son of the great Governor of Massachusetts Bay. Born in the manor house at Groton, Suffolk, bred at Bury St Edmund's Grammar School, Trinity College, Dublin and the Inner Temple, he was a travelled and experienced manager of his father's English affairs and had always stood out. We have come across him as the agent for the Warwick patentees at Saybrook and he was also a prospector for minerals. At the age of fifty-two he was coming to be recognized as one of the outstanding New Englanders of his time. Connecticut was thankful to have captured him as governor. He had needed some persuading to come and live in Hartford with his family: a small committee, appointed to negotiate his terms of office, had arranged for him to be provided with the house and grounds of the late governor, John Haynes, as an official residence and to furnish him with horses and men to grace his welcoming journey. More important, there was talk of altering the colony's constitution to enable the governor to be re-elected annually without, as hitherto, having to stand down for a year. This would be done in two years' time, in May 1660, thereby ensuring that the colony should enjoy Winthrop's services as Governor, in effect, for his lifetime. This was to prove a particularly perspicacious move: in six months' time the Lord Protector of England, Oliver Cromwell, would die and uncertainties about the succession and a possible restoration of the monarchy would have anxious reverberations throughout Puritan New England; but few that morning in Hartford imagined that it would be as a result of the exertions of their own versatile and talented Governor at King Charles II's court three or four years hence that the remote little colony would be granted its royal charter, the most liberal for any colony in its time. Still less could any of his acquaintance this morning foretell that their new Governor's energetic and inquiring mind, with its well-known bent towards natural philosophy, would lead to his election, on that same London visit, to a fellowship of the newly founded Royal Society, the first colonial Englishman to be so distinguished.

On that March morning the assembly in Hartford courtroom was concerned mainly to see how their new Governor would handle the business of his first meeting of the General Court. The agenda was the usual mixture of large and small matters: one of the deputies was sworn in as constable of Stratford; William Phelps and Matthew Allyn of Windsor, among others, were re-appointed magistrates; several people were exempted, on grounds of health or age, from militia training or watching and warding; the magistrates were instructed to hold probate courts in their respective plantations; someone from Pequot was permitted to rent some land from Uncas, the Indian sachem; under strict conditions; John Bissell had his contract renewed to run the ferry across the Great River at Windsor, with special provision that Windsor people should go over for half-price and troopers and their horses carried free. The court also resolved that the plantation of Pequot should be renamed New London. As the citation had it:

> Whereas . . . this Country hath its denomination from our deare native Country of England and thence is called New England, so the planters in their first settling of most new Plantations have given names to those Plantations of some Cities and Towns in England . . . as Boston, Hartford, Windsor, York, Ipswich, Braintree, Exeter – this Court, considering that there hath yet no place in any of the Colonies been named in memory of the City of London, there being a new plantation within this jurisdiction of Connecticut settled upon the fair River of Monhegin, in the Pequot Country, it being an excellent harbour and a fit and convenient place for future trade, it being also the only place which the English of these parts have possessed by conquest and that but a very just war upon the great and warlike people, the Pequots, and that therefore they might thereby leave to posterity the memory of that renowned city of London from whence we had our transportation, have thought fit, in honour to that famous City, to call the said Plantation, New London.

Since the new Governor was a founding planter of Pequot and still had property there, it is reasonable to suppose that this was his own personal proposal.

Finally, there were two agenda items, each of more than routine importance. Judging by the length of the secretary's minute, the first took up the greater part of the court's time that day. It concerned the scandal of the church in Hartford where dissidents were in revolt against the ministers and elders over church government and membership. This conflict, clearly already recognized as grave, would continue to wrack the Puritan community and spread to the other river settlements. For the moment, the

General Court was still hoping to defuse the issue by instructing both sides to desist from agitation and by calling a special meeting of the court together with the church elders to try to discover a means of reconciliation.

The remaining item on the court's agenda concerned defence. The court resolved to augment the colony militia by establishing a troop of horse. The proposal had been mooted at the meeting of the court the previous May; the names of those who had volunteered were reported to the court and they were formally recruited to constitute a troop. Their choices of officers were confirmed and commissioned. The troop was to serve directly under the commander-in-chief.

The commander-in-chief was present at court that morning in his capacity as magistrate. He was, of course, our old friend Sergeant-Major General John Mason, 'the Major' for short. For the last twenty years he had retained his pre-eminence in military affairs and, as the colony grew, so he had acquired increased stature, both military and civil. He had been a magistrate since 1642 and in two years' time he would become deputy governor. He had left Windsor to take command at Saybrook ten years before and he would shortly become a principal founder of a new plantation in his old Pequot campaigning country, to be called Norwich. At the age of fifty-eight he had seen Connecticut Colony establish itself prodigiously since its precarious hold on the Great River at the time of the Pequot War. From a population of about 800 in three plantations at the close of 1636, it had grown to upwards of 3000 in nine plantations in 1658. Although the sequestration of the Pequots had established the English ascendency on the river, Indian relations continued to be problematic. Hardly a year went by without some threatened outbreak of hostility with or between the Indian tribes, particularly the Narragansetts' repeated attempts under Miantonimo and more recently Ninigret to destroy Uncas and his Mohegans, and latterly against the Montauk Indians on Long Island. Of recent years the situation had been complicated by the machinations of the Dutch from the Hudson which would have resulted in full-scale war a few years back had not Massachusetts as usual failed to co-operate and Cromwell's defeat of the Dutch fleet ended official hostilities. In most of these alarums and excursions Mason had played a principal role, as soldier, negotiator and commissioner for Connecticut to the New England Confederation. Within the past year he had led yet another investigating mission to the Long Island Indians and he had made a full report to the General Court concerning yet another action in defence of Uncas at Niantick. At the moment he was at work on a historical account of the Pequot War, as was his old comrade in arms, Lion Gardiner, now living in retirement across the Sound at Easthampton, Long Island. It is a fair assumption that it was Mason's initiative that had led to the establishment of the troop of horse on that March day in 1658.

After the improvised expeditionary force had returned from its baptism of fire against the Pequots in 1637, Mason as the newly appointed commander-in-chief had set about instituting a militia system based on the one they had left behind in Massachusetts. Each town established a trainband of all able-bodied men between sixteen and sixty who elected their officers (for confirmation by the court) and drilled on the town green. There were six regular training days a year; two in September were eventually devoted to a general muster of all the trainbands under the command of their Major; and a search was made for land suitable for an 'artillery yard' for the purpose. The duties of the town trainband included providing an armed guard of forty men for Sunday meeting and, in emergencies, nominating recruits, sometimes volunteers but more often impressed men, for mobilization against the Indians or, as in 1653, against the Dutch.

Such forces were still foot companies. There were mounted militiamen but they had been deployed hitherto only individually as scouts. In New England's earliest days, horses were too scarce and the country too unfamiliar for a cavalry arm to be practicable; but in time the possibilities of fast movement against Indians and no doubt the example of Cromwell's cavalry made the institution of the troop of horse a more attractive proposition. Massachusetts had established its first troop in 1648 and now, ten years later, Connecticut was following suit. The troop of thirty-seven men, seventeen from Windsor, fourteen from Hartford, six from Wethersfield, was only about half the strength of a cavalry troop of the day, for the settlements could still boast only a limited number of able-bodied men with the means to support the horse, armour and accoutrements of a trooper. Nevertheless, the event represented the birth of a cavalry arm for the militia and this was to have both military and social significance for the colony.

It is the social significance of these volunteers that is for the moment our principal concern, for their relationships reveal much about the social structure of Windsor and the colony. The horse, like the foot, had its roots in the English shires, but, by a long-standing tradition which can be traced back to the Middle Ages, recruits came from the gentry and superior yeomanry, with an obligation and the means to provide their own mounts, accoutrements and weapons. They were thus set apart from the foot by being socially select volunteers. It was in something of this spirit that in the late 1630s some young gentlemen in the Boston area had come together as a sort of club, called the Artillery Company, to practise the martial arts, and that Massachusetts and now Connecticut had established their first troop of horse.

Most of those thirty-seven troopers were men of good family with intimate connections in the Great River neighbourhood. Six were in the meeting house that day as members of the court. Apart from Major Mason, there was Lieutenant Daniel Clarke, the deputy from Windsor who next August would become secretary of the colony; Cornet John Allyn, deputy from Hartford who in turn would succeed Clarke as colony secretary; the captain of the troop, Richard Lord, and troopers James Steele and Jacob Mygatt were also deputies from Hartford; and if the other thirty-odd were not present, except perhaps as members of the Governor's guard or as spectators, they knew each other well.

Their official connections were impressive. Samuel Wyllys, a magistrate at twenty-six, was son-in-law of the colony's first Governor; Thomas Welles was the son of its second. George Phelps's brother was a magistrate and a founding commissioner as was James Steele's father. Richard Treat was a magistrate's son; Captain Richard Lord was the son of a prominent Hartford deputy who had been a close friend and neighbour in England of both Governor Haynes and Thomas Hooker. Daniel Clarke was and John Allyn would be colony secretary and magistrate, and Allyn would marry the grand-daughter of the formidable William Pynchon, founder and overlord of Springfield up the river; Jonathan Gilbert was the colony's marshall, and John Porter's uncle the colony's London agent. Equally striking were the troopers' relationships with the clerisy. Stephen Terry was John White's nephew and John Chester was Thomas Hooker's great-nephew; Thomas Allyn was married to John Warham's daughter and John Strong would marry Ephraim Huitt's daughter; John Hosford was the son of a ruling elder and Nathaniel Loomis and two of John Bissell's brothers were deacon Moore's sons-in-law. Troopers were also intermarrying with the families of their comrades-in-arms. John Bissell had just become betrothed to the daughter of his commander-in-chief; John Allyn's daughter would marry the son of Lion Gardiner, ex-governor of Saybrook Fort; Corporal Nicholas Olmstead was married to one of the Loomis girls, sister to troopers Nathaniel and Thomas; Thomas Allyn's sister was married to Captain Benjamin Newberry and Lieutenant Clarke's wife was Newberry's sister; Simon Wolcott married the daughter of his fellow trooper Aaron Cooke;

Corporal Samuel Marshall married the daughter of his fellow trooper David Wilton; and, for good measure, Daniel Clarke's son would marry the daughter of another trooper, Daniel Pratt.

Most of the troop were sons of the first settlers, up-and-coming young men of a second generation. With possibly two exceptions, they had been born in England and vividly remembered their childhood there as well as the voyaging, trekking and settling, first on the Bay and then on the Connecticut, that had since been their life experience. They were, in fact, virtually the first New England generation of colonial Englishmen. In their remote and improvised little settlements, their backs were to the wilderness and their vision still looked down the Great River, across Long Island Sound to the north Atlantic and Old England. At the General Court that March day, these Englishmen, meeting in their rough formality on that remote American river settlement, took for granted the habits and assumptions of the local self-government which they and their parents had practised and brought with them from the old country thirty years before. The epic nature of their Puritan migration might have wrought a sea change in the system of English law, custom and belief which they inherited, but the river planters still considered they were conducting their affairs as Englishmen in accordance with English custom. However, they did not all come from the same part of England. Most came from the eastern counties, the Hartford people by way of New Town, those of Wethersfield by way of Watertown, Massachusetts; but the Windsor people were overwhelmingly West Country, in origin, habit and religious conviction distinct from their East Anglian neighbours. Let us look more closely at those Windsor troopers and their connections.

Three weeks later on a spring day in April the Windsor contingent rode out by way of the upland highway towards Hartford to take part in the troop exercises on the first training day of the season. The going was heavy so early in the spring, though the road was now passable for carts as well as for livestock, and the bridges over the swamps had survived the winter in reasonable condition. The upkeep of that highway had been a bone of contention between Windsor and Hartford ever since it was first surveyed in 1638, as one of the troopers, Stephen Terry, well remembered: he and young Henry Wolcott had been the two Windsor men in the original survey party; and there had been complaints, usually from the Hartford people, on and off ever since. Riding together in rough cavalry formation, they must have felt exhilarated as they eyed one another's mounts and accoutrements. These were not exactly New Model Army standard but their breastplates and uniform scarves gave them a sense of a shared and privileged identity. Each owned his own horse and the colony would provide compensation if it were killed under him in action; they enjoyed free ferriage for themselves and their mounts and were paid 6s 8d a day, a unique privilege; above all, they were free from duty with the town trainband; drilling with pikes as foot soldiers was no longer their lot, thank the Lord.

They were seventeen, more than Hartford could muster and many more than Wethersfield. They looked forward to acquitting themselves well in this first exercise under the Major's eye. Although the troop's captain, quartermaster and cornet were all Hartford men, their own Daniel Clarke was the lieutenant and rode at the head of the column. They knew one another more or less intimately. Most were second generation in their early to mid-thirties; all were married with small children; most had grown up together, sharing a West Country background and, often, childhood memories of shipboard and Dorchester; they spoke the same language – literally, a West Country drawl; figuratively, in instinctive reactions based on a common experience and leaving so much unsaid. There were exceptions: two or three were much older and four had come to Windsor with the Huitt party; but all in all they were a homogeneous company of similar English origins and similar social standing in Windsor.

Their lieutenant was one of the exceptions. We have come across Captain Clarke as that young man of about eighteen who had arrived with the Huitt party, married John Warham's stepdaughter Mary Newberry and started a family on a substantial homestead behind the Warhams on the way to the mill. He quickly made his mark as a lettered young man of energy and drive. He had joined the church a year before he married, was executor of Huitt's will, a juryman in 1646, constable in 1651, a deputy in 1657 and, having shown his skill as a draftsman, appointed colony secretary the following year. He became a magistrate in 1662 at the age of about forty and was named one of the Assistants in the new royal charter of 1662. At this point his career received a check. He was accused by a fellow trooper of breach of his oath, unfaithfulness in his trust, infringement of the royal prerogative and contempt for the authority of the colony. This probably had something to do with an allocation of land at Hammonasset from which he had benefited; and there was enough in it for the General Court 'to find him so far faulty as to put him out of the secretary's place until the next Election Court'. The following year, whether or not through pique, he declined to serve as a magistrate; but the year after that, 1665, he was back again both as magistrate and as colony secretary, serving as the former for three years and the latter for two, and during this time he continued to play a full part in the affairs of the court, even acting as attorney for the Governor, John Winthrop, and being granted 100 acres of land at Middletown. Yet at the Court of Election in 1668 when he was proposed, as usual, as a magistrate, he failed, unaccountably, to be elected, and thereafter never returned to the General Court either as magistrate or deputy. It may be that he remained under a cloud, or simply that his military career was proving too demanding; in any case the latter appears not to have been affected. On 12 May 1664 he was promoted captain of the troop and he retained this command in the events leading to King Philip's War. At the outbreak of fighting he was a member of the Council of Safety, the colony's executive in prosecuting the war.

He was a considerable family man. Mary Newberry bore him ten children only two of whom died in infancy. After she died in 1688, in his mid-sixties he married Martha Pitkin, the widow of his fellow Windsor trooper Simon Wolcott. One of his sons was a problem to him, like Tahan Grant to his father; he was convicted of 'notorious, reproachful, contemptuous speeches' threatening Major Treat, Connecticut's commander-in-chief during King Philip's War, fined £20 and imprisoned. The sentence was remitted on Major Treat's plea. That apart, Daniel Clarke died in 1710 a greatly respected man of about eighty-eight. He left among his effects a number of books chiefly of a devotional kind, Bibles and psalm books, including a Bible and four other books in Latin, evidence of a grammar school education.

The man who replaced Daniel Clarke as colony secretary on his temporary disgrace in 1663 was John Allyn of Hartford. He and his brother Thomas of Windsor were both troopers. They were the sons of Matthew Allyn whom we may remember as having moved up from Hartford to buy the Plymouth trading post in Windsor. Matthew, with his wife, their younger son Thomas and daughter Mary, became one of the most well-to-do families of Windsor. The Allyns were a West Country family of some consequence in Braunton near Barnstaple, Devon. Matthew appears to have emigrated about 1633 to Charlestown, where his standing is indicated by his considerable acreage there and in Cambridge, where he is reputed to have been the largest landholder and had been a deputy to the Massachusetts General Court. After moving to the Connecticut River in 1635 he was granted or bought over the years 100 acres and the mill in Hartford, the Plymouth lands in Windsor and extensive tracts in Killingworth and Simsbury. One reason for his moving up from Hartford to Windsor was that he had been excommunicated by Hartford church, probably for some doctrinal dispute with Master Hooker. As owner of the Plymouth lands in Windsor he had the arrogance to claim that he should be free of Connecticut taxation. He was also in court a good deal and usually lost his cases. He was a member of the General Court for over twenty years, a commissioner to the United Colonies, moderator of the committee to petition for the royal charter and named in the latter as one of the Assistants. He was distinctly a grandee.

John, Thomas and Mary Allyn were born in Devon and crossed the Atlantic as small children. Thomas, born in 1626, must have had vivid memories of the voyage, of Dorchester and the trek to Connecticut; but he grew up in Windsor where his playmates in the Island neighbourhood were Newberrys, Wolcotts, Loomises and Porters, all of whom must have attended their neighbour Mr Branker's 'school' at his home on Little Meadow. He learned farming, land management and trade in a household which boasted a servant or two as befitted a magistrate of means. As a young man he suffered a traumatic experience. On a training day in October 1651 he accidentally killed his neighbour in the ranks, the elderly and respected Henry Stiles. The Particular Court charged him: 'Not having that due fear of God before thine eyes for the preservation of the life of thy neighbour, [thou] didst suddenly, negligently, carelessly cock thy piece, being charged and going off in thine hand, slew thy neighbor to the great dishonour of God, breach of the peace and loss of a member of this Commonwealth, what sayest thou, art thou guilty or not guilty?' He pleaded guilty, was convicted of homicide by misadventure, sentenced to a fine of £20, bound over and prohibited from bearing arms for twelve months. This did not, however, prevent his being made a freeman the following May along with the two Bissell boys and John Hosford. At that first troop muster he was still a bachelor but in six months he would marry one of the girls down the road, Abigail, the eldest of John Warham's daughters by Jane Newberry who would bear him eight children. When their old schoolmaster died and his widow conveniently married father Warham, the Allyns fell heir to the Branker place where they lived until old father Allyn died. They then moved into the spacious Allyn family home on Plymouth Meadow, the original part of which was reputed to have come prefabricated from England and erected as the Plymouth trading post. Though a captain in the Windsor trainband Thomas was not, like his father and brother, conspicuous in public affairs but he inherited a great part of the family property and when he died in 1696 was worth some £1200.

We have not exhausted the connections of the Warham household with the young military of Windsor. Thomas Allyn had a younger sister Mary who at the age of eighteen long before the first troop muster had married another childhood friend and neighbour, Benjamin Newberry, brother of Mary Newberry married to Daniel Clarke and of Sarah married to Henry Wolcott. It will be recalled that the Newberrys were prominent among the West Country families who settled Dorchester. Thomas, who had so unfortunately died on the eve of the departure for Connecticut, was of the lesser squirearchy of west Dorset. His grandfather held a substantial manor at Netherbury called Othe Francis. His father, who was a younger son, married a wife who brought him a small estate in Yarcomb twelve miles away in Somerset and here Thomas was brought up. Also a younger son, he tried his hand at reading for the Bar in London but, finding it not to his taste, married Joan, daughter of Christopher Dabinot (of Huguenot extraction) who settled on them a property called Coweleyes in Marshwood Vale a few miles west of Netherbury. After Joan died, Thomas married her cousin Jane, another Dabinot, and it was with her and his seven children that he set forth from Marshwood Vale for New England in 1634.

That Thomas had strong Puritan leanings may be confidently inferred. His first cousin Walter Newberry, who had inherited the family manor at Netherbury and extensive properties in Dorset, had taken orders and settled into the valuable living of nearby Simonsbury. He married successively daughters of two local squires, both subscribers to the Dorchester Company, and his widow married into that prominent Puritan family, the Stoughtons, two of whom were *Mary and John* passengers. Cousin Walter must have been a strong influence on Thomas Newberry's religious faith and in prompting him to embark on the New England adventure.

Of the Newberry children, the unfortunate John, as we saw, was hanged in 1647, and Joseph the eldest returned the following year to the family home in Dorset; so Benjamin remained the only son in Windsor. Brought up under the wing of John Warham who had married their stepmother Jane Dabinot, Benjamin and his two sisters were not unprovided for; and although, in a suit against the town of Windsor in 1669, they claimed they had been given short measure in the original land assessment of 1640 in relation to their father's capital investment in the enterprise, they each owned a nicely balanced holding of meadow, upland and land across the river which Benjamin, taking to himself Joseph's and John's holdings and dealing in real estate on his own, gradually built into a useful property.

One surmises that Benjamin, as an orphan, though endowed with land and benevolent stepparents, had to make his own way in the world. His marriage in 1646 at the age of twenty-two to Matthew Allyn's daughter was a first step, and he succeeded in his farming, trading and land deals. He learned to hold his own. He was found guilty of defamation and fined 20 shillings in 1647, but the following year he won an action for debt and promptly sued his former plaintiff for slander and won again. He was clearly ambitious. In 1655, aged thirty-one, he was proposed for nomination as captain of the trainband but was closely defeated by Aaron Cooke, becoming lieutenant as a consolation prize. Two years later he achieved this ambition and was elected captain. Two years after that he was made a selectman, a position he held for five years and again twice in the 1670s. He began to have ambitions for office in the colony. In 1663 the General Court made him a member of a committee to lay out lands at Massaco for Windsor people and the following year of another committee to adjust the boundaries with the Bay and Rhode Island. He did not succeed in being elected as a magistrate in 1664, and failed again the following year, but this time he was at least elected a deputy and thereafter was regularly a member of the court.

However, it was as a soldier that he made his name in colony affairs. In 1658 when the troop of horse was formed he was captain of the Windsor trainband. His duties, particularly for training, must have prevented him from volunteering with his peers and he was not gazetted among the troopers from Windsor; but he was so closely associated with them that he must be included in any account of their companionship. He was a success as captain of the Windsor trainband, a commission which he held from 1656 until, as we shall see, the events leading up to the next great confrontation with the Indians, called King Philip's War, took him to higher things; and in 1666 the General Court appointed him to its new Committee for the Militia. This body seemed to have assumed responsibility for reorganizing and strengthening the Connecticut militia and, in particular, for mounting a proportion of the foot as dragoons as well as for establishing cavalry troops in all the counties. In a war-scare with the Dutch in 1673, the committee was reconstituted as the Standing War Council and two years later, when hostilities broke out with the Indians, it was activated on a day-to-day basis. Apart from the Governor and the other ex-officio officers, Newberry was, throughout, the principal member of this council. He thus became over the years the colony's chief staff officer. As we shall see in the final chapter of this narrative, he played an important military role in King Philip's War.

By the end of King Philip's War, Benjamin Newberry was one of

Windsor's principal citizens. In 1658, as a true son of his long-dead Puritan father, he had followed his wife Mary into full membership of Windsor church and, as a gesture, undertook to provide new sills for the meeting house. He was a member of a committee to reorder the seating and of another to find a new minister, both tasks of peculiar responsibility. In 1685 he was the first on a list of seven prominent citizens petitioning the General Court for a town patent for Windsor. When he died four years later he left an estate inventoried at £563 which brought him well into the first quarter of Windsor affluence. The Newberrys had two sons, Benjamin, also a captain of militia, and Thomas, who married a daughter of Thomas Ford, and five daughters, one of whom married the son of trooper Thomas Strong, and another John Maudsley, her father's lieutenant in the campaigns of King Philip's War.

Like the Wolcotts, he kept a link with the old country. Along with his brother Joseph who had returned to Dorset, Benjamin had a life interest in the Coweleyes property in Marshwood Vale, left them by their grandfather Dabinot, and other land bequeathed by a Dabinot aunt. But in 1686, shortly after Joseph's death, a Newberry cousin would write from Chardstock, Dorset, to his 'loving cousin' Henry Wolcott in Windsor to inquire for legal purposes if 'cousin Benjamin' were still alive; so by this time the Newberry link was becoming attenuated.

The Wolcott connection deserves the separate treatment it will receive in the next chapter. Suffice it here to note that while Henry, the oldest Wolcott of the second generation, was not a military man, his younger brother Simon was a member of the troop. Simon Wolcott had the year before married Joanna, the daughter of one of his fellow troopers, Aaron Cooke, with whom he must have felt a special bond that morning as they rode together to Hartford: his bride had tragically died six weeks after the wedding. At the troop's foundation Aaron Cooke was forty-eight and, like Henry Wolcott, at the older end of the second generation. Indeed Henry and he, then aged nineteen and twenty, had been young companions on *Mary and John* all those twenty-eight years before. It will be remembered that Aaron had been on that voyage with his mother and his step-family, the Fords. Thomas Ford, former merchant of Simonsbury and Dorchester, had grants from Windsor plantation which made it its fourth richest man. In 1637 young Aaron married his stepsister Mary Ford and set up house near the Fords at the lower end of Main Street with the Pomeroys, Hosfords and Denslows as neighbours, all from the Brit Valley, Dorset.

Aaron Cooke became noted for his military bent. He was a formidable wolf hunter and regularly claimed the town bounty of ten shillings for each one slain, though once he was only allowed half this rate 'for seven young wolves taken out of an old one'. By 1648 he was the lieutenant of the Windsor trainband and five years later he was commissioned by the colony as commander of a small force mobilized in a war-scare against the Dutch. Two years after that he was promoted captain by an overwhelming number of votes over all the other candidates, with Benjamin Newberry as his lieutenant. As captain he was responsible for training and for guard mounting on Sabbaths and lecture days. He took his military duties seriously and owned an up-to-date military manual, *The Complete Body of the Art Military* by Lt. Col. Richard Elton published in 1649. He is said to have befriended the regicide judges, Goffe and Walley, when they were on the run in New England after the Restoration. By this time his first wife had died and he had married the girl next-door-but-two, Joan Denslow, whom he had probably also known as a child on the *Mary and John* if not before in Allington, Dorset; her mother, like Mary Ford's, was a Way from Dorchester.

Captain Cooke had the reputation of being a vigorous and restless fellow so it was not surprising that he should have speculated in land. In 1653, perhaps in recognition of his recent command against the Dutch, he was granted fifty acres of land to the west, by the Rivulet at the falls of Massaco. After 1660 he moved up there and spent most of the 1660s developing his property and that of his father-in-law. Despite this, he never settled permanently. Instead, though holding on to the land, he moved with the Fords up to Northampton about 1672 and then on to Westfield where, as an old man, he would be commissioned by Governor Andros as Major, the highest military rank in the colony.

At forty-eight Aaron Cooke, though second generation, was one of the oldest of those troopers riding to Hartford on that April morning in 1658. Four others of the first generation were his near contemporaries: William Hayden, George Phelps, Stephen Terry and David Wilton. All these five were old enough to have fought the Pequots but only Hayden, who had saved Captain Mason's life in the Mystic fight, was a veteran of that war. A Somerset man, he appeared in Windsor from Hartford about 1640 and bought land from the Stiles's up towards Pine Meadow, a neck of the woods which became known as Haydens. He was a farmer and also had a quarry on nearby Rocky Hill. He had a row with his litigious neighbour John Bissell, served as a rating commissioner and, as a responsible citizen on the edge of town, took in as lodger at the behest of the townsmen a notorious delinquent called John Bennet to keep him out of mischief. After his wife died he, like one or two other troopers, would move away to a new colony, in his case down the river to Hammonasset on the Sound, leaving a son, Daniel, in Windsor who, in turn, would become a trooper and lieutenant in the next generation.

George Phelps was the younger brother of William, the magistrate and founding father of the colony, also from Somerset. Unlike his elder brother, George never made much mark in Windsor though he was a townsman for a couple of years. He lived on the Island and married a daughter of Phillip Randall of Allington, Bridport, whom he had known first on the *Mary and John*. He migrated upriver to Westfield in 1670, an inauspicious moment to move to a frontier exposed to Indians, but he survived, and died in 1687. He was unique among this connection in having to sign his name with a cross.

Stephen Terry, who was fifty on that ride to Hartford, had a family provenance that takes us back to the original impulse for the whole West Country migration. His father, John Terry, one-time fellow of New College, Oxford, was vicar of Stockton, Wiltshire and a noted anti-Catholic writer. His mother Mary was John White's sister. White, also a fellow of New College, had recruited his brother-in-law as a member of the Dorchester Company. When Terry died his widow moved with her five sons to Dorchester to be under her brother's wing. One of her sons, Josiah, was set up as a haberdasher and became a prosperous merchant and burgess; he was constable, a member of the common council, twice mayor and lieutenant of militia under the Parliament. His younger brother Stephen was only seventeen when they moved to Dorchester and he was no doubt marked down by uncle John White as a suitable recruit for his New England venture. At any rate, he sailed on the *Mary and John* with a wife and child. A young man of some standing, he was an early freeman and paralleled his elder brother by becoming constable of Dorchester, Massachusetts. The Terrys moved to Windsor with the Warham hegira and settled on lower Main Street next to the Fords. He was not prominent in local affairs though he served as a rate commissioner and as a townsman. In due course he followed a son to the settlement at Massaco, which became Simsbury, where he probably ended his days. That son married a Wadsworth girl from Hartford and would die worth more than £500 which put him well up in the first quarter of Windsor property owners in the first two generations.

David Wilton was exceptional in deriving not from the West Country but from East Anglia, from the village of Tipcroft near Norwich; he crossed the Atlantic with the main body of the Winthrop fleet. In Windsor he lived in the south-west corner of the Palisado and looked after the burial ground. He added to his holdings and worked a useful farm with land in Great Meadow, Northwest Field and across the river. He was also something of a trader and was once fined for illegally exporting lead. He was, however, a greatly respected citizen, a devout church member, in demand as an executor, a rate commissioner, a long-serving townsman and a deputy. A month after that cavalry muster he would be in Hartford again as leading juryman in the trial of Elizabeth Gullick for witchcraft. (They found her not guilty.) He had a strong military bent. Four years before, the General Court had nominated him for the invidious job of deciding who in Windsor should be pressed into service against the Dutch; two years later he was ensign and then lieutenant of Windsor trainband. He was to serve as a lieutenant in King Philip's War and as member of the Committee of Safety in Northampton where he had moved in 1660 and where he became a leading citizen. He left a silver bowl to Northampton church of which he was a founding father, and £10 to Harvard College.

Unusually for that generation, David Wilton had only one child, a daughter Mary (he also had a scapegrace younger brother Nicholas who must have been a great trial to him). Mary Wilton was married to another of those troopers riding to Hartford that morning: Samuel Marshall. Young Marshall was becoming a person of mark in the second generation. His English background is obscure; his father was a tanner and the first shoemaker in Boston, Massachusetts, and he was probably brought up to that trade. At the time of the Pequot menace he had a lot in the Palisado which he exchanged for Major Mason's more prestigious home by the Rivulet ferry when the latter moved down to Saybrook. He dealt in land, though he appears not to have been much of a farmer. Instead he acquired the licence to sell strong liquors, which was renewed over the years. As befitted the son of a tanner, and possibly as one himself, he was appointed sealer of leather. He appeared in the Particular Court as an attorney for several, especially English, clients. He was made a freeman on the same day as his fellow troopers Simon Wolcott and the Loomis brothers and he would act as constable of Windsor. In 1663 he was elected corporal of the Windsor trainband, a rank he held for ten years before being promoted to quartermaster at the outbreak of Indian hostilities, in recognition of which he was awarded a grant of 150 acres. Two years later, in May 1675, on the mobilizing of the river towns against King Philip, he was made ensign of dragoons for Hartford County and the following November promoted captain of the Hartford County force which, as we shall see in the last chapter, was about to set out on a critical winter expedition to Narragansett Bay. On 19 December he led his men with great gallantry into attack at the famous Narragansett swamp fight and was killed in the assault. He left his widow Mary with nine children. His affairs after his death were handled by his brother officers Benjamin Newberry, John Allyn, Daniel Clarke and David Wilton. His son Samuel was to marry Benjamin Newberry's daughter Rebecca.

Samuel Marshall was not the only tanner in the troop. There was also Thomas Strong whose father, John, came from the tanning family of Chard, Somerset that we came across earlier. John Strong had married Thomas Ford's daughter Abigail as his second wife in 1638 and the Strongs and the Fords settled down together on adjacent home lots on the lane to the ferry in the Palisado; here Strong developed his tanyard and young Thomas, our trooper, grew up. On that April morning in 1658 Thomas was still a bachelor but two years later he was to marry the Rev. Ephraim Huitt's daughter Mary. By this time, however, the family had undergone another upheaval. The year 1660 saw a considerable exodus from the bottom end of the Palisado. John Strong, his father-in-law Thomas Ford, David Wilton (as we have seen) and ultimately Strong's brother-in-law Aaron Cooke all elected to move again, this time up the Connecticut Valley to become founding families of Northampton. John Strong was ruling elder and, like David Wilton, a prominent member of its church. Son Thomas went with his parents to Northampton but his brother Return Strong remained in occupation of the Palisado homestead with its tanyard where he continued the family business. He would marry Sarah Warham the minister's daughter and thus join the charmed circle of the Warhams. He became a Windsor citizen of note and property.

Among the troopers that April morning there were therefore many brothers-in-law, and several fathers-in-law and sons-in-law, but there were only two brothers. Thomas and Nathaniel Loomis were the sons of Joseph Loomis who, like David Wilton, came from East Anglia; he and his family of five sons probably came with the Huitt party in 1638. He was a man of substance, receiving from the plantation grants valued at £675 which placed him among the most wealthy. His large home lot of 26 acres was prominent on the Island next to old Henry Wolcott on the Rivulet bank of Plymouth Meadow. He did not, however, play any notable role in Windsor's affairs nor indeed, with one exception, did his sons, save that three of them served as town constable. The exception was the second son, John, who was a townsman and a deputy and, with a family of thirteen children, inherited his father's homestead. His true importance was as a deacon of Windsor church, an office which he exercised with authority for many years. Neither of our troopers, Thomas and Nathaniel, achieved distinction, though they lived respectably and comfortably, Thomas with four and Nathaniel with twelve children. Nathaniel married deacon Moore's daughter. This marriage, together with that of his brother Joseph to Mary Chauncey, daughter of Warham's successor as minister, and brother John's becoming a deacon, were to bring the family well within the ambit of church dignity and influence.

The Loomis boys had as a fellow trooper a first cousin, John Porter junior. His father had come from Felsted in Essex, a neighbouring village of the Loomis's town of Braintree. Porter and Loomis had married sisters and the two families emigrated together, probably with the Huitt party in the summer of 1638, and settled near each other on large home lots on the Island. Like the Loomises, the Porters were a large, established family of means. There were nine children and John Porter's initial land grant of 400 acres rated him almost in the top quarter of land ownership; and when he died, an elderly man, ten years later, he left a sizeable estate of £470 in land and chattels. He was a prominent citizen in Windsor, following Henry Wolcott as the town's second constable and acting as grand juror and deputy to the General Court. He traded overseas and sent his second son James to London where, as we noted, he was to become a prosperous merchant and colony agent. The eldest son John had inherited the family homestead on the Island and was to live a long and prosperous life, dying in 1688 leaving twelve children and an estate worth nearly £1000. He does not appear to have followed his father into civic life and, apart from serving along with his peers as a dragoon in King Philip's War, he was to achieve no active military standing.

The father of John Bissell, another trooper, is supposed to have come from Somerset; little is known of John senior until he arrived in Windsor with his family in the late 1630s when he acquired 774 acres in grants from the plantation which made him the largest landowner in Windsor after the Wolcott family, greater even than the Stiles family, whose lands marched largely with his own at the northern edge of the town on the way to Pine Meadow. As we have seen, he acquired the franchise of the ferry over the Connecticut. This gave his family a strategic position in the town and the impetus to develop their landholdings over the river; John Bissell senior was probably the first to settle on the east bank. He was important in Windsor, sought after as an executor, rates commissioner and deputy. He was also somewhat notorious, even for that litigious age, for being named in thirty-one separate court actions in the Particular Court between 1639 and 1663. His eldest son, John the trooper, was born in England but grew up in Windsor. In April 1658 when he rode to Hartford with the troop he must have been at least in his early twenties and looking forward to his wedding which was to take place on 17 June. He was betrothed to Isabel Mason, whom he must have known as a child before the Major and his family moved to Saybrook. On his marriage his father was to hand over to him the ferry which he kept for ten years, though perhaps not all the time willingly; in 1663 he unsuccessfully petitioned the court to be relieved of it. In the end he handed it on to his younger brother Nathaniel, who was also his partner in running a sawmill on the east bank, and four years later he himself moved across the river. John Bissell was to see active service in King Philip's War and would subsequently be appointed quartermaster of the troop of horse. He would die, a widower of well over seventy, in 1693, in the family homestead surrounded by his eight children.

There remain three members of the troop riding to Hartford that spring morning yet to be accounted for. One, John Williams, is a shadowy figure notable chiefly for an early conviction for some sexual offence, for a son who took after him in that respect and for leaving little land and few possessions, though he must have had the wherewithal to keep a saddle horse. The second, John Moses, was more substantial. Nothing is known about his English origins or his movements until he makes a sudden appearance in Windsor in 1647. He first lodged with his fellow trooper David Wilton, whose daughter Mary he was fined for importuning by that busybody Particular Court; but in 1653 he married and bought a home lot in Silver Street; that spring of 1658 he was starting to raise what was to be a large family and he was to become a man of some standing. He would serve as collector of rates and when he died he owned 355 acres and left a total estate of £575, well up in the first quarter of wealth. Like Henry Wolcott, he specialized in cider making.

The last member of the troop was John Hosford. Unlike the others of the second generation, he was not connected by marriage to other trooper families; but in other respects his background and family circumstances were similar. As we have noted, the Hosford family came from that valley of the Brit in Dorset which provided so many settlers' families for Windsor. His father was William, the ruling elder who had left Windsor for Springfield and thence returned home to the West Country three years before that cavalry muster. His mother had long before succumbed to the rigours of those first winters on the Connecticut and his stepmother, Jane, had followed his father back to Devon. One sister, Sarah, was dead, the other, Hester, was married to another Beaminster man in Windsor, Richard Samways. Young John was largely on his own.

There was one fortunate consequence for him of this isolation; apart from the original homestead which his father had deeded to his sister's husband, he inherited all his father's property including not only the original grants from the plantation which, as befitted an elder, were considerable, but substantial holdings brought by his stepmother Jane ffoulkes when she married his father. These included the attractively situated homestead and meadow, just west of the Palisado by the Rivulet, where he had grown up. John rounded this out by buying the adjacent home lot and orchard and other parcels of land; his own father-in-law was to deed him a farm of 50 acres across the river to supplement the 240 acres there from his father. Altogether, by the time of his death, in addition to two houses and barns and two orchards, John was to possess upwards of 450 acres, much of it in improved land in prime areas like Great and Hoyte's Meadows and Northwest Field. In 1658 he was taking these holdings in hand and on his way to becoming a very substantial farmer. By the time of his death he had a milking herd, herds of store cattle, sheep and hogs, and was cultivating a fair acreage of arable with two plough teams, with oxen, cart and cart-horses (as well as his saddle horse), and raising a variety of crops: winter wheat and rye, Indian corn, peas, barley and hay. True to his Brit Valley birthplace he also grew and spun flax and as a West Countryman cultivated his orchards commercially with a cider mill and press; at the time of his death he had forty barrels of cider in stock.

Such farming demanded labour and, perhaps in reaction to being the only son in a small family, and like so many of his own, second, generation, he was to go in for a big family. His wife was Philippa, daughter of William Thrall, an early settler who had fought against the Pequots but was otherwise of unlettered and obscure background; he made a living from a smallholding up in Hoyte's Meadow and from quarrying stone out of Rocky Hill. Philippa bore John Hosford nine children of whom six were able-bodied boys who grew up to work the family farm. Of these Hosford children, Timothy and Samuel both married daughters of Nicholas Palmer and Nathaniel, Obadiah and Sarah all married children of Joseph Phelps, a grandson of the magistrate.

Hosford appears to have been too committed to farming to have had time or inclination for civic affairs. He did his duty as constable but was never townsman or rates commissioner, let alone deputy or magistrate; and though he was to serve in the dragoons in King Philip's War he remained a private soldier. He appeared in court in minor cases involving neighbours. Walter Filer prosecuted him for failing to maintain their common fences and they were involved in a boundary dispute. He sued Nicholas Palmer for imprisoning his cattle. His fellow trooper Aaron Cooke prosecuted him for a similar offence, an incident which appears to have led to high words if not blows with John's father-in-law William Thrall prosecuting Cooke in turn for 'threatening John Hosford tending to the breach of the public peace'.

All this was the small change of village and farm life. However, John Hosford also appears to have been increasingly at odds with Windsor church; and this was the more serious in the son of that church's original ruling elder. The year before the troop muster he, along with five others including Nicholas Palmer and John Denslow, had suddenly opposed the renewal of the pension voted annually to old Mrs Huitt, widow of the church's long-dead and lovingly remembered minister. They failed, but there may have been some inwardness of church politics involved. In 1660 his seat in the meeting house was paid for not by him but by his stepmother who was a devoted member of the church. There is no evidence that he became a full communicant himself or presented any of his nine children for baptism. It is presumed that he was in favour of the half-way covenant and that in the controversy of the late 1660s which, as we shall see, led to a split and the forming of a second church, he belonged to the break-away party; and, when in 1680 the inhabitants of the east side of the Great River petitioned for a separate church, John Hosford was one of the signatories. All this is telltale evidence that in religious matters he was something of a rebel against the church and perhaps against the pure Puritan doctrines in which he had been brought up by his pious father and stepmother. In addition, however, something more mundane and venal, there was a matter of church property.

Before he 'went for England', old William Hosford had made a new will bequeathing all his property to his son, save for small bequests to his Samways grandchildren, and £40 to his wife Jane should she stay in New England, though he hoped she would follow him back to the West Country. This she did the following year; and before she left she made a will of her own which was to be the cause of protracted controversy. When she maried William Hosford she brought with her the sizeable estate of her first husband Henry ffoulkes. As the law then stood this automatically became her new husband's property unless specific portions had been reserved to herself before marriage. This had been done; but, whether through vagueness or cupidity, William seems not properly to have recognized it and, 'some dissatisfaction arising thereupon' between wife and husband, he was persuaded at some point 'to discharge in part what he was engaged to' by formally designating one piece of land which had belonged to her late husband, twenty acres in Hoyte's Meadow, to be her own 'reserved estate'. In the one substantive clause in her will Jane bequeathed this land in perpetuity to Windsor church 'for the use of a pastor or teacher as the Church shall see most need and when one is dead to go successively to another'.

Ten years later, on 3 March 1665, William Hosford in England complicated matters further by converting his bequest to his son into an outright deed of gift of 'all my housing, lands, cattell, debts whatsoever due unto me', without any reference to Jane's reserved portion of Hoyte's Meadow, and shortly afterwards, it is assumed, he died. A few years after this, Jane, still very much alive in Tiverton, Devon, must have begun to wonder what was happening to her prime meadowland, because on 15 January 1672 she confirmed her bequest to Windsor church in a new instrument, witnessed by two Tiverton justices, which also gave power of attorney in Windsor to her stepson-in-law Sarah's husband, old John Witchfield, William's brother elder in the church, and Walter Filer, an old friend and next-door neighbour and a man to be reckoned with. These three promptly went to work to investigate the matter. It seems that Jane had allowed John to use the land but he had neglected to pay the rent so her attorneys sued him in the county court for £80 arrears and damages. The jury found against him, though cut down the penalty to £12. On appeal the same October the General Court raised this to £50 and costs. However, John Hosford remained stubborn and Filer had to take him to court again two years later to establish Jane Hosford's right to the ownership of the Hoyte's Meadow land. There was a hung jury; whereupon plaintiff and defendant agreed to withdraw the action. In an out-of-court settlement, John Hosford recognized an obligation to pay rent but the whole question of the freehold was side-stepped.

The matter appears to have rested in this unsatisfactory state until after John's death in 1683; it is significant that the inventory of his real estate lists '20 acres at Hoyte's Meadow' valued at £100, clearly implying that he and his heirs still regarded the land as theirs and Jane's bequest invalid. At any rate, for some years afterwards John's widow and children continued to crop the meadow with impunity. However, in 1692 two overseers of Windsor church, our friend Daniel Clarke and Henry Wolcott the third, took the matter once again to the General Court in order to establish the church's right to the endowment. The Hosford family first took the line that there was no evidence that Jane was dead and any bequest was not therefore operative; but the court sensibly decided in favour of the petitioners' view that, since she 'was an ancient woman when she went away and hath been gone wellnigh forty years and nothing heard from or concerning her in twenty years past but that she lied under a tombstone in Tiverton', she must be deemed to have died unless evidence could be produced to the contrary. No evidence was produced; whereupon young John Hosford the second on behalf of the heirs tried to argue in a long memorandum that Jane at best had had only a life interest in his grandfather's estate, that her will was legally void because that parcel of land had not been specifically reserved before her marriage to William, and that the subsequent conveyance was invalid because it was between husband and wife and 'under coverture'. However, the General Court dismissed or ignored this argument and on 10 May 1694 finally approved Jane's will and granted administration to Henry Wolcott. Even after that, Wolcott had to go back to the court to force John Hosford the second to surrender the land; and as late as October the following year, 1695, Windsor's new minister, Samuel Mather, was sueing John's widow Philippa and two sons-in-law for harvesting hay and barley on the Hoyte's Meadow land. They were found guilty of trespass and had to pay heavy costs, though the widow was allowed to keep the barley.

John Hosford's role in the sorry story of his stepmother's bequest to Windsor church is strangely reminiscent of the role of a forebear of his, an earlier John Hosford of Netherbury in Dorset's Brit Valley, who disgraced himself in Queen Elizabeth's time as a trustee of the Netherbury Free School by holding on to the income from its estate. He was brought to book by local notables who included a Newberry, a Hoskins and a Denslow. More than a century later, our John Hosford in Windsor might well have been taken to task, not as he was, by Henry Wolcott, but by the latter's brother-in-law, a Newberry; he might also have been joined by a Hoskins and a Denslow, also from Dorset's Brit Valley.

The two instances reveal a striking continuity. Both John Hosfords had a yeoman's stubborn drive to acquire and hold on to land. In our Hosford's case, his motive may have been reinforced by a filial reaction against the piety of a Puritan father and the intense atmosphere of a small home with an only son and two elder sisters. At any rate, his own style was different: here was an acquisitive, rough, down-to-earth farmer with a healthy wife who would bear him six sons and three daughters. He remained close to the land and unlike some of his contemporaries had no marked leaning towards trade. Reacting against his father, he was probably anti-clerical and responsive to the more liberal attitudes towards church order of the second generation. He died a rich man for Windsor, with an inventoried estate valued at £1203, the fourth wealthiest person in those first two generations for whom there are inventories. But, unlike others of similar affluence, Hosford's wealth was overwhelmingly in land, stock, farm buildings and implements. In contrast to the Wolcotts, Newberrys, Allyns and Stiles, the Hosfords lived simply. Apart from the usual table and forms, beds and bedding, kitchen implements and utensils, there was little in the way of furniture and hangings and the rooms of the house, upstairs and downstairs, were cluttered with dairying equipment, farm stores, barrels, hogsheads and sacks. He boasted only one silver spoon and no pewter ware. Although John himself was literate – he may well have been taught respectable letters by his father's friend Branker who saw to it that the son could draft an articulate legal document – his books were limited to a Bible or two and a few other items valued only at £1. Even discounting the fact that his widow may have had clothing, furnishings, linen and trinkets not included in the inventory, his was hardly a family like the Wolcotts who aspired to re-establish in the New World the more cultivated standards of the Old. Goodman John Hosford remained a transplanted yeoman, successful, even relatively rich, but still a husbandman. In New England terms, we find here the representative of a second generation on its way from English yeoman to hard-nosed Yankee farmer.

The foregoing account of Windsor troopers and their family connections is, it is hoped, largely self-explanatory, coming after the narrative of their origins, voyage and travels to the Connecticut frontier. However, it may be worthwhile to summarize the character of them as a group.

First, they belonged overwhelmingly to that central core of families who contributed the greatest material resources to this Puritan experiment. Our soldiers represented seventeen families (including Benjamin Newberry). Of these, fourteen were among the most well-to-do quarter of Windsor families of the first and second generations. Put another way, seven of the first ten of Windsor's families in wealth could boast a founding member of the troop of horse. Of these seventeen families the great majority had settled as neighbours in the most sought-after parts of Windsor: seven were near if not next-door neighbours on the Island; three lived in the Palisado, that citadel at the heart of Windsor; two other families lived nearby at the lower end of Main Street and only three, one in Backer Row, two up by Rocky Hill, were somewhat removed from the central community, though, of the latter, the Bissell family could hardly be classed as outsiders. Of these families, several derived from the English minor gentry or yeomanry, others from the merchant class and at least one, Stephen Terry, from the Puritan clerisy.

These seventeen families comprised most of the ruling oligarchy of Windsor; and the troopers, their parents and relations assumed as a matter of course the principal offices in town and colony. Out of our eighteen individuals, one was to be a magistrate and secretary of the colony, four were to be deputies, four were sons of magistrates or deputies and one was the brother of a distinguished magistrate and founding commissioner of the colony. Almost all in their time served their year as constable of Windsor and many were townsmen and other key officers. Equally striking were their connections with the church. Ten had clerical relations, either as the son of a minister or an elder or through having married the daughter or stepdaughter of a minister or a deacon or through being a deacon's brother or brother-in-law.

These interrelationships ramify with such complexity as to defy arithmetic, and may best be traced by the kind of descriptive vignettes which have formed the substance of this chapter. For instance, four of our soldiers were one way or another brothers-in-law through their marriages with the Warham–Newberry families (Daniel Clarke, Thomas Allyn, Benjamin Newberry and Simon Wolcott). Simon Wolcott was also son-in-law of trooper Aaron Cooke, Samuel Marshall son-in-law of trooper David Wilton, and John Bissell son-in-law of commander-in-chief John Mason. John Porter was first cousin to the Loomis brothers. The cumulative effect of such relations was a powerful, close-knit family network influencing the affairs of Windsor and, to a lesser degree, the colony. Despite the demands of their growing families, many did their duty in civic affairs as magistrate, deputy, townsman or constable. They also became involved with the problems of church order which, as will be seen in the next chapter, were to beset Windsor church. A number professed the half-way covenant, even some who by their upbringing and commitment could have claimed to have their children baptised; and some joined the more liberal second church. They were also among those instrumental in new enterprises. In 1673 four of the five members of the committee set up to provide a school were troopers: Samuel Marshall, John Porter, John Bissell and Daniel Clarke were, after all, fathers of many school-age children. This was also a time when Windsor people were again starting to have itching feet and to look for greener pastures; and among those who left town to colonize were several trooper families. The first settlers of Northampton up the river included Aaron Cooke, Thomas Strong and David Wilton; and, as we shall see in the next chapter, several troopers were to be involved in the drive to develop the rich meadows there by the falls of the Tunxis, Aaron Cooke, Simon Wolcott, Benjamin Newberry and John Moses prominent among them.

This family network, moreover, was characterized by a marked and persistent West Country dimension. Nine of these eighteen people were born, and the older of them raised, in the English West Country; and two others, Daniel Clarke and Nathaniel Loomis, married West Country girls. Further, of the nine West Countrymen, all except Thomas Allyn, who was a Devonian, hailed from those parishes of south Somerset and west Dorset which have been the centre of our attention: Aaron Cooke, John Hosford, Benjamin Newberry and Stephen Terry from Dorset and William Hayden, George Phelps, Thomas Strong and Simon Wolcott from Somerset; and at least five of them had been passengers on the *Mary and John* twenty-eight years before.

And so these younger members of the Connecticut troop of horse were to act as tracers for the significant activities of Windsor in its second generation, between the troop's formation and, after thirty or so years of comparative tranquillity, that outbreak of Indian hostilities which history will call King Philip's War.

CHAPTER 11: THE WOLCOTT FAMILY

A S WE SAW IN THE LAST CHAPTER, PROMINENT AMONG THE WINDSOR families represented in the troop of horse were the Wolcotts. It was trooper Simon's elder brother Henry who, by marrying Benjamin Newberry's sister Sarah, linked the Wolcotts to what I have called the Warham cousinhood. Henry and Sarah Wolcott were the older end of that cousinhood. Henry had voyaged with his parents on the *Mary and John* when he was nineteen. In Dorchester he had been made a freeman when he was a mere sprig of twenty-three, and in Windsor, when he was only twenty-seven, he had already been singled out by the General Court (no doubt through his magistrate father) to distribute to the town that precious supply of grain sent down from Springfield at the time of the severe dearth of 1638. In 1662, the year of Connecticut's royal charter, which may conveniently be taken as marking the close of Windsor's first generation, he was fifty-one; he and Sarah had been married for twenty-one years and the eldest of their eight children was twenty years old. Since the deaths of both his father and his elder brother in England seven years before he had been head of the family. His elder sister Anna had long been married to Matthew Griswold in Saybrook; only his younger sister Mary, married to Job Drake, and his youngest brother Simon remained in Windsor. By now Henry was already following in his father's footsteps as one of Windsor's principal men of affairs. He was one of Windsor's deputies on the General Court and had just been named Assistant in the royal charter and was thereby a magistrate, an office he would hold for the rest of his life. Alongside this, he was the manager of the family properties, and these, together with his magistracy, his seniority and the fact that he had a cadet brother to represent the family, were reasons why he never joined the troop of horse and why, when he had been elected lieutenant of the trainband, he had 'refused to accept the place'. He was too busy and had no ambition for the military title. An able man of affairs, he had mastered the novel art of shorthand which he used to good effect, not least to take down sermons in Windsor's meeting house. He also kept accounts and diaries some of which survive and enable us to know more about him than most of his contemporaries.

His father Henry, it will be remembered, came from a family of clothiers in Wellington, Somerset. Early in Henry VIII's reign his great grandfather held tenements of the manor of Gaulden in the tiny village of Tolland on the western side of the Vale of Taunton towards the Quantocks. Here in Queen Elizabeth's time Henry's father, John, built up a good 'living' not, it seems, as a clothier like his cousins, but as a farmer and miller; he also worked a stone quarry for roof tiling with his sons, labourers and four or five horses. He was a prosperous and much-respected yeoman in the neighbourhood with extensive holdings in the manor and nearby parishes. In 1619, a few years before his death, his eldest son Christopher, by this time a mercer in Wellington, was financially in a position to buy from the lord of the manor all his father's and another tenant's copyhold lands and messuages in Tolland, thus converting them to freehold. It was a significant step for a family on its way up into that borderline between yeoman, merchant and gentry from which such an important minority of our emigrants came. Henry, born in 1578 and the second of three sons, was brought up to a comfortable country life and its pursuits. He early acquired property of his own, notably from a clothier uncle, and subsequently other holdings in Tolland and its neighbourhood. In 1607 he married Elizabeth Saunders of a neighbouring family of clothiers in Lydiard St Lawrence and they were to have seven children.

At some point the family became tinged with a Puritan religious outlook. In the case of the second son, Henry, under the influence, it is said, of one Master Edward Elton, this became a radical conversion, and he determined at the advanced age of fifty to foresake Tolland and Somerset for the New World. After making a reconnoitring voyage to New England on his own in 1628, he embarked with his family on the *Mary and John* as one of its principal adventurers. He sold a considerable part of his property to help finance the enterprise. With his talents and energy and his substantial means, Wolcott with Roger Ludlow, Edward Rossiter and Thomas Newberry provided the principal lay leadership for the *Mary and John* enterprise; and in New England it appears that it was Wolcott, Ludlow, Newberry and Israel Stoughton who put up most of the money to found Dorchester and then Windsor. He was arguably the most prominent citizen of the town throughout his long life and one of its wealthiest.

The Wolcott family owned lands in Windsor, by grant or purchase, amounting to some 600 acres, choice holdings chiefly in Plymouth and Great meadows and large tracts on the east bank of the river. These he and his sons, no doubt with hired hands, developed into a prosperous farming enterprise with beef and dairy cattle as well as extensive arable crops. They grew hops for their beer and true to their Somerset origins they also established orchards for their cider and perry. Young Henry especially was famous for his apple and pear orchards which became probably the largest on the Connecticut River. His trees were bearing as early as 1649 and his cider presses were at work the following year. Thereafter, for thirty years he purveyed apples by the bushel, young apple trees by the hundred and cider by the hogshead to his Windsor neighbours, to Hartford market and its annual fair, to other plantations and, in time, to other colonies. As early as 1649 he was selling at least six varieties of apples: summer, winter, London and Holland pippins, pearmains and bellibones. In the next three years, among other deals, he sold 100 bushels of apples to the deputy governor of New Haven for £20, 50 bushels to the ex-governor of the Dutch fort for £11 17s 6d, 500 young apple trees to a customer in Hartford at 6¼d a tree, and another 500 at 2d a tree in wheat and peas to his Island neighbour from Somerset, George Phelps. He was shipping barrels of cider downriver by the score running up a sizeable bill with the cooper at Hartford. In 1663, on a voyage to England, he boasted to a fellow passenger with whom he messed at the captain's table 'that he made five hundred hogsheads of cyder out of his orchard one year'. At his death he owned some 34 acres of orchards in Windsor.

Old Henry Wolcott kept close links with his brother John in Tolland. He continued to be interested in political events in England and in the progress of true religion, inquiring about the 'teaching of the Word' in Somerset and disappointed that, according to his brother, there was no longer a mid-week lecture in Tolland and in some parishes only one sermon a month. The tenor of their correspondence reflects the high devotional seriousness of their Puritan ties, including the occasional prayer: 'We do daily pray for your prosperity, beseeching the almighty God to bless you all and send you his kingdom of grace and the kingdom of glory in Heaven through Jesus Christ our only saviour and redeemer, Amen'. However, in 1639 their eldest brother Christopher died, unfortunately for family harmony, intestate. The Wolcott properties he had inherited therefore fell to Henry as the second son. John, the youngest, who was in possession at Tolland and had had some sort of deathbed promise that the property would go to his own son, was understandably bitter, especially when he learned that Henry in New England intended to hold on to his inheritance as an absentee landlord. In the event Henry took on his nephews as tenants for his two properties in Tolland and Longforth, in Wellington. The rents from these provided him with a sizeable income which was the foundation on which the Windsor Wolcotts built a comfortable mercantile business.

As early as 1640 Henry Wolcott was in partnership with Thomas Marshfield of Windsor and Samuel Wakeman of Hartford with shares in two ships, the *Charles* of Bristol and the *Hopewell* of London; however, this was at the beginning of the slump of the 1640s and Marshfield shortly got into financial difficulties, both in Bristol where he had to sell his whole estate to pay his debts, and in Windsor where he was virtually declared bankrupt; as the receiver appointed by the general court, Wolcott's time was taken up over the next ten years sorting out Marshfield's debts. Whether it was this experience or the fact that the remote upper Connecticut was not the best place for a ship-owning business, he did not persevere with it. Instead he developed a prosperous import business through Boston. The rents from Tolland and Longforth were of little use to him as specie on the Connecticut frontier; instead he instructed his tenants to convert the income into goods needed for his own family, for neighbours in Windsor and then commercially. It probably began with West Country cloths. One commercial schedule ended: 'the rest is in cloth', those kersies, serges and dowlas woven in his own neighbourhoods of Wellington, Taunton and Wivelsicombe and probably bought from Wolcott relations and neighbours. In 1655 Elizabeth Wolcott's nephew George Saunders wrote to Henry from Lydiard St Lawrence about the state of the cloth trade and offered himself as an agent. Over the years the Wolcott cargoes became more various and in addition to textiles there was a wide range of dry goods needed by the colonists, from kitchen ware to farm implements, made up into packing cases and consigned by one or another trusted ship captain for delivery to a Mrs Blake in Boston to be trans-shipped up the Connecticut River.

The English end of the business, which involved London as well as the

West Country, was normally handled by agents, not always satisfactorily. Henry Wolcott senior became too old to make the gruelling Atlantic trip; in any case he had deeded his Tolland property to his son Henry as early as 1642 and increasingly the business was in his son's hands. From time to time young Henry, and then in turn his son John, crossed the Atlantic to supervise the annual buying in person and to look after the Somerset properties. Young Henry was probably in England about 1654 and certainly in the winter and spring of 1671–2.

On the latter trip, he sailed from Boston on 10 October 1671 in the *New Supply*, 190 tons, master Captain Fairweather. Apart from an early storm when the passengers were fearful of being driven on to Cape Sable, the voyage appears to have been uneventful and quick. The passengers contributed to a purse nailed to the mainmast as a prize for the first ship's boy to see land from the masthead and they sighted the Scillies at three in the afternoon of 1 November. They made Deal on the 24th, rounded into the Thames at Gravesend two days later and on 1 December, a Saturday, tied up in the Pool of London. One of his fellow passengers recorded that he 'cleared [his] goods, shot [London] Bridge and landed at the Temple about 7 of the clock . . . the voyage homeward 7 weeks and 4 days'.

There is no record of Henry's movements on disembarking but it may be assumed that he made his way down to the West Country to stay with his kinsmen and inspect his properties over Christmas and the New Year, and no doubt ordered bolts of the local cloths. He was back in London by mid-February energetically buying the cargo of trade goods which he carefully itemized in his shorthand accounts. There was a wide variety of clothing: suitings, shirts, dresses, silks, stockings, gloves and hats and of notions such as ribbons, tapes, collars, hooks and eyes, pins, needles and household stuffs like rugs, curtains, valances and blankets. There were dry goods like nails by the firkin, kitchen utensils, farm implements such as bill hooks and scythes by the dozen, cases of knives and brushes. There were reams and quires of writing paper and ink horns; and personal purchases such as a pair of pistols and holsters, three yards of lute string and books, including two Bibles, one in Latin, Wild's and Wither's poems, Culpeper's *Physic for the Poor* and Lily's *Almanack*.

These were bought from a variety of shopkeepers who included John Hibbert of the Three Chairs in Smithfield, Chofer Bannister at the Three Brushes in Southwark and Daniel Wallace at the Three Blackbirds in St Clement's Lane. He bought the bulk of his haberdashery from the James Porter, son of John Porter of Windsor, who was to become agent for

Connecticut. Henry also bought two trunks from Mrs Brown on London Bridge and into these and other cases he packed his purchases, had them carried aboard the ship *Sea Flower* in the Pool of London and early in March sailed for home.

This was a slow and no doubt tedious voyage: it was only on 16 May that he unloaded his cases from *Sea Flower* in Boston harbour and trans-shipped them to Mr Belcher's ketch for the Connecticut River. Two days later he settled with Captain Smith for his passage and that of his 'boys' or servants and for the freight of his goods, at £13 which he borrowed from a Mr Usher (he must have run short of cash by this time). The total cost of the purchases he made in London came to about £70 which was about equal to the rents he was reputed to have received from the Somerset properties. He finally 'came home to my house', in his own words, on 23 May 1672. The phrase is significant. Although Henry Wolcott had been born and brought up on Tolland Water in Somerset and had been a young man of nineteen when he sailed in the *Mary and John* and although he had several times revisited his childhood haunts, 'home' for this second generation Wolcott was Connecticut, not Somerset.

When he arrived home in Windsor Henry Wolcott was sixty-one and this would be the last of his visits to England. In future, like his father before him, he would send his son in his stead. Also the early 1670s were not a propitious time to be away from home. Hostilities loomed with both Dutch and Indians, the river plantations were being placed on a war footing and the able bodied were volunteering or being pressed into service. But the Wolcott family business must be carried on and three years later, on 25 October 1675, when his uncles Simon Wolcott and Benjamin Newberry were on active service with the dragoons, Henry's son, aged thirty, set out from Hartford with his servant Pope for England on business. After a few days in Boston he sailed on 11 November. The voyage took five weeks. He landed at Deal on 15 December and two days later was in London. After a week or so there he made his way down to Somerset, arriving on 25 December to stay with his West Country cousins over Christmas. He remained in Somerset looking after the rents in Tolland and Wellington and laying out purchases in Taunton for the rest of the winter. At the end of April he returned to London for further weeks of business. He made a late summer passage home, arriving in Boston on or about 9 October.

John Wolcott's visit to Somerset is especially pertinent to this account of Windsor family relationships. Since this was presumably his first visit to England, he had never met his English kinsfolk and on his horseback journey from London up the Thames Valley and across the downs into Somerset, he must have speculated as to how he would find them for an extended visit. He had two sets of cousins. There were the Wolcotts – his second cousins – John of Tolland and Hugh of Wellington, tenants of the properties he had come to inspect. But there were also his mother's Newberry cousins; there was his uncle Joseph who had lived at the family home of Coweleyes in Marshwood in Dorset ever since he left Windsor as a young man nearly thirty years before; and there was that other Newberry, his mother's first cousin John, son of her uncle Robert who had inherited the family home at Yarcomb nearby in Somerset. It was to Yarcomb that John Wolcott went that Christmas and although he paid several visits to the Wolcotts at Tolland and Wellington and to uncle Joseph Newberry at Marshwood, his base for the winter months was with his less immediate cousin John Newberry. There was a reason for this. The Wolcotts had to rely on a local agent to look after their Somerset properties, to collect the rents and convert them into goods for shipment to New England. There had been at least two agents, 'farmer' Venn and one Tucker, but neither evidently satisfactory in a delicate situation where Wolcott cousins were tenants. So at some point Henry Wolcott had decided to make his wife Sarah's cousin, John Newberry of nearby Yarcomb, the Wolcott agent and it was natural therefore that young John Wolcott should make Yarcomb his base. Thus the childhood friendship which had blossomed into marriage between Henry Wolcott and Sarah Newberry had its ramifications in the Wolcott family interests back in Somerset and Dorset.

Henry Wolcott's last act before leaving for Boston and England, on 2 October 1671, had been to revise his will, confirming the disposition of his properties in Windsor, Wethersfield and Somerset and his business interests among his sons, to bequeath lump sums to his daughters and to make suitable provision for Sarah. When he died nine years later, his real and personal estate amounted to nearly £4000 which made him the wealthiest man in Windsor.

The younger Henry Wolcott, a church member from old Dorchester days, retained his father's Puritan cast of mind, as did Sarah whose only books when she died were a Bible, a psalm book and six books of catechism, no doubt kept to provide a proper religious instruction for her children and grandchildren. Yet the inventories of their possessions suggest that even in this, the oldest of the second Windsor generation, a certain amenity, if not worldliness, was beginning to creep into the Puritan style of living. Sarah may have been a Puritan lady but she was the wife of a prosperous importing merchant and her wardrobe when she died in 1686, aged sixty-two, valued at £56, included half a dozen cloaks, two of silk, seven coats, one of satin, five petticoats, twenty coifs, silk sleeves and aprons and taffeted waistcoats, as well as such telltale fashions as gloves, a muff, a fan, a dressing case and four gold rings. She also left a canopied feather bed with curtains and valance, and a positive storehouse of bolts of cloth of all kinds valued at £33. Her husband left silver, gold and plate to the value of £75 and a library valued at £13. This contained not only 'several divine' books, doubtless including the Latin Bible he bought in London and two Books of Martyrs inherited from his father, but some history books, evidence of a reading household which included Henry's youngest son Josiah whom his father gave a classical education. An even greater sign of worldly affluence was the fact that Henry owned a negro slave called Cirus who was valued at £30.

'Young' Henry died in 1680, a year which may conveniently mark the beginning of the end of Windsor's second generation of which he was one of the oldest. His immediately younger brother died without children, so that the only other Wolcott male line, an important one as it turned out, was that of the youngest brother Simon, the trooper. As a sickly five-year-old, Simon had been left behind for a year or two with his aunt and uncle in Tolland before being fetched to join his family in Dorchester and he was only ten on the trek to Connecticut. As the youngest, he was the most completely Windsor-bred of all that kin. He was thirty and still a bachelor when his parents died, his father leaving him as his portion the extensive Wolcott land across the Connecticut River. Two years later, as we noted, he married Joanna, the eighteen-year-old daughter of his fellow trooper Aaron Cooke, who tragically died within weeks. But Simon was too eligible a bachelor to remain for long unmarried. Three years later, in 1661, there arrived in Hartford, on a visit to her brother William Pitkin, his sister Martha. William Pitkin was a young Englishman who had only recently come to the colony and was making his mark as an attorney. Their father was headmaster of Birkhamsted School and, according to her son, Martha was 'a gentlewoman of bright natural parts, which were well improved by her education in the City of London'. Martha was a lively young woman who appears to have captivated this little colonial society on the New England frontier. As another chronicler put it: 'This girl was too valuable to be parted with. It was a matter of general consultation what young man was good enough to be presented to Miss Pitkin. Simon Wolcott of Windsor was fixed upon; and beyond expectation, succeeded in winning her hand; her brother favored the proposal, and the results showed that they had judged worthily.'

They were married on 17 October 1661. Martha was clearly a catch, a lively, educated woman; but she also did her family duty by bearing Simon nine children. At first they lived in the house Simon bought opposite his father's old home on the Island. However, perhaps because Simon, as the youngest son, had inherited his father's great tract of unimproved land across the river, Simon raised his eyes to broader horizons. For some time there had been talk of, and speculation in, the rich meadowlands up the Tunxis River at Massaco. As we saw, two of the troopers, Aaron Cooke with his stepfather Thomas Ford, and John Bissell, had been the first to receive grants there from the General Court in 1653. It may well have been a popular topic of conversation among the Windsor troopers on that morning's ride to Hartford in 1658 because, of those seventeen troopers, the families of seven were in due course to be represented among the first investors. They included Daniel Clarke and Simon Wolcott who shortly afterwards bought land there, as did Benjamin Newberry; so it looks as if the Wolcott–Newberry connection had decided to speculate together. Benjamin's allotment was to be called Newberry Plain for generations; and he and Simon were to have the chief responsibility for founding Massaco, to be called Simsbury; with deacon John Moore they constituted a committee of three appointed by the General Court to make the initial land allotments for the would-be settlers from Windsor.

Of the three, Simon was the only one actually to settle in Massaco, a move he had made with his family by 1671 when he was elected one of Simsbury's first deputies to the General Court. In the same year he was licensed to retail wines and spirits in the absence of an ordinary in that frontier settlement; and two years later he was appointed captain of the Simsbury trainband. By this time such a commission was no honorary accolade; hostilities had broken out with the Indians and Simon would soon be on active service to protect the English settlements. These efforts were in vain so far as the exposed little community of Simsbury was concerned; it was evacuated and the Indians burnt it down. After King Philip's War Simon decided not to return, but to write off his expensive investment and to settle, in 1680, on his other property on the east bank of the Connecticut in what would become South Windsor. Here he spent the last seven years of his life. Although as a Wolcott he was comparatively well off – he was rated in 1686 at £214, high up in the first quartile of Windsor wealth – and he enjoyed an attractive wife and nine children, he appears to have been given to melancholy. Perhaps the disasters and uncertainties of his latter years at Simsbury proved too much for him; he became depressed by the political prospect of Sir Edmund Andros becoming governor of Connecticut and it was said that this hastened his death in 1687. He rests in Windsor burial ground with an inscription which reads:

> HERE LYES WAITING FOR YE RESURRECTION OF YE JUST
> MR. SIMON WOLCOTT BORN 1625 DYED SEPT. 11TH
> 1687

to which a later mason added: 'Also Martha Pitkin Wife of Simon Wolcott Born 1639 Dyed Oct. 13 1719'. Martha, a good vigorous woman of forty-eight, had another thirty-two years to live. She promptly married again: our old acquaintance and Wolcott brother-in-law Daniel Clarke whose wife Mary Newberry had just died and who, at the advanced age of about sixty-eight, still, it seems, managed to command Martha's affections.

Simon was the youngest in a family of seven. His own youngest son, Roger, was born in 1679 and would become a prominent citizen and Governor of Connecticut Colony. In a family memoir he had this to say about the Windsor in which he grew up:

> About this time I began to take notice of the people, their manners and way of living, and according to my remembrance there was much simplicity and honesty in the generality; their buildings were good to what they had been, but mean to what they are now; their dress and diet mean and coarse to what it is now; they were strict in keeping the Sabbath and paid a greater reverence to their magistrates and ministers than now; their blemishes were too much censoriousness and detraction, and as they had much cyder many of them drank too much of it.

And who better than a Wolcott, who brewed the cider, to say so.

CHAPTER 12: THE SECOND GENERATION IN WINDSOR 1662–1675

O F THE TROOPERS RIDING TO HARTFORD THAT SPRING MORNING IN 1658, ten belonged to Windsor's second generation. They were all young married men, half of them with small children. They were all to have large families. The smallest was that of Aaron Cooke who already had seven children, the largest that of Thomas Strong who was to have fifteen; but Nathaniel Loomis and John Porter were to have twelve each and the average for the eleven families was to be an impressive ten. This second generation was clearly taking to heart the biblical admonition to 'be fruitful and multiply and replenish the earth'.

In this spirit they baptised their children with a limited number of biblical names, mostly from the Old Testament. The 57 boys born to these families had only 28 names among them. Of these, 18 were Hebrew, most frequently Samuel, Benjamin and Nathaniel, and including Josiah, Hezekiah, Jeremiah, Moses and Ebenezer, all fashionable Puritan names. The 46 girls had only 21 names among them of which 10 were Hebrew including 17th-century revivals like Esther, Hannah, Ruth, Abigail and Rebecca. The rest were mostly severe Puritan creations such as Mindwell, Waitstill and Submit. The only names not deriving from the Bible, apart from William and Henry named after grandfathers Hosford and Wolcott, were Simon Wolcott's sons Charles and Roger, two secular names perhaps indicating the English Restoration and the fact that this next generation of Wolcotts was moving on from its Puritan phase.

By the mid-1660s, seven years after that cavalry muster at Hartford, the children of our trooper families were growing up. Aaron Cooke's four eldest were already in their twenties and two other Cookes, two Clarkes and two Porters were teenagers. Most were younger, but of school age, and their parents were faced with the problem of their education: of handing on to their children that schooling in reading, writing and figuring which their own parents had seen to it should not be neglected in the vicissitudes of rough New England living. This high duty was reinforced by law. Roger Ludlow's Code of 1650 enjoined heads of families to teach their children and apprentices to read, to know the colony laws and the catechism, as well as to learn a trade. Beyond such rudimentary instruction, the Code also made provision for schools. As the preamble has it, following Massachusetts: 'one chief project of that old deluder Satan is to keep men from the knowledge of the Scriptures, as in former times keeping them in an unknown tongue, so in these latter times by persuading them from the use of tongues so that at least the true sense and meaning of the original might be clouded with false glosses of saint-deceivers'; and so in order 'that Learning may not be buried in the grave of our forefathers in Church and Commonwealth', the court laid down that any township of fifty householders must appoint a schoolmaster who should be paid by fees or from the town rate. In Windsor, as we saw, this role was first filled by elder John Branker. Shortly before he died in 1662 he was succeeded by one James Cornish, a shadowy figure who seems to have made an usher's living up and down the river settlements. He was paid a stipend of £36 a year from pupils' fees.

This school population was growing so fast that classes could no longer be contained within the master's homestead. In 1667 it appears that a schoolhouse was at least projected and Nathaniel Loomis's father-in-law, deacon Moore, billed the town for ironwork for it. However, the actual accommodation remains obscure; even seven years later Master Cornish was teaching his classes alternately five months on the south side of the Rivulet for the Island children and seven months on the north side for Main Street and Backer Row.

By this time the cohort of second-generation children had reached their teens and some at least were ambitious for more advanced schooling than the reading, writing, arithmetic and Scriptures which were the primary fare of the town school. Ludlow's Code, in addition to primary education, had the foresight to provide for Latin or grammar schools, 'the masters thereof being able to instruct youths so far as they may be fitted for the University'. When a township reached the size of 100 households it was under an obligation to establish such a grammar school on penalty of a fine of £5 a year. This was an ambitious stipulation and did not prove easy to meet. In 1672, therefore, to provide an incentive, the General Court allotted 600 acres to Hartford, the county town, as an endowment for a Latin school and about the same time fined Windsor, which long before had passed the 100-household size, £5 for not having started one of its own, which sum was to go to the Hartford school. Whereupon Windsor, determined not to be outdone, was galvanized into action. The following November a special town meeting set up a committee to promote a grammar school for Windsor. Three of its four members were troopers, Corporal Samuel Marshall, John Bissell and John Porter, and they were instructed to consult with a fourth, their brother officer Captain Daniel Clarke. All four of them by this time were prominent Windsor citizens of the second generation and among them they had thirty-two children to educate, a large schoolroom-full.

The project was overtaken by the events of King Philip's War, but it was clearly a town issue. On 30 August 1675 John Fitch, a widower with no children who was pressed into service against the Indians, made a will leaving 'the small estate God hath given . . . for the promoting of a school here in Windsor'. As we shall see poor Fitch was mortally wounded in the swamp fight against the Narragansett fort. He was a humble and obscure inhabitant not unacquainted with house of correction and whipping post; and after his debts were paid it was unlikely there would be much left for the school; but the town was sufficiently touched by his death in action and the terms of his will to add £3; in the event, the sum amounted to £31 5s 4d. The following December when the town was picking up the pieces again after the war, Windsor was still in trouble over the pressing matter of its school. Cornish had departed and there was difficulty finding a successor. In the end Daniel Clarke himself was persuaded to take the job on for a year at a stipend of £40, still on the basis of six-month classes on each side of the Rivulet. To what extent he undertook to teach a grammar school curriculum is unclear, but he was qualified for it.

This second Windsor generation were also becoming concerned about their offsprings' state of spiritual grace. Windsor church, like her New England sisters, consisted of disciples gathered together, from whatever their occupations and walks of life, by the experience of conversion to the spiritual truth of Christ crucified, and governed by the precepts of early

Christian discipleship practised in a wilderness insulated from the corruptions of superstition. This Calvinist covenant, entered into in March 1630 in the Free Hospital in Plymouth, had sustained the Dorchester pilgrims on their journey from England to the Bay and onwards to the Connecticut River. Owning the covenant was a desperately serious matter only achieved by both introspective and publicly demonstrable conversion to a state of spiritual grace; and church membership was a privilege jealously guarded.

This presented few problems for the first pioneer generation of founding 'Saints', or for their elder children such as young Henry Wolcott brought up in the intensely religious atmosphere of those epic days; they had little difficulty in achieving the requisite conviction for church membership. But as time passed, fewer Windsor people of the second generation, either from lack of conviction or waning pressure from family and ruling elders, steeled themselves for the open testimony and rigorous cross-examination demanded for full church membership. To be sure, they were baptised into the church and painstakingly educated in its beliefs and practices; but this was a different experience from the blinding flash of adult conversion; and as this second and much larger generation grew to maturity, only a minority felt that welling-up of grace which justified owning the covenant. Hence, by the 1660s, church members, those who came to the Lord's table, were a diminishing minority of the congregation, not many more than 50 male members in a community of upwards of 150 households; even among our second-generation troopers with their clerical connections, only four were to become full church members. Most of Windsor's second generation, though themselves baptised, were not members of the elect and therefore not privileged to have their children baptised, even though these infants' grandparents had been founding Saints and the family remained in good religious standing. The original mystique of the gathered church had not anticipated such a spiritually uncontrolled growth of population.

There developed, therefore, throughout the river settlements a groundswell of unease which erupted into angry waves of unrest focusing on the problem of baptising the infant children of non-communicants. It was a general New England problem; and as early as June 1657 a council of ministers and elders in Boston faced up to it by resolving that it was the duty of adults who had been baptised into their church in infancy to recognize the covenant they had made and, even if they did not consider themselves 'fit for the Lord's supper', they had the right to claim baptism for their children. This was the celebrated half-way covenant. However, though it had the seal of approval from the council of churches, confirmed by a subsequent synod in 1662 and endorsed by civil authority in the form of resolutions of the General Court, and although it was the minimum concession compatible with changing times, it was by no means accepted without continuing friction and strife. There were many who felt in the marrow of their bones a threat to that New England Way which was their dedicated purpose in this New World.

So far as Windsor was concerned, John Warham had been a member of the Boston council of 1657 and approved of its resolutions. After all, as an ordained clergyman of the Church of England had he not long ago argued with the Separatist Samuel Fuller that God's church embraced sinners as well as saints? And so on his return from Boston he set about baptising the children of any person, husband or wife, who, though not a communicant, had satisfied the elders in private concerning his or her knowledge of the principles of religion and the covenant. He practised this from the end of January 1658 for some seven years, admitting a number of adults into half-way membership and baptising numerous children. However, scrupulous, brooding, indecisive in his faith as we have found him to be, he came in time to be uneasy about the practice and on 19 March 1665 he startled his congregation by announcing that as a result of weighty arguments put to him he had developed scruples of conscience and was therefore going to suspend it. Matthew Grant reported him as saying, 'not that he intended to cast off the practice wholly but only to delay it for a time till he could be better able to answer his present scruples, for if he should act and not of faith, Romans 14 would be a sin to him.' Poor Warham may have felt this a mere temporary suspension until he could sort the matter out in his mind; but, in the event, he was never again to baptise the children of his half-way-covenanted flock and for three years that sacrament was denied to most of his congregation.

Perhaps because of the respect in which he was held, there was no open rebellion and matters remained in a state of suspense until the next summer. By this time Windsor had become acutely aware that their old minister was failing and needed pastoral support. John Witchfield, the one remaining elder, and the deacons duly sent to the Bay for suggestions for an assistant minister. The name that came back was Nathaniel Chauncey, son of the president of Harvard College. Perhaps because Chauncey had argued so forcibly against the half-way covenant at the synod of 1662, his son's candidature was bitterly contested. The proposal set aflame a smouldering marsh fire of resentment which went far beyond the issue of baptism for non-communicants. The children of the Saints might feel concerned that their children were kept outside the pale of Christ's church because of their own spiritual limitations; but there was now a wider constituency for whom the spiritual exclusiveness of the elect was becoming intolerable. By this time the inhabitants of Windsor included a growing number of people who had joined the plantation after the Warham hegira and whose motives for transplanting were less religious and more mundane, with only rough, ready and Anglican assumptions about the church's role. These demanded the same rights of church membership as they had been baptised into in their English parish. Also, though such people might stomach compulsory attendance at the meeting house on the Sabbath which they had, in any case, had to endure in England, and even the mid-week lecture, they came to resent having to contribute to the upkeep of a minister without any say in his terms and conditions of appointment or in church government. What began as an expedient to protect the spiritual grace of infants broadened into a conflict about the nature of the church itself. The half-way covenant implied first and second class church membership and, when to this there was infused more traditional assumptions of a broadly Anglican character, the threat to the purity of Calvinist doctrine in both faith and order became manifest.

There is also a sense in which Windsor church was a special and confusing case. It had been grounded, not on an abrupt separation from the Church of England like the Plymouth Separatists, but on a return to pure and uncorrupt practices within that church. The Dorchester emigrants had been conservative Puritans who conformed to the Church of England while shunning those papistical practices associated with the name of Laud. Warham's church kept a strong sense of continuity with its English past. No wonder that Warham was confused in his conscience about a church which had been a gathered community but which looked as if it might revert to being a parish.

The issue was rudely put in March 1664 by two Windsor inhabitants. Michael Humphrey, the distiller of turpentine, and James Eno, the barber, were two Johnnies-come-lately, having only arrived in Windsor in the 1640s, and they had no commitment to the high purposes of the Puritan dedication. They wrote an offensive paper to the General Court demanding their rights as members of the Church of England. The court dismissed this with contumely; but they had raised an issue which would not lie down. The same fall the court received another petition, this time signed not only by Humphrey and Eno but by five others and skilfully drafted in good

Parliamentary language by William Pitkin of Hartford, Simon Wolcott's brother-in-law. With a preamble which made pointed reference to the Church of England, to our Sovereign Lord Charles the Second by God's Grace King of England and to the royal charter of 1662, it eloquently rehearsed the case for an orthodox ministry according to the faith and order of the Church of England, including not only baptism of children but access to the Lord's table, and with references to sheep scattered, having no shepherd, a situation which both God and our King would have different; and furthermore, the seven requested that for the future

> no law in this corporation may be of any force to make us
> pay or contribute the maintenance of any minister or
> officer of the Church that will neglect or refuse to baptise
> our children and to take care of us, as of such members
> of the church as are under his or their charge or care.

Despite the General Court's sympathetic attitude to the half-way covenant they gave short shrift to Anglican sentiments of this kind which must have struck as cold steel into the hearts of Puritan Congregationalists. The petition was before its time. Three years later when Windsor was rent with opposition to the nomination of Nathaniel Chauncey, the General Court again took a hand and instructed Windsor town meeting to take a vote on his candidature under the chairmanship of the local magistrate, Henry Wolcott. The freemen and householders of Windsor and its satellite, Simsbury, were instructed to bring their votes in the form of 'papers' or ballots in writing proposing Mr Chauncey or blanks. Chauncey was chosen by 86 votes to 52.

The dissatisfied minority were not, however, prepared to abide by this result. They pushed the matter a step further by petitioning the General Court to be allowed to appoint a separate minister of their own choice. The court, while recognizing Chauncey as the duly appointed minister, gave permission to the minority to appoint 'an able orthodox minister' of their own. By the following spring, the dissidents had nominated the Rev. Benjamin Woodbridge; the General Court recognized him only as a lecturer but stipulated that he might preach every other Sabbath if Mr Warham should 'so far condescend' to agree. This compromise satisfied no one. The atmosphere in Windsor in the early summer of 1668 was tense. On 21 June Chauncey, the newly appointed minister, attempted to defuse the situation by himself reintroducing the half-way covenant and baptising a number of infants, thus breaking the log jam of baptism which had existed ever since Warham's *crise de conscience*.

However, the gesture failed to propitiate the opposition. For the issue had become a fundamental matter of faith and order and they were not to be bought off. The anti-Chauncey faction were so incensed by the stubborn refusal of the orthodox ascendency of Windsor church to recognize their right to appoint Woodbridge as their pastor in the full sense that they determined to call an extraordinary town meeting to railroad through a resolution authorizing him to preach on the Lord's Day. The meeting was summoned for 8 August by townsmen at the wish of 'several inhabitants', and the proposition was accepted 'by a full vote'. However, it seems as though the meeting had been irregularly summoned and the vote packed; for the minute was drafted not by Matthew Grant, the town clerk, whose duty it was, but by George Griswold, a leading member of the Woodbridge faction. As a townsman Griswold had called the meeting himself, had conducted its business and then, with 'some others', had gone to Grant's house in the Palisado and demanded that the minute of a vote in favour of Woodbridge's Sabbath preaching be duly inscribed in the official minute book. Matthew Grant refused. 'I told him', he wrote, 'I would have no hand in the business nor enter their vote'. Whereupon Griswold, with his authority as a townsman, demanded the minute book. Grant laid it on the table and Griswold wrote the minute in his own hand. That town meeting had been irregularly engineered in order to achieve the vote the dissidents wanted. It was the act of exasperated and no doubt unscrupulous men. George Griswold further evinced his bitterness two months later by appealing to the court against Mr Chauncey's refusal to baptise his child on the ground that he was a Woodbridge supporter.

That fall the General Court tried again, by appointing a committee of four external ministers. These also failed to reconcile the differences, contributing only the suggestion that both ministers might be dismissed and an entirely fresh one appointed to effect a union of the parties. Finally in the fall of 1669 the court, in despair and 'to their great grief that the differences and dissensions at Windsor yet continue', admitted defeat and acknowledged that they saw no reason 'to deny liberty to those dissenters to meet distinctly and . . . to embody themselves in church state according to law'. On 18 March 1670, therefore, Benjamin Woodbridge was formally ordained minister of the second church and the old town house was fitted up as their place of meeting. A fortnight later, on 1 April, John Warham died.

This formal recognition of a state of schism was no solution and for another decade there continued to be bitterness and recrimination between the two congregations. The serious depth of feeling was revealed in 1673 by yet another petition to the Governor and Assistants signed by thirty-three lay members of the second church. This was a time when the colony was on a war footing against the Dutch. The old congregation had refused to accept the second church's invitation to join in a solemn day of fasting for the impending hostilities. The petitioners referred to 'a deep rooted spirit of bitterness boiling in the breast of some of those of the old congregation . . . that we are guilty of treachery, perjury and apostacy, that those that had a hand in the ordination of our minister were styled sacrilegious thieves', that Mr Chauncey had 'publicly preached and asserted in the pulpit . . . that our Minister is no Minister of Christ and can expect no blessings on his labours . . . comparing our differences to the differences between papists and protestants, dealing with persons that have occasionally communicated with us as having thereby fellowship with the unfruitful works of darkness'. So suspicious were they, not to say paranoid, about the old church establishment that they proceeded to tell the court they considered it 'unsafe and dangerous for us to be joined in arms with them' against the Dutch because they would have 'as great enemies in our camp as those we go out against'. They were therefore petitioning the court that 'either we or they be exempted from going out' to war. In clarification they added: 'We would not in this motion be understood any way to hinder the weal of the Colony or discourage the sending out against the enemy, in which design we are willing to hazard our lives; but we count it dangerous to go forth with such as will give us more bitter and evil speeches than the enemy himself and through some false conceited opinion cannot pray with us for the prosperity and blessing in going forth.'

The outbreak of hostilities against the Indians two years later found the two congregations still in this state of enmity with furious arguments about the refusal of the townsmen to pay for repairs to the old town house as well as the meeting house and with protracted negotiations about the terms on which the second church and its minister might be reabsorbed. In the upshot it was only in 1681 after Chauncey had left Windsor for a new call that a town meeting, weary of the whole business, voted unanimously to appoint a fresh minister, Samuel Mather, son of Warham's successor at Dorchester, and to leave it to him to find a formula for reconciliation and union. This he did, retaining the half-way covenant and easing the conditions for admission to full communion. Woodbridge, virtually redundant, left for Boston consoled with a grant of 200 acres from the colony.

How did our nexus of families divide on this issue? It is hardly surprising that Matthew Grant the town clerk, as a venerable member of the old guard 'that came from Dorchester in full communion', deliberately omitted from his list of church members in 1677 those who had 'joined themselves with the other company'. Our knowledge of the members of the second church is, therefore, partial. However, from thirty-five signatures to various petitions addressed to the General Court it appears, not surprisingly, that they belonged to the second generation and, more interesting, that at least ten were sons of communicating members of the old church. One, John Hosford, was the son of a ruling elder, another, Andrew Moore, of a deacon, and all but one of the ten, James Eglestone, belonged to West Country families of the original transplanting, six of them, Pinney, Phelps, Gaylord, two Drakes, Terry and Moore, of the *Mary and John* vintage. They could not be said to be at odds with the Windsor establishment. Their decision to brave the obloquy of joining a suspect and rebel congregation had other motives, perhaps a second generation revolt against Congregational exclusiveness and sympathy for a more liberal concept of church fellowship. The Windsor members of the troop of horse were to be found in both congregations. John Moses and John Hosford, whose Thrall father and brother-in-law were particularly close to Benjamin Woodbridge, were members of the second church, as were two sons of troopers, Daniel Hayden and John Terry. But the weightier majority remained of the orthodox party. That trio of brothers-in-law, Henry Wolcott, Benjamin Newberry and Daniel Clarke, were repeatedly called upon in the late 1670s to serve on committees to negotiate between Chauncey and Woodbridge; in December 1679 the trio were principal members of a committee which included two other troopers (George Phelps and John Bissell) and four others who were their brothers, brother-in-law and son. The old trooper freemasonry continued to exert its influence at the centre of Windsor's affairs.

As we have seen, an underlying cause of the urgent concern for more formal schooling and of the distressing turbulence which impelled Windsor into schism was the burgeoning of the town's child population.

On 7 March 1670, a week before Benjamin Woodbridge was ordained minister of the second church and a fortnight before old John Warham's death, Matthew Grant's son Tahan, who was that year's constable, made a return to the General Court for tax purposes of the number and size of Windsor families and the amount of wheat and corn they possessed. This list was the first census, not only for Windsor but for the whole Connecticut Valley. According to this, Windsor comprised 135 taxable households with a total population of 754. Five years later, a special rate to support the Rivulet ferry revealed 147 taxable householders, a figure which, allowing for five years' growth, matches the 1670 number. This is also consonant with comparative figures for households in earlier decades. There is a regular sequence of figures beginning with the original land grants, ending with the rateable list for 1686 just referred to and sustained at irregular intervals in between by other returns of which the most important are those of the rating commissioners sent each year to Hartford for taxation purposes. For a significant number of years in the late 1650s and the 1670s the latter returns record the number of ratepayers. From these sources a fairly consistent graph of Windsor's population growth may be drawn. The 54 family heads who made the trek from Dorchester to Matianuk in 1635 grew to the 94 who had received land grants before the end of 1641, to the 112 who had received such grants in 1645. This, in turn, matches the 116 houses or more which are recorded as existing in 1650; there was virtually no immigration during the 1640s which was a period of consolidation. On the other hand, the 1650s were years of increase. By 1654 the number of householders had risen rapidly to 165 and remained roughly at that level for the rest of the decade. There is little evidence for the 1660s but by 1670 the number of taxable householders had fallen back again to 132, rising again only slowly to 147 in 1675, then on a rising curve to 220 in 1679 and a high of 277 in 1686.

Estimates of total population growth are less easy to arrive at. We may be confident of the 'grain census' figure for 1670 of 754; but the total for Windsor's first settlers is more a matter of guesswork. Assuming a rather arbitrary family size, Windsor began with a population of about 220 which by 1640 must have reached at least 360. Allowing for a conservative increase in family size, the total population may have been just over 500 in 1650 and 800 in 1660, but dropping back to 750 in 1670. Seven years later, on the same basis, the population would have been 1200. This compares with the comprehensive list of births and deaths which Matthew Grant compiled in that year. According to this, 1025 persons had been born in Windsor 'from our beginning hitherto', of whom 128 had died and 122 had removed elsewhere, leaving 775; adding to this an allowance for the few original settlers still alive and later immigrants, Windsor's chronicler, Stiles, calculated that the population of 1677 could hardly have been less than 1000. As a generalization, the population of Windsor from its first settlement to the close of this study forty years later may have multiplied five times. With more confidence, we may guess that during the thirty years from 1640 to 1670 Windsor roughly doubled in size.

An increase in population on this scale exerted its inevitable pressure on the land. The river-meadows of Matianuck which had beckoned the Dorchester planters were still fair but such land was becoming scarce. In any case it looks as if Windsor's acres were not quite as rich as those of her neighbours. In 1676 the home lots of Wethersfield and Hartford were valued at 40 shillings an acre, but those of Windsor at best at 25 shillings and 'worser' at 20 shillings; Windsor's improved uplands, at 17½ shillings an acre, compared unfavourably with Wethersfield's and Hartford's at between 25 and 20 shillings; as for meadow, Wethersfield's was valued at 47½ shillings an acre, Hartford's at 45 and Windsor's at only 43.

The more established and well-to-do for the most part responded to this pressure on the land by subdividing their own ample home lots and building a second homestead for a son and daughter-in-law next door or buying a nearby lot for them. Families like the Moores, Porters, Wolcotts and Newberrys continued to live in and about the Island, the Loomises especially dominating one end of it; and this was true of many more modest families on Main Street and Backer Row. In 1670 as many as thirty-five of the original settler families were still living on the home lots they had been granted by the plantation thirty or more years before.

However, for a long while Windsor people had had their eyes on additional land to accommodate their growing progeny and as a speculation. Their immediate object was the land on the east side of the Connecticut. Most of the original grants from the plantation had included an extensive ribbon of wilderness stretching from the river a notional three miles eastwards to the Windsor bounds and varying in width from a mere 10 rods (55 yards) to 58 rods (320 yards) in exceptional cases. In early years these were left as a growth investment save for the meadows between Podunk and the Scantic; these were grazed, sometimes planted with corn and cropped for hay which was stacked and brought across the river by barge or, in a winter freeze, by sled. The Great River remained a formidable barrier and for a generation no one essayed to settle on its east bank. As we saw, the first to do so was John Bissell who had large holdings and built himself a homestead about 1658. By this time there was a track through the water meadows for farm work and a landing stage for carts and barges at

Bissell's ferry; but it was another decade before there was any pronounced movement of settlers across the river. By 1672, however, there were a score or more families on the east bank improving their rough homesteads along the upland which overlooked the river-meadows. Twenty-seven men were listed by the town with the duty of keeping in repair a highway along the upland brow. They included John Bissell's brother Thomas, John Porter's son John and John Hosford's brother-in-law Stephen Taylor. Two of our other principal figures also had a stake in this enterprise, though not as settlers. The General Court had granted Benjamin Newberry and deacon Moore extensive tracts over and above their original holdings, in Newberry's case 250 acres. Windsor apparently took exception to this; whereupon the court resolved that if Windsor released its own township rights east of the river to enable a separate, daughter plantation to be settled, Newberry and Moore would waive their rights. This appears to have called Windsor's bluff because nothing more was heard at that time of a separate township and the court subsequently confirmed Newberry and Moore in their grants.

It will be recalled that several of our troopers were also deeply involved in that other development up the Rivulet at Massaco which was to become the settlement of Simsbury. The settlers had been conscious from earliest days of the charms of the blue hills of Massaco with their rich, enfolded valley above the falls of the Tunxis, some ten miles upstream from Windsor. Here were winding river-meadows and thickets of hops and wild vines flanked by a wilderness of pines and hillside richly forested with all kinds of hardwoods. It was the resort of local Indians who cultivated patches of corn and succotash, hunted deer, moose and bear, caught otter and beaver and in season fished for salmon and shad in the river and brooks.

The Tunxis was Windsor's hinterland and as early as 1642 the General Court had invited the Governor and his deputy to allocate lands at Massaco to Windsor people; but no Indian title was acquired and no grants made. It was left to Michael Humphrey and John Griffen six years later to take the first initiative by acquiring rights to Massaco's pine forests for their tar and turpentine enterprise. In 1648 a Windsor Indian was convicted of setting fire to Griffen's stocks of tar. The Indian's friends at Massaco redeemed him from a heavy fine and imprisonment by granting Griffen extensive land rights there, known as 'Griffen's Lordship'. In the same year, perhaps prompted by this, the General Court decided to buy Massaco for the colony for subsequent sale to Windsor people. Five years later the first allotments were made. These consisted of three grants of fifty acres of meadow each to Thomas Ford, his stepson Aaron Cooke and John Bissell. Ford or his stepson was already at work up there because he had already improved forty-four acres for ploughing and mowing. For Ford and Bissell who were among the wealthiest of Windsor's first generation this was a speculative venture rather than an attempt at settlement; but in the next few years Aaron Cook worked on their lands above the falls. His name survived as a place name. But Aaron never settled there and sold his holding to Simon Wolcott. The first permanent settler was John Griffen who was living there as early as 1663 at work on his turpentine business.

Meanwhile the General Court regularized the situation by getting Indian confirmation of title and, in 1663, persuading Griffen to exchange his rights for a grant of 200 acres, ostensibly in token of his pioneer work in tar and turpentine. This legitimized the activity of the court's committee which by 1660 had already made grants to some nine Windsor individuals. In 1663 when the committee was revamped to consist of Benjamin Newberry, Edward Griswold and John Moore, to be joined later by Simon Wolcott, it was responsible for laying out the remaining undivided lands. Newberry, Wolcott and Moore all had useful holdings of their own there. In a February thaw in 1666 the three of them rode up to the Massaco falls to measure the upland lots from Newberry's own lot to Bissell's Brook. These they allocated to fellow committee members Wolcott, Moore and Griswold and to the Bissells, all in the category of preferential shareholders, as well as to fellow troopers John Moses and Samuel Marshall and to Michael Humphrey the turpentine distiller. The recipients had to plough, mow and fence their land within two years and were not to sell before they had lived there for three. Settlement proceeded apace. The following year there were sufficient settlers for separate provision to be made for them to vote in the election of Chauncey as Windsor's minister. In 1668 at a meeting in deacon Moore's house in Windsor twenty-five were awarded grants on settlement terms; in 1669 a return of freemen lists thirteen from Massaco, formerly of Windsor; and by 1670 nearly twenty had taken up their allotment.

The thirty or so people who took out the first grants at Massaco on these settlement terms were all of the second generation and they included a smattering of West Country names like Drake, Pinney, Gibbs, Denslow, Hoskins and Holcombe. Few, however, could be said to belong to the inner core of dominant Windsor families. What is striking is the number who had rebelled against the hegemony of the old Windsor church. Michael Humphrey and John Griffen may have gone upriver to exploit the Massaco pine forests but they had also been the first explosive protesters against a church which would not admit them to communion, and in that first group of Massaco settlers over a dozen family heads belonged to the Woodbridge party who seceded to form the second Windsor church. The religious impulse, rebelling against an authoritarian church, was once again significant.

In October 1668 the General Court reappointed Newberry, Moore and Wolcott as its committee for Massaco and gave them extended terms of reference. Instead of Massaco being 'an appendix to the town of Windsor', they were to plan to establish it as an independent plantation. The following year the court exempted Massaco plantation from the colony rate for three years and appointed its first constable. In May 1670 it was recognized as an independent township, renamed Simsbury, its bounds defined and its first deputies admitted to the court. The following year Simsbury was allotted its cattle brand, and two years later Wolcott and Griffin were appointed to organize its trainband. In three years' time Simsbury would pay her colony taxes like all the rest.

Why the new settlement was named Simsbury is obscure. Maybe it was after Simon Wolcott. As a member of its planning committee, a principal first settler, first deputy to the general court, captain of its trainband, licensed to dispense its wines and spirits and a Wolcott to boot, he was its most important citizen. (Many years later, his son Roger would suggest the Wolcott family name of Tolland for yet another Windsor offshoot.) But to give a settlement a Christian name other than a royal one would have been unusual, and an alternative suggestion is that it was named for another member of the troop of horse, Aaron Cooke who, it will be remembered, had been the first to develop his own and his stepfather's lands at Massaco in the early 1650s. Both Cooke and Ford came originally from the village of Simonsbury, pronounced Simsbury, three miles from Bridport, Dorset.

Simsbury was now a fully fledged town, Windsor's first colony. That was the extent of it so far as the General Court was concerned. But the court would have reckoned without the Indians. It might have been a matter of routine in 1673 for the court to appoint Wolcott and Griffen to organize the Simsbury trainband; but two years later matters were no longer by any means routine. Members of that trainband were on twenty-four hour alert for active service; and on 14 October, the court had perforce to give the Simsbury settlers a staggering ultimatum: a week's notice 'to secure themselves and their corn there, and the end of the week from this date, the souldiers now in garrison at Simsbury shall be released their attendance there'. In other words, the town was to be evacuated because it could not be defended from an imminent Indian attack. Simsbury, up the Tunxis on the edge of the wilderness, was indeed especially isolated and exposed; but, by December, the new Council of Safety was ordering the nearby Windsor people on the east side of the Connecticut to leave their homesteads and return with their cattle and grain to Windsor and the shelter of the Palisado; and those who remained were to kill their swine and maintain strict garrison discipline. For the first time since the Pequot War in their parents' day nearly forty years before, the Windsor planters were in a state of crisis bordering on panic from the threat of Indian attack. Even then, they could not have conceived that within six months their own local Indian neighbours would put their abandoned Simsbury homesteads, so recently and painstakingly built and furnished, to the torch.

CHAPTER 13: CAPTAIN NEWBERRY AND KING PHILIP'S WAR 1675

O N 9 AUGUST 1675, IN THE PARLOUR OF HIS OFFICIAL RESIDENCE AT Hartford, old Governor, John Winthrop, had just approved the draft of a dispatch to Major John Pynchon up at Springfield. This had been the principal business of the day for the Standing Council. This council of war, activated by the General Court a month before to deal with the new Indian menace, had been meeting almost every other day, so urgent were the events crowding in on the colony. Not since that far away time nearly forty years before when the Pequots erupted had there been so critical a threat to the safety of the river towns.

It was worrying enough at the beginning of July when 'King Philip' and his Wampanoags attacked the Plymouth village of Swanzea and they had to rush those dragoons to protect Connecticut's eastern frontier beyond New London and Stonington. Even the Narragansetts were a problem and Winthrop was worried lest his inexperienced son Wait, by impetuously taking his New London force into their country, might stir them up; and though they were all relieved at the so-called 'treaty' with the Narragansett sachems, the Governor suspected they had not heard the last from that quarter.

Infinitely worse had been the turn of events in the past week. It was now clear that the flash at Swanzea had started a trail of Indian arson, pillage and murder which was spreading like wildfire through the Massachusetts back country, so that even the Nipmucks were infected and the loyalty of our own river Indians was in doubt. The ambush of that scouting party from the Bay and the siege and partial burning, less than a week before, of those twenty or so huddled families at Quabaug (Brookfield) on the Bay Path only a few miles up into the Nipmuck country, struck cold fear to the hearts of the river settlements. If this could happen to Brookfield, what about the equally exposed frontier settlements on the river itself at Hadley, Hatfield and Northampton? It must be assumed that Springfield remained sound; the people there were confident of the loyalty of their local Indians. This was the Bay's responsibility; but Springfield was only those few miles upstream from Windsor and the news of the Brookfield disaster brought five nights ago by that Springfield messenger had been a shock. For the Governor, elderly and ailing, to have to call a meeting of the Standing Council at one o'clock in the morning was an emergency he hoped not to have to repeat. However, he was thankful he did, and that on the early morning of 5 August the council had managed to dispatch that company of forty dragoons under Lieutenant Watts up to Springfield, and the next day put in train the raising of a force of 100 dragoons under Captain Newberry to be fully equipped and on an hour's alert. Today it had been reassuring that Uncas' son Joshua should offer his services with thirty or so Indians, 'longing to be employed', as he reported to Pynchon at Springfield, and to be able to send them upriver after Watts's dragoons.

So far so good; but it was hard to know what to do for the best. After the ambush of that troop from the Bay and given the Indians' notorious talent for erupting and then melting away into the forest, it seemed clear that English militia, even well mounted and armed with the new flintlock musket, were vulnerable to attack and must be carefully deployed. Most worrying was the sheer lack of information about the Indians and especially their own river tribes whose loyalty they had taken too much for granted. As his own dispatch to Pynchon put it: 'Want of intelligence puts us to a loss what to do . . . We stand tiptoe for intelligence and earnestly desire as any comes to your hand it may be posted away to us'.

Winthrop and his colleagues would continue to be largely in the dark for the next ten days. The council, meeting again the next night, sent the colony's marshall up to Springfield to liaise with Pynchon, watch over Joshua's Indians, and give them a dram or two of liquor to keep up their courage; and two days later they would send Major Talcott with a guard of ten troopers to assess the situation and if possible make contact with the New Yorkers at Albany on the Hudson. On the 18th they decided they should meet in virtually continuous session, that as many of the assistants as possible should stay in Hartford throughout the emergency and that John Allyn, the colony secretary, should not go to Boston for the meeting of the New England commissioners but that the Governor should go instead.

This had come as a relief to Winthrop. In his seventieth year, he had for some time been feeling his age. But his mind was as sharp as ever and his instincts for politics as sound and shrewd; indeed this latest emergency reassured him about his own judgment of men and affairs; *politique* that he was, the empirical, moderate approach to problems which had been his metier was what was needed now. Despite his Puritan inheritance he was no root-and-branch man and in this new Indian crisis he was as worried by the fire eaters among the English as by the unreliability of the aborigines. He had been long enough on the river to distrust Bay solutions to problems, especially in Indian affairs where the stakes were against poor, isolated Connecticut. The last few weeks reminded him of Lion Gardiner's fury when in 1637 Endicott stirred up those hornets and then left Saybrook and the river settlements to feel the Pequot sting. How he remembered, over forty years before, first meeting Gardiner, that young engineer officer hired by the Warwick patentees to build Saybrook Fort; and how he missed John Mason! For Winthrop, Mason's death three years before was the end of an era. Connecticut had, for a generation, relied on Mason as commander-in-chief, deputy governor and diplomat–negotiator to keep the Indians peaceful. The younger generation had no consciousness of those dangerous days of 1637. Thanks to Mason and others, they had come to take for granted, condescendingly and complacently, that one Englishman was a match for ten Indians.

Winthrop was conscious that he had outlived most of his contemporaries and was ageing. He had spent the greater part of his life in public service in the taxing conditions of the New England frontier and he was weary. Because of the public demands on his time and energies his private affairs remained a mess and there was much to sort out. He would dearly like to make one more voyage back to England, to the Suffolk of his childhood and youth. His health, never robust, had recently become precarious and he was distinctly frail, suffering, as he put it, from 'troubles and pains and some infirmities'. The previous August he had not made his usual journey back to the Bay but contented himself with resting in the Hartford neighbourhood. For some time he had been determined to retire. The court had re-elected him governor as usual the previous May; this time, however, he had demurred and, though allowing himself to be sworn in, had submitted his resignation in writing the following week; he had followed this with another formal letter of resignation with his seal affixed and had executed a power of attorney in anticipation of his voyage to England. For most of July he had taken no formal part in colony affairs and this Indian business had brought him only reluctantly back into executive leadership. The suggestion, therefore, that he should take Allyn's place as commissioner at Boston had come as a godsend. The next day he would chair his last meeting of the Standing Council; thereafter, his deputy William Leet would have to take charge and he would make his preparations to leave for the Bay.

About nine days later John Winthrop said his last goodbyes and embarked with his daughters Martha and Anne on the pinnace that was to take them round the coast to Boston. As the ship dropped down the Great River, the governor watched the bluffs of Hartford recede from view for the last time. He died in Boston on 5 April the following year.

That same spring, the English colonists on the Connecticut had little idea of the violent eruption of Indian tribes which, for a second time, was about to threaten their very existence. Ever since their parents had conquered and dispersed the Pequots, they had learned to live with their neighbouring tribes, purchasing their lands and trafficking with them on uneasy but familiar terms. But gradually, as they established their plantations and grew in numbers, the Indians became conscious that the kind of co-existence that they had enjoyed was no longer so mutually beneficial. The English were coming to dominate the landscape and the future for their Indian neighbours was at risk. Or so thought the chief sachem of the Wampanoags who came to be known as King Philip and whose territory lay east of Narragansett Bay. For several years he had been trying to form a tribal coalition against the English and, despite the continuing loyalty to them of many tribes, particularly the christianized or 'praying' Indians, he felt sufficiently strong and desperate in June 1675 to take the offensive. The result was the most devastating war New England was ever to experience, with reverberations far beyond the Wampanoag territory flanking Massachusetts Bay and not least in the upper Connecticut Valley.

At that critical meeting of the Standing Council on 6 August following the news about Brookfield, the officer appointed to command the force of dragoons for immediate service was our old acquaintance Captain Benjamin Newberry. He had been the principal officer of the Standing Council since its reconstitution on 9 July (apart from the Governor and the other ex-officio members) and he was to serve as such throughout the war save for a few weeks in the early summer of 1676 when he was commanding troops in the field and his brother-in-law Daniel Clarke substituted for him. He was so important to the council's deliberations that within three weeks he was released from his command of the dragoons, 'being of the Council and his attendance being necessary'. At fifty-one he was at the height of his powers as an active and experienced militia officer. Nine years before he had been an original member of the Standing Council's predecessor, the Committee for the Militia, along with his brothers-in-law Henry Wolcott, Captain John Allyn and Captain Daniel Clarke, all of whom were or were to be his colleagues on the Standing Council. It was the usual, close-knit group of peers, most with military experience. Of the council's sixteen members, nine were or had been captains of their town trainband.

Military tactics had changed since their parents had faced that first showdown with the Indians forty years before. The English had learned something, if not enough, from the Indians' guerilla fighting in the forest, of tracking, dispersal, ambush and hand-to-hand fighting. The English militia were now more mobile, less encumbered and had more wieldy weapons. The 14-foot pike, though used for training, was virtually obsolete on active service and the matchlock was being replaced by the handier flintlock musket and the light and more accurate carbine. Men marched more lightly accoutred and had greater appreciation of the need for speed and surprise. The use of the horse was also better understood. Something had been learned, no doubt from the English Civil War, but more from the wilderness, of the impracticality of the cavalry charge, the dangers of close formation fighting and the possibilities of fast mounted movement through forest trails unimpeded by much brushwood and thicket.

In the eighteen years since the Connecticut troop was formed, the horse had become increasingly important. In 1672 each county was instructed to raise its own troop on the model of Hartford County whose captain, Daniel Clarke, had been authorized to augment it to its full strength of sixty troopers. However, it was not practical to have regular cavalry exercises at county level and troopers trained with their local town foot. It is doubtful whether they saw much action as regular cavalry in King Philip's War. Although they were deployed in guards of ten or a dozen or in twos or threes for reconnaissance, their classic weapons, the sabre and pistol, were of no special advantage against Indians who had acquired firearms. Instead Newberry and his colleagues were increasingly impressed with the advantage, in terms of surprise, of arming horsemen with 'long arms', half-pikes or lances, and with muskets for rapid employment over a distance, or in other words as mounted infantry, named 'dragoons' from the smoking dragon mouths of their muskets. By the fall of 1675 most of the horse had been so converted and the General Court resolved that any trooper who did not provide himself with a musket or carbine must revert to being a foot soldier: clearly some cavalrymen were reluctant to change their ways.

As early as 1667 up to a third of the foot companies had been provided with mounts. This may have been over-ambitious, because Newberry and his colleagues then reduced them to foot companies, to be remustered only in an emergency. In 1673 there came just such an emergency when the Dutch appeared to be about to recapture their New Netherlands possessions on Long Island and west of the Connecticut. That August the newly named Grand Committee of the Militia raised 500 dragoons, fully horsed and at an hour's alert. Captain Newberry commanded Hartford County's contribution of 160 dragoons, 38 from Windsor. Fortunately, news of the peace with the Dutch in Europe forestalled open hostilities; but the exercise proved a useful rehearsal for the outbreak of war with the Indians two summers later. On 6 August 1675 the Standing Committee was able without hesitation to order the mobilization of 230 dragoons. Thereafter, the campaigning that fall was largely dependent on them.

There was plenty of work for dragoons. By the end of August it was becoming clear that the situation on the upper Connecticut, though still confused, could no longer be contained. A rather panicky letter from Pynchon in Springfield reported outlying settlements in great fear and hostile Indians between Hadley, where Watts's dragoons were stationed, and Northfield, where a guard of twenty was too weak; and on the 25th Pynchon wrote that 'a war [was] already begun': in a skirmish between Hatfield and Deerfield the Indians were blooded and nine English killed or mortally wounded. The following day the Standing Council ordered the Hartford County dragoons to be ready to march at the weekend and promulgated a Day of Humiliation, Prayer and Soul Affliction once a month until further notice. Four days later Major Robert Treat was appointed commander-in-chief of the colony forces and on the last day of the month started with his dragoons on their way up to Westfield and Northampton.

How did the people of Windsor respond to this emergency? They were well served by Henry Wolcott (who remained a civilian) and Captain Newberry on a Standing Council otherwise dominated by Hartford people. These two Windsor men, who were present almost every day at these council meetings, must have either ridden endlessly up and down that highway between Windsor and Hartford or have had an arrangement with the Hartford ordinary. Windsor, the northernmost Connecticut settlement, with scattered homesteads thronged about with Indian settlements, was in a state of apprehension; and although Springfield shielded them, Windsor people must have been concerned about the frontier outposts further up the river to which some of their own neighbours had recently migrated, like the Fords, Aaron Cooke and David Wilton at Northampton and George Phelps at Westfield. Early in September, Wilton as lieutenant of militia and member of Northampton's Committee of Safety, was urgently inquiring of his old comrades-in-arms at Hartford the reason for delay in sending that relieving force of dragoons up the river. When it arrived a few days later it included his son-in-law Samuel Marshall who was ensign of dragoons with Treat's force. And there were also their other exposed friends up the Rivulet at Simsbury, not least Henry Wolcott's brother Simon who, as captain of Simsbury trainband, must have been a very worried man indeed. Windsor men were already serving with the dragoons, fourteen with Lieutenant Watts's advance company at Hadley and now a further twenty-five on their way up with Major Treat. Trooper John Bissell's brother Nathaniel was acting as a messenger between the Standing Council and Major Pynchon in Springfield.

Such anxious speculation was overtaken by worries closer to home. Treat's force had barely covered the ten miles to Windsor on their way north when two Windsor men said they had been shot at, one on the Simsbury road, and there were reports of Indians skulking on Hartford North Meadow. Whereupon the Standing Council, concerned for the safety of their headquarters, summoned Treat back to Hartford and ordered him to send three companies of thirty dragoons each, as a show of force, one up the east bank of the Connecticut, another down from Hartford to Wethersfield, the third from Hartford up to Windsor. This accomplished, Treat reverted to his original objective of Northampton, followed in a few days by two further companies, one of twenty Windsor men under Sergeant John Grant, Matthew's son.

After their departure, the Windsor constable acting on instruction from the Standing Council put the town on to full alert. A quarter of the able-bodied men aged from sixteen to seventy were to constitute an armed day and night watch; those in the fields were to work in armed companies, not less than six to a company if they were more than half a mile from the Palisado green, with severe fines for non-compliance; patrols were set up on the roads to Hartford and Simsbury; there were rules for conserving powder and shot. As the news from up the river grew bleaker a defence committee was organized and stores of wheat and corn were conserved and protected. During the 1660s, the town had built a fortified stone house, the Stoughton House, towards the upper end of Main Street and this provided a fort to which the inhabitants could retreat, better protected than in the old Palisado; but in October the Standing Council was still worried about Windsor's exposed position and recommended doubling the patrolling watch.

And so the people of Windsor became accustomed to the routines of war. They were conscious that the wilderness to the north contained charred and silent homesteads and indeed whole frontier villages. By the end of September Northfield, Deerfield and Brookfield had all been abandoned and horrifying accounts of slaughter were filtering back, like that of Captain Lathrop at Bloody Brook and Captain Beers and his troop near Northfield, and reports of their severed heads mounted on poles. These were Bay troops, but English, and their destruction shattered morale; the only compensation was the news that their own Major Treat and his Connecticut dragoons were keeping their nerve and acquitting themselves well in the field.

There was worse to come. The people of Springfield remained confident of the loyalty of their neighbourhood Indians who lived in and about a fort a mile from town. But on 4 October that fort suddenly received about 300 of Philip's warriors plotting to take the unsuspecting town. The same evening, down the river in Windsor, an Indian called Toto who was a servant in Henry Wolcott's household revealed the secret to the Wolcotts who sent warning expresses immediately up the river to Springfield and to Major Treat at Westfield. Unfortunately the complacent Springfielders did not heed the warning. On the morning of the 5th, they suffered a furious and murderous attack on their town. Treat, acting on Toto's intelligence, rushed across from Westfield and, despite being hindered crossing the Connecticut, arrived in time to prevent a massacre and the destruction of the town. But Springfield was a ruin. Over thirty homes, apart from outhouses and barns, were burnt to the ground and the town was crowded with refugees and troops. Within a fortnight, Treat, who was back at his Northampton base with reinforcements from Hartford, had to face another attack. The Indians, flushed with success, assembled a force of some 800 in the area of Hadley, Northampton and Hatfield. Outguessing the Bay commander-in-chief Appleton, they subjected Hatfield to a furious assault. Here, however, the garrison resisted vigorously, other Massachusetts troops came to the rescue and, once again, Treat and his dragoons, moving quickly from nearby

Northampton, routed the attackers and put them to flight.

The sack of Springfield brought the shock of war home to the lower Connecticut townships. The treachery of the Springfield Indians led them to suspect their own Indians and to fear an immediate attack. Treat was ordered down to Hartford in a hurry with sixty men; little Simsbury was put on notice that its garrison would be withdrawn within a week; and it was fortunate for the relief of Hatfield that an order to send Treat east to protect Norwich was countermanded. The three river towns organized garrison houses for women and children and moved their stocks of grain for safe keeping. The General Court recruited a further 120 men as reinforcements, ordered each county to raise a troop of sixty dragoons, forbade any able-bodied man to leave the colony, prohibited the export of food without a licence and imposed a swingeing sixpenny rate to pay for war supplies.

However, as so often in war, the tide, unobserved by the people of Windsor or indeed by members of the court or its standing war council, was beginning to turn. The Indians' defeat at Hatfield appears to have shaken their morale and by the beginning of November Appleton, Treat and their fellow officers suspected that Philip's belligerent warriors were moving back from the upper river valley to Narragansett country. On 17 October Appleton was confident enough to release the Connecticut troops from his command. They promptly marched down the river to their home towns. The people of Windsor must have been as joyfully relieved as their parents had been in 1637 to see their men riding through Pine Meadow and down Main Street to the Palisado green that day. At their head was the ensign of the force Samuel Marshall, bringing to his wife Mary the loving greetings of her father David Wilton still up there in Northampton.

Five days later Major Treat presented his compliments in person to a full meeting of the Standing Council in Hartford and informed them that, 'finding no footsteps of the enemy, by all [our] search made by scouts for many days past, up this River of Connecticut, and so judging the enemy were removed, with the consent of Captain Samuel Appleton, commander-in-chief, [I] have moved [my] army hither'. Whereupon the council appointed 2 December as a Solemn Day of Public Prayer and Humiliation, 'to supplicate the Lord's pardoning mercy and compassion towards his poor people and for success in our endeavours for the repelling of the rage and insolency of the enemy'.

But this was a Day of Humiliation still, not of Thanksgiving; for the war was by no means over and a critical winter campaign lay ahead to the east in the Narragansett country. Philip and his Wampanoags were one enemy, but there was a growing suspicion, especially in Massachusetts, that the Narragansetts were not only sheltering Philip's men but planning a *demarche* of their own which would threaten all New England. To forestall this, in Boston that fall the united commissioners decided the best recourse would be a pre-emptive strike into the Narragansett country to cow their sachems and at least keep them neutral. This was bold thinking; indeed old Governor Winthrop thought it foolhardy because it risked forcing the Narragansetts into the war and involved a winter campaign fraught with formidable problems of physical hardship, supply, and of tackling the Indians in remote, well-defended winter quarters. In any case, Winthrop's old instincts were against provoking tribes which had for so long been a useful barrier and which, turned hostile, would divide New England and isolate Connecticut. But his view did not prevail and the commission resolved to mobilize an army to force the Narragansetts to observe their treaty obligations and to return some Indian fugitives they were sheltering. Plans were concerted to raise an army a thousand strong with contingents from the three colonies; these were to converge on the Narragansett country with a show of force. It was to be the most ambitious military force New England had yet succeeded in mustering.

Consequently in that same meeting at Hartford when Major Treat reported the end of the campaign on the upper Connecticut, the Standing Council approved the commissioners' proposal for a winter campaign and resolved that Connecticut should contribute upwards of 300 men under Treat's command. He himself would be under the orders of Major Winslow of Plymouth, as commander-in-chief. Hartford County's share was 110 men including those already on active service and just returned from the upper valley. Windsor's quota was twenty-eight men.

Windsor's early chronicler, Stiles, estimated that about 125 Windsor men served in King Philip's War, mostly as dragoons. Of the twenty-eight serving in the winter campaign we only know the names of those who were killed or died of wounds. For the rest we are dependent on mentions in dispatches, petitions for pensions and an old book of rates which lists eighteen troopers each entitled to receive 6s 8d on war account. The latter include original members of the troop of horse (Daniel Clarke, Samuel Marshall, Thomas Strong, Nathaniel Loomis, John Porter, John Bissell, John Hosford and John Moses) together with two sons of old members (Daniel Hayden and John Terry) and four brothers or nephews (Nathaniel Bissell, Joseph Loomis, Thomas Moore and Henry Wolcott the third). Of the other nine original members, six had removed to other settlements and of these at least three were on active service. Members of the troop of horse, of both first and second generation, continued to be in the thick of it.

Especially in the thick of it was Benjamin Newberry. When the Indians had first erupted in the upper Connecticut Valley he had been the Standing Council's choice to command the initial force of dragoons to be sent upriver; but a fortnight later he was judged so valuable a member of the Standing Council that he was replaced in the field. Throughout that late summer and fall he had sweated it out in Hartford as a staff officer at those daily meetings of the council which had directed and supported Treat and his troops in their successful campaign. But he still yearned for an active command in the field and now seemed to be his opportunity. On 25 November the Standing Council gazetted him senior captain and deputy commander-in-chief in the new expedition against the Narragansetts. One can barely imagine his chagrin and disappointment when, a second time, he was baulked of his opportunity. On 30 November John Allyn recorded that Captain Newberry was 'disabled to go forth in this expedition'; and he was absent from council meetings for the next two weeks. From what we know about his career this probably means that he was struck down by some disabling illness such as was all too common at that time. He was back in harness on 17 December and in the end his time would come; but for the time being he was to remain an armchair soldier.

The command of Newberry's company went to his fellow officer and original trooper, Samuel Marshall, who was promoted captain. Marshall's soldiering record was long and solid: corporal of the Windsor trainband for ten years, then county quartermaster and now ensign of dragoons with an intensive season of campaigning behind him. His was one of five companies, two from the river towns and one each from New Haven, Fairfield and New London. John Mason, son of the old commander-in-chief, was to command the New London company and Nathaniel Seely that of Fairfield. The only exception to this locality rule was the New Haven company which went to John Gallop of New London, probably because the commander-in-chief was a New Haven man and Gallop, from frontier Stonington, knew the terrain of the campaign in prospect. Of the Hartford contingent Thomas Watts, who had taken that first dragoon company up to Springfield, commanded the senior company, the core of which was the thirty men from Hartford town, just as the core of Marshall's company were the twenty-eight men from Windsor.

No one was under any illusion about the formidable nature of such an undertaking at the onset of what promised to be a severe New England winter; and preparations were thorough. New London was to be the forward base for the Connecticut force and 10 December the deadline for its assembly. This was less than three weeks away so that things had to move fast. Wait Winthrop at New London had already been instructed to kill and salt down whatever cattle he could and to grind and bake their store of wheat. An immediate consignment of powder, lead and flints was shipped to New London to augment a stock of ammunition already there, as well as cheese and corn; in addition 300 bushels of wheat were to be procured, ground and baked into biscuit. No provisions were to be exported from New London for two months and ships were to be inspected to enforce this. A commissary was appointed for the army who went about his business of issuing warrants for commandeering supplies and quartering men and horses. Smiths and farriers were much in demand and on 1 December Watts and Marshall were sent on ahead from Hartford to see to the supply of ammunition.

Meanwhile men who had enlisted or been conscripted to fill the quotas were saying goodbye to their families and mustering in their county towns. Care was taken to see that they came protected by extra warm clothing and boots as well as corselets, leather jerkins, bandoleers, belts and pouches, and that their muskets were well found. Unlike the previous summer on the Connecticut, this campaign was conceived largely as an infantry affair. Winter actions in a frozen and marshy wilderness did not lend themselves to fast dragoon movements; and in any case the supply of mounts would probably not run to such a sizeable force. The Connecticut contingent was essentially of foot. Officers were to be mounted; otherwise, apart from a troop to protect their commander-in-chief, there was to be only one horse to every three foot soldiers. These were mainly pack-horses, not mounts.

These various units appear to have foregathered at New London according to plan within a day or two of the 10 December deadline, and the entire force of just over 300 in their five companies, together with some 150 Indian auxiliaries recruited from neighbouring Pequots and Mohegans, moved off in columns from their encampment on the bluff above New London harbour (which had been the old Pequot fort) on their way to Stonington and beyond into the Narragansett country. With them went the earnest prayers of a whole colony deeply aware of how dangerously exposed were all their communities and of how much depended on the good fortune and steadfastness of their militia. The observance on 2 December of a Solemn Day of Humiliation had been no conventional formality; indeed an apocalyptic sense of divine intervention and of the urgent need for redemption from sin so far permeated affairs that the Standing Council instructed the elders and ministers to search out the sins which had brought down the Lord's anger on the colony. It was a Puritan enterprise in the most solemn and dedicated sense.

Meanwhile the expeditionary force was on the march along the old Pequot trail in freezing December weather. Their rendezvous with the Massachusetts and Plymouth troops was supposed to be at Wickford half-way up Narragansett Bay; but their immediate objective was a small settlement on an inlet of the Bay's west shore called Pettaquamscut, with a stone garrison house belonging to a trader called Bull where they expected to be welcomed and to shelter overnight. But the enemy had forestalled them. When they arrived they found the garrison house and its cluster of outbuildings a charred and silent ruin. Their hosts, ten men and five women and children, were dead at Indian hands.

Winter had come early that year. Even before the soldiers left home the Connecticut River towns were frozen in. That evening the weather was cold and stormy and the troops had to camp in the snow around the ruined buildings. The following day it was a relief to welcome the Bay troops whose commanders, hearing of the Connecticut force's tardy arrival, had moved down from Wickford to make Pettaquamscut the jumping-off point for their attack. And so the next night the whole army slept rough in the wet and bitter cold. They were thankful when dawn came, the trumpeters sounded the order to form columns and the march began. The Great Swamp, in whose secret depths the Narragansetts had constructed their winter quarters, lay some fifteen miles to the west and towards it, through a snowy waste of woodland and marsh, the long slow columns wound their way in the freezing weather. There were to be no stops for warmth or food and such rations as the men had – they were already beginning to run short – were gnawed at on the march. It was afternoon on this short December day when they were brought by their Indian guide to the mysterious and lonely fastness of mere and marsh which was the Great Swamp. There, in the afternoon light, they could discern on some raised ground in the midst of the swamp what appeared to be a large Indian village. This turned out to be a fortified town of maybe five or six acres, protected not only by its marshy moat but by a tall, solidly built palisade, circumscribed by a thicket fifteen feet wide and, at intervals, blockhouses for infilading fire. It was a formidable achievement of Indian fortress engineering.

Fortunately for the attackers, the heavy frost had frozen the mud and marshy water of the swamp and the Indians, who had counted on the unaccustomed and heavily accoutred English foundering in the swamp, were deprived of this advantage; and the first units reached the palisade in short order. Fortunately, too, though there was now no question of surprise, the English had the good luck to happen on the one place where there was a gap in the palisade, blocked only by a tree trunk placed horizontally some five or six feet above the ground. Here the first Massachusetts companies hurled themselves into the attack, braving lethal fire from a covering blockhouse. Despite heavy casualties, they forced the Indians to give ground; but they could not penetrate far into the palisade before they were forced back into the swamp. By this time the main body of troops had arrived and formed up for a concerted assault on the tree trunk gap. This time they forced a way through and carried the attack well into the interior of the fort. Here the fighting was fierce among the lines of wigwams, with muskets flashing and smoke obscuring the waning light of that winter afternoon. The confusion in those confined spaces with hundreds of women and children cowering from the line of fire was intense. It appears that the battle remained bitterly and evenly contested until a handful of English, seeking a diversion, found their way through a hole in the thicket to the rear of the action and suddenly subjected the Indians to musket volleys from behind. It was probably this attack which first gave the English an edge and forced the Indians to retreat. Then, as at the Mystic Fort thirty years before, the order was given to set fire to the wigwams in order to hasten the destruction of the fort. This not only resulted in heavy casualties to women and children but deprived the English themselves of the shelter and food they so dearly needed. However, once the decision was taken and the torch lit, the end was inevitable. The village became a holocaust in which maybe hundreds of Narragansetts, women, children and the infirm, perished in the flames. The experience was so appalling that many of the English were haunted by it and asked themselves afterwards 'whether burning their enemies alive could be consistent with humanity and the benevolent principles of the gospel'.

After some three hours of fighting, the Indian warriors retreated into the swamp; and amid the acrid smell of burnt wigwams and human flesh, the English counted their dead, succoured their wounded and faced the grim prospect of marching back to the nearest food and shelter in the gathering darkness of another bitter winter night. The journey bore more the character of a retreat than a victory and it was only in the early hours of the next morning that an advance party straggled into Wickford. It snowed hard that night and many of the wounded died from loss of blood and frostbite; even the unharmed suffered frozen and swollen limbs. Only next day could the force commanders make a clear-eyed assessment of casualties. It looked as if about a score had been killed in the action itself and a similar number had died of their wounds on the march back to Wickford. But this was to be only the beginning of a death toll from wounds and exposure which the primitive surgery and nursing of the day could do little to alleviate. In the end it is thought that some eighty were killed or died of wounds as a result of what they were calling the Great Swamp Fight. In addition there were about 150 wounded who recovered, this out of a total of about 1000 Englishmen. But the immediate position was even worse. At Wickford after the battle as many as 400 troops were incapacitated from active duty by weakness and exposure and all thought of further action against the Narragansetts had to be abandoned.

The plight of the Connecticut troops was particularly severe. They had had further to march than the others and had suffered two nights in the open before the battle. It also seems that, though they were in the rear, they arrived at the tree trunk blockhouse when the fighting was at its height and consequently suffered disproportionate casualties. Of their 300 troops, forty were killed or died of wounds and a further forty were more or less seriously wounded. Among the killed were three of their five company commanders and a fourth was subsequently to die of his wounds. It was no wonder that Major Treat decided his force was not fit for further action and must return immediately to their home bases to rest and recover. Those that were fit enough marched back along the Pequot trail; the wounded and the weak were carried on ships pressed into service to transport them round Cape Judith to New London, Saybrook and doubtless New Haven on their way to be nursed at their home hearths.

As the people of Windsor must have been asking, what news of the Windsor contingent? Of Captain Marshall's company, about a quarter (fourteen in all) were casualties; but of the twenty-eight Windsor men nearly a quarter died, five in action and a sixth soon after from wounds. Most of these half dozen were more or less obscure private soldiers whose only claim to historical fame is that they followed their captain in the assault on the tree trunk blockhouse and died honourably in a decisive battle against the Indians. But three of them merit more than a passing mention as an elegiac conclusion to this narrative. There was John Fitch who before leaving home for his unit had made that will bequeathing all he possessed to endow a school in Windsor; and there were two officers. One of the five

Connecticut captains was John Mason. Although commander of the New London company and a resident of Norwich, he was the son of the great John Mason, victor of the Mystic Fort Fight of 1637 and Connecticut's first and great commander-in-chief. The younger John Mason had been born and raised in Windsor where his childhood playmates were second-generation members of the troop of horse, like John Bissell who had married his sister Isabel. He was to die of his wounds within the year. The other officer was none other than our trooper acquaintance Captain Samuel Marshall himself. He was killed outright in the thick of the action as he led his company with courage and elan into the assault over that log at the blockhouse entrance. So ended the life of an able and experienced amateur soldier, typical of the best of Windsor's trooper generation. He died in place of his brother officer and friend, Benjamin Newberry, who by grace of God and illness, lived to take a field command at last in the closing stages of King Philip's War the next summer.

RETROSPECT

To understand in retrospect the story of those West Country people who in the 1630s left their villages and country towns in west Dorset and Somerset for Massachusetts Bay and thence to the Connecticut River, it is important to cleanse one's mind as far as possible of all knowledge of what was to come and specifically of the anachronistic assumption that theirs was just a first chapter in that odyssey which was to lead ultimately to the growth of the American nation.

A useful exercise is to examine the language and discard the nomenclature which subsequent generations have used to describe the experiences of these 17th-century West Countrymen. For example it would be natural for us to describe them as 'emigrants'. However, emigrant is a concept they would not have understood; the word only entered the language a century later, in 1754 in relation to the Pennsylvania Germans. In the 1630s there was no word to convey the sense of a one-way voyager. The only term they would have used to describe themselves is 'planter', that is to say he who went abroad to plant, as opposed to the 'adventurer', who invested his money but stayed at home. They would not have recognized the term 'settler' which only dates from the 18th century. As for our planter's relationship with England, he may have become used to the term 'colony' but he did not yet see himself as a 'colonist' let alone a 'colonial' which was a term his old-country cousins were only to apply to him somewhat pejoratively just before the American Revolution. If he classed himself at all it was as a 'New-Englishman' or 'New Englander'. As for the word 'American', this was applied exclusively to the aborigines, more usually called 'the natives' in contradistinction to 'the English'. If one is searching for a word to describe our voyagers it would be 'pilgrims', that is, those who went on a journey in search of a land where the true principles of faith and morality could be practised as distinct from the corruptions of the old world. The fact that this word was much later hijacked for the founders of Plymouth Colony should not prevent our using it as an accurate description of the subjects of this narrative.

Having undergone some such exercise let us try to interpret the minds of our West Country voyagers.

To begin with there can be no denying their adventurousness. They were as much a part of that great age of discovery as the Earl of Warwick who surveyed and manipulated its potential rewards from his privileged position in Whitehall Palace. As those ships' companies of West Country people rounded Rame Head into the Channel towards the open Atlantic they carried mental maps of a shadowy New England littoral beyond the heaving ocean which was tinged with myth; but they sailed with a confidence based on generations of practical seamanship. 'How useful a neighbour is the sea', exclaimed John White and both he and John Higginson believed that those English who did not love their chimney corner too much could find honour and glory in the wonderful works of Almighty God beyond the sea. Such people were possessed of a high courage in facing that voyage into the unknown.

But that was the extent of their adventurousness. They were impelled by mixed motives: some, in White's terms, by 'necessity' or home circumstances from which ocean flight was the only way out, others by what he called 'novelty' or a spirit of adventure and still others by 'hopes of gain' in a land which, if not flowing with milk and honey, promised a better life than people of small means could enjoy in England; but for most the motive was religious: to worship according to a more reformed and purified Church of England than was proving possible in the England of Charles I. For the moving spirits, especially the Puritan ministers who had been ejected from their livings for conscience's sake, there was little choice; it was a matter of seeking a refuge in flight from adverse discrimination if not actual persecution. But it would be anachronistic to attribute to those Dorchester people on their forlorn Massachusetts shore the immigrant frame of mind of later generations. The experience of uprooting from their ancestral West Country must have been traumatic and the decision to leave in varying degrees a radical commitment. Henry Wolcott had not only undergone a Puritan conversion but he and Thomas Newberry liquidated considerable properties for the expedition and many other family heads must also have sold up to finance their removal. Among the Dorchester people, even at their weakest and most exposed, 'the discourse . . . was not, "Shall we go to England?" but "How shall we go to Heaven?"' Yet after experiencing those first winters a few did take ship home and more must have harboured an *arrière pensée* that if circumstances in England altered, they would return to resume their lives in a purified religious and civil polity. Several later did so, not least Roger Ludlow.

It would also be anachronistic to think of our pilgrims as contemplating an experimental future. Their 17th-century minds may have enjoyed a new and exhilarating global view of the world but they had no concept of 'progress' in a 19th-century sense. For our Puritans the key to utopia lay in continuing the work of an incomplete Reformation in a virgin wilderness, insulated from corruption and looking, not forward to a temporal future of progress, but backwards to New Testament values. Everything they wrote testified to the singular providence of God under whom they were to establish a new way in the wilderness. In the words of William Bradford of Plymouth Colony, paraphrasing Scripture:

> Our fathers were Englishmen which came over this great
> ocean, and were ready to perish in this wilderness, but
> they cried unto the Lord and He heard their voice and
> looked on their adversity.

They were agents for God's preordained plan. Such a world view renders unthinkable any concept of man-made progress.

These were a special sort of English people voyaging abroad, New-Englishmen, New Englanders in a literal sense, taking with them their own values, institutions and social order. In Dorchester, Massachusetts and then in Windsor our people practised the forms of government and political habits they had known in Dorchester, Beaminster or Crewkerne. The Assistants of the General Court were equivalent to the gentry from whom Members of Parliament were drawn; and the same men, acting as magistrates in the Particular or County Court, governed the Connecticut River towns in much the same way as the justices of the peace governed Dorset and Somerset through the quorum or at quarter sessions. At the township level, there were the constable, the town clerk, the townsmen who were English burgesses and vestrymen writ large, and an array of petty officers such as the clerk of weights and measures, the leather sealers and the way wardens, those Dogberrys and Verges of the New World, all regulating the town's affairs in a familiar paternalistic and mercantilist way. The town's militia company, too, with its compulsory service, professional muster master, amateur officers, complex drills, field days and its volunteer troop of horse for the quality, was modelled on that of the English shires.

Although Windsor church in its Puritan Congregational form followed the pattern of its neighbours, its founding father had been John White who had protested in the *Humble Request* that its congregation might be voyaging to the New World but were not separating from the Church of England; and it remained the church of John Warham who had so stubbornly asserted it to be the church of sinners as well as saints and who, until he lost his nerve, pioneered the half-way covenant.

Windsor's social order was also recognizably that of provincial England. Its ring of interrelated families of property and social position, with disproportionate amounts of choice land in and about Windsor's Island, holding the principal public offices, connected with the clerisy, distinguished by formal modes of address and sumptuary privileges – these constituted a governing oligarchy the members of which were the New World equivalent of English squires and burgesses.

This nexus of families was predominantly, though not exclusively, of that strain which had its origins in the West Country, its shared experiences of the *Mary and John* and the other ships and of that sojourn at Dorchester on the Bay. They held these loyalties in common with many less well-connected Windsor neighbours. Many of these, too, had settled both in Dorchester and then on Windsor's Main Street with home lots and field strips next door to neighbours from the Brit Valley or the Crewkerne district. Such common folk memories were an effective substitute for the customary communities they had left behind. Although only a few families such as the Wolcotts may have had the means to preserve and cultivate their family connections in Somerset, the way of life of most, with apple orchards and cider, Devon cattle rearing and dairying, hemp and flax, preserved a West Country flavour. If one reads aloud items from the inventories of Windsor planters, taken down and phonetically spelled by barely literate neighbours, one hears the echo of a West Country burr.

Yet, however much these pilgrims continued to regard themselves simply as West Country English in New England, influences were at work which would subtly alter their attitudes, habits and ultimately their institutions.

From the beginning they were never a characteristic sample of the English or even of West Country people in the rough and the round. They were a purposeful and highly eclectic version of English society, a self-selected group who, for a congeries of reasons connected with the need to worship God in their own way, deliberately chose to come together to live in a separate community in the New World. This set them apart and continued to define the perameters within which their own lives and those of their children were shaped. They were also singled out by the fact that they were predominantly a community of families with children and, largely, within a comparatively limited age range. Moreover, this character was enhanced by a second generation of large families which made Windsor a community of well-defined and interconnected family groupings. The social profile was also sharper and more limited than that of the west of England as a whole. There were relatively few servants and at the other end of the scale few, and only minor, gentry. The aristocratic or even the gentle strain did not transplant. Lords Saye and Brooke and Sir Richard Saltonstall never made their landing at the mouth of the Connecticut and even George Fenwick abandoned the place after poor Mistress Fenwick's death. Our pilgrims consisted, in fact, predominantly of that middling range from husbandman and master craftsman to substantial yeoman, merchant, seafarer and cleric which fitted Richard Eburne's prescription for a successful Puritan plantation.

Politically speaking, also, the New England climate was different. Our planters were governed in Massachusetts under the authority of a royal charter; but this was the charter of a trading company which the Governor and Assistants had brought with them and these circumstances subtly altered the attitudes of governors and governed from those they had grown up with in the West Country. In the first place, the seat of government was not over a hundred miles away in a royal establishment at the Palace of Westminster, but at a very different kind of court a few miles down the road, in Boston and then in Hartford; and once Connecticut set up its own government it became one remove further still from an external authority which remained somewhat shadowy until the restoration of the monarchy in 1660. Government was a neighbourly affair. Moreover, according to trading company rules, the Governor and Assistants were elected by the freemen whose status was based on that of the freeholder of an English shire or the freeman of an English borough but was in Connecticut achieved probably by many, if not most, substantial citizens. At the town level this sense of immediate participation was even more direct because the franchise for town offices and affairs in Windsor was in the hands of all 'inhabitants', that is, householders of good repute, exercised through the town meeting. It is anachronistic to think of this as in any sense 'democratic'. Government remained an oligarchic affair but these representational ground rules were psychologically charged for the future.

If political affairs underwent a sea change, climate and topography effected a kind of wilderness change. After the shock of the first winters and the heat and mosquitoes of summer our planters responded well to the New England climate and came to boast that it was healthier than that of the old country. But they had many adjustments to make before they settled to a viable domestic economy. The few mariners took easily to the albeit dangerous business of fishing and coastal trading but the great majority who must support themselves on the land underwent many trials and errors before adjusting their husbandry to the demands of the wilderness. They benefited immeasurably from taking over from the Indians their cleared lands and maize culture; but it was years before they could acclimatize English grains and find nourishing fodder for their livestock. They adjusted to the need to share scarce manpower, draft animals and ploughs to clear land for tillage by reverting to a form of the old English open-field system, and in other ways preserved a communal element in their village economy. They settled as a matter of course according to an English village plan within range of the meeting house; but the plenitude of land provided them with the luxury of home lots which were sizeable smallholdings so that the New England main street quickly took on the spacious character it preserves today. Similarly, though they built their houses according to English practice, the danger of fire forced them to build stone chimneys and to substitute wooden shingles for thatch, and they made other innovations like the lean-to kitchen as a result of which emerged the characteristic New England house as it still survives. Already in that first generation the English village became the New England township.

Church affairs also went through a sequence of changes in these two generations after the gathering of Warham's church in Plymouth that March day of 1630. Its members may have continued to think of their church as being still in some sense in communion with the Church of England and one of their elders, William Hosford, eventually returned during the Commonwealth to take a parish living in Devon; but their gathered nature, their topographical separateness and their government by ministers and elders tended inevitably towards a Congregationalist frame of mind and away from that of an English parish church. The church's rigid, Puritan discipline was essential in sustaining its pilgrim community in the unpromising soil of Massachusetts Bay and in the weary work of renewal on the Connecticut frontier; but it was a discipline difficult to maintain beyond that first generation of church members who had undergone the full rigours of a spiritual conversion. In time, and especially after the death of its revered pastor, Windsor church failed to withstand the strains of an inevitable cooling of evangelism's white heat and the emergence of a prolific second generation of potential church members. However, such was the dominance of the idea of a gathered church that there could be no return to the old English concept of the parish, only the half-way covenant and a replication of churches beginning in Windsor with Woodbridge's second church. The English parish never took root and the state, in the form of the General Court, gave up trying to impose a single church for each township.

Yet the disciplined Puritan way of life persisted. It would be a mistake to anticipate or over-emphasize the extent to which a diminution of the hardships of pioneering and the amenities of a more settled life induced in the second generation a greater worldliness of outlook or liberality of values. Mistress Sarah Wolcott may have amassed a rich and varied wardrobe which even her husband's status as a magistrate and import merchant could hardly justify under the sumptuary law, but the only books she left were psalms and catechisms for the instruction of her grandchildren. If the language had lost the earnest intensity of her Wolcott father-in-law's early, prayerful letters to his brother in Somerset, both rhetoric and content were Puritan still. Sermons were in the style of those Sarah's husband had taken down in shorthand as a young man and the habit of introspective diary keeping persisted; indeed, with Matthew Grant, it prompted a remarkable standard in the keeping of public records. Imbued as they were with a religion which enshrined 'the Word', literacy was paramount. Although it was a struggle to maintain a school, there were regular town subscriptions to support that college in Cambridge, Massachusetts to which they looked for their future ministers of that Word. Negative but telltale evidence of Windsor's continuing Puritan character is the absence of aspects of culture other than the literary. None of over a hundred inventories of the first two generations of Windsor people which itemize meticulous details from pewter plates to the last kitchen knife and farm tool record a single musical instrument, no recorder or fiddle, not even a fife, and there are no pictures, even portrait sketches. Could it have been that, over time, as with the English Quakers, music and the visual arts were, as it were, being bred out of this Puritan strain? At the outbreak of that new Indian revolt of 1675 which came to be called King Philip's War, the inhabitants of Windsor and the other river towns faced the crisis in true Puritan spirit. On a Solemn Day of Humiliation before the winter campaign of that year they were exhorted by the court

> to make diligent search for those evils amongst us which have stirred up the Lord's anger against us, that they, being discovered, may by repentance and reformation be thrown out of our camp and hearts.

It was still a very Puritan society.

The course of that campaign also proved that in the forty-eight years since the Pequot War they had learned a good deal about forest lore and about soldiering against the Indians in the wilderness. They had quickly made the militia a more serious military force than it had ever been in England. Training days might be cheerful masculine diversions from the drudgery of farm work or the exercises of the meeting house but over the years the foot came to be better armed and more sensibly drilled, more knowledgeable about the terrain and the enemy's methods and led by more experienced officers. And latterly the horse had come to be used, not as cavalry, but for scouting and intelligence and as mounted musketeers or dragoons. Yet when it came to the sticking point at the Great Swamp Fight in the December of 1675 the difference between defeat and victory lay not so much in the soldierly qualities of the English or their fire-power – the Indians had themselves acquired muskets – as in the decision, as in the Mystic Fort Fight all those years before, to smoke the enemy out by burning down his fort with all its inhabitants. And it was characteristic that they should justify such ruthless action to their consciences in the language and by the arguments of the Old Testament.

So, too, in those four decades the English had learned to know the Indians better; but in doing so they had developed ambivalent attitudes towards them. When they first landed in Massachusetts Bay they had looked on the unknown savages with curiosity and a certain dread but not without those missionary thoughts which had been a strong motive for a Puritan colonizer like John White; and although a Christian conversion into 'praying Indians' was more a feature of Massachusetts than Connecticut, Windsor people came to know and appreciate the friendliness of their Indian neighbours and with Puritan consciences they scrupulously acquired legal titles for their lands. Yet it was probably inevitable that the tribes should become increasingly uneasy about the way in which the increasing numbers of English were encroaching on their hunting territories; and, on the other hand, the sudden eruption of the maverick Pequots in 1637 brought home to the English how small and vulnerable they were and how easily they could be wiped out. So far as the Pequots were concerned it was thought to be 'them or us', and the only solution, their virtual extermination. That example gave the English the best part of four decades of uneasy coexistence with the other tribes but the memory of it complicated English attitudes towards the Indians whom they came to regard, however affectionately, as primitive and inferior peoples in much the same way as their 19th-century successors in a latter day Empire were to regard African natives; and is it too far-fetched to think of Major Mason as one of the first of a long line of colonial administrators with responsibility for tribal policy? When a second and prolific generation of English planters grew up demanding land of their own to settle on, the interests of the Indians received scant shrift.

In the settlement of New England, as we have seen, an antiphonal theme to the quest for a Puritan refuge was the appetite for land. John White had recognized this in *The Planters Plea*; dissatisfaction with the stony soil of Massachusetts Bay and the lure of those rich meadows along the Connecticut led to Dorchester's second swarming; and when the children of the Windsor planters grew up they, in turn, had to be accommodated, either with land carved out of their parents' holdings, especially on the east bank of the Connecticut, or with new lands still further afield. Notable among such were those Indian-cleared meadows and upland some ten miles upstream at the Massaco falls of the Tunxis, which were settled by Ford and Cooke, and the younger Wolcott, Newberry and company, and called Simsbury. Simsbury, which survived King Philip's War, was only the most notable place to be colonized from Windsor. As the reader may have noticed, individual family groups had been leaving Windsor for supposedly greener pastures ever since Roger Ludlow led his little band to found Fairfield in 1639. Several went to other places on the Sound or, as they put it, 'at the seaside', such as Hammonassett, Killingworth (a corruption of Kenilworth), or Bray Rossiter's Guilford; others were attracted to newer settlements up the Connecticut River like Thomas Ford and David Wilton to Northampton or George Phelps and Aaron Cooke to Westfield. And after the period of this narrative Windsor would colonize other settlements east of the river such as Hebron and Tolland. As with the founding generation's uprooting from the West Country, there was often a mixture of motives behind such departures. In addition to a desire for new and more fertile land such defectors often went for religious reasons like the folk who went to Northampton and those Anglican-minded people among the founders of Simsbury.

It is difficult to distinguish between those who went and those who stayed save to note the obvious fact that among the first settlers those most likely to stay in Windsor were the well established in terms of property and position and many of these were of West Country origin. However, a significant number of notable West Country people, such as those instanced in the previous paragraph, did in fact choose to go and for them this was a third uprooting. Could it be that the experience of uprooting, first undergone in 1630 in Dorset or Somerset, had perhaps become progressively less traumatic with each move and that the children of our band of West Country pilgrims were on their way to becoming, geographically and psychologically, pioneers of America's moving frontier of settlement, bonded together more by the intimacies of a travelling neighbourhood than by ancestral folk origin?

Thus the character of our West Country families was being altered in a variety of ways by their experience of migration. In their self-selection, their Puritanism, their political habits, their fortitude in voyaging and trekking, in bracing themselves for climate and wilderness, in their husbandry, in skills relearnt, in their soldiering and relations with the Indians and in their experience of rapid change, in all these respects they were no longer quite the West Country people they or their parents had been in 1630. England was still their old country but for the younger Henry Wolcott 'home' was Windsor in New England. They had become provincial English of a new kind. Were they becoming 'American' without knowing it?

APPENDIX I
FIRST GRANTS FROM THE PLANTATION
(registered by the end of 1641)

Total acreage in orders of magnitude

Name	Acreage	
Newberry family	789	Top 12 per cent own 6220 acres = 37.4 per cent
Bissell, J.	774	
Stiles family	763	
Ford, T.	703	
Loomis, J.	675	
Wolcott family	593	
Gaylord family	588	
Warham, J.	485	
Hosford, W.	429	
Stoughton, T.	421	
Porter, J.	400	Top quarter own 9555 acres = 57.5 per cent
Haynes, J.	368	
Witchfield, J.	350	
Hill, W.	348	
Drake, J.	338	
Rossiter, B.	332	
Terry, S.	320	
Hull family	307	

Hoskins family	285	
Phelps, W.	285	
Hayden, W.	358	Second quarter own 4008 acres = 24 per cent
Gibbs, G.	244	
Filer, W.	241	
Rockwell, W.	237	
Grant, M.	231	
Gunn, T.	219	
Pomeroy, E.	209	
ffoulkes, H.	208	
Pinney, H.	207	
Eglestone, B.	193	
Wilton, D.	193	
Cooke, A.	192	
Moore family	192	
Mason, J.	179	
Griswold, E.	178	
Winchell, R.	178	
Hawkins, A.	176	
Hoyte, S.	160	
Randall family	159	
Oldage, R.	153	
Branker, J.	147	Third quarter own 2254 acres = 13.5 per cent
Buckland, T.	141	
Williams, R.	141	
Hulburd, W.	140	
Taylor, J.	126	
Holcomb, T.	122	
Ludlow, R.	122	
Allyn, S.	116	
Gillett, J.	115	
Carter, J.	115	
Rockwell, J.	110	
Voare, R.	104	
Barber, T.	102	
Marshfield, T.	102	
Denslow, N.	99	
Hawkes, J.	94	
St. Nicholas, J.	94	
Bassett, T.	91	
Gillett, N.	88	
Clark, J.	85	

Phelps, G.	83	Fourth quarter own 795 acres = 4.8 per cent
Buell, W.	78	
Bascomb, T.	70	
Birge, R.	61	
Palmer, N.	60	
Dewey, T.	59	
Williams, A.	48	
Parkman, E.	45	
Weller, R.	40	
Dibble, T.	37	
Phillips, G.	33	
Hillier, J.	33	
Tilley, Edith	32	
Alvord, B.	30	
Stuckey, G.	26	
Try, M.	21	
Thrall, W.	20	
Hannum, W.	10	
Samways, R.	9	

TOTAL ACREAGE   16,612

Omission: the Rev. Ephraim Huitt. Near total omission: Roger Ludlow

Note: There is a discrepancy between the total number of grants in the text (94) and in the above table. This is because the number in the table (79) includes eight families with more than one grantee, usually a son or sons. The list was computed thus in order to show the holdings by family rather than individuals.

APPENDIX II
WINDSOR INVENTORIES

Total amounts (£s) in orders of magnitude

First generation

Name	Amount	Birth	Death
Newberry, Thomas	1520	1594	1636
Warham, John	1239	England	1670
Marshall, Samuel	902	England	1675
Pinney, Humphrey	780	England	1683
Wolcott, Henry	764	1578	1655
Elsworth, Josiah	655	England	1689
Huitt, Ephraim	633	*c.* 1590	1644
Filer, Walter	629	England	1683
Moses, John	575	England	1683
Bissell, John	520	1592	1677
Branker, John	502	*c.* 1600	1662
Moore, John	489	England	1677
Porter, John	470	England	1648
Allyn, Matthew	466	1604(?)	1671
Nowell, Thomas	368	England	1649
Pinney, Mary (widow)	356	England	1684
Buckland, Thomas	346	England	1662

Hoskins, John	338	England	1648
Drake, John	324	c. 1600	1659
Osborne, John	315	England	1686
Gaylord, William	296	1585	1673
Tudor, Owen	294	England	1691
Holcombe, Thomas	294	1601	1657
Witchfield, Margaret (widow)	280	England	1669
Eno, James	278	England	1682
Gillett, Jonathan	273	England	1677
Rockwell, John	244	England	1662
Maudsley, John	228	England	1690
Alford, Benedict	229	England	1683
Stiles, John	222	England	1662
Gibbs, Katherine (widow)	220	England	1660
Denslow, Henry	215	1615–20	1676
Dewey, Thomas	213	England	1648
Chapman, Edward	184	England	1675
Loomis, Joseph	178	England	1658
Birge, Richard	174	England	1651
Phillips, George	174	England	1678
Thrall, William	158	England	1679
Buell, William	147	England	1681
Barber, Thomas	132	1614	1662
Pond, Samuel	129	England	1655
Warham, Abigail (widow)	126	England	1684
Filer, Jane (widow)	122	England	1690
Grant, Matthew	118	England	1682
Eglestone, Bigod	116	1587	1674
Hoskins, Ann (widow)	113	England	1663
Randall, Phillip	113	England	1662
Hill, William	111	England	1649
Samways, Richard	110	England	1650
Bancroft, John	110	England	1662
Sexton, Richard	107	England	1662
Wilton, David	101	England	1678
Hayward, Robert	96	—	1684
Clark, Daniel	95	England	1710
Skinner, John	90	England	1651
Vore, Richard	81	England	1683
Allyn, Samuel	76	England(?)	1648
Clarke, Joseph	71	England	1641
Sexton, Sarah (widow)	69	England	1674
Denslow, John	62	England	1689
Moses, Mary (widow)	62	England	1686
Winchell, Robert	61	England	1668

Dibble, Thomas	60	England	1700
Hull, George	58	1590(?)	1659
Denslow, Susannah (widow)	57	England	1683
Taylor, Stephen	49	England	1683
Fitch, John	46	England	1675
Wilton, Nicholas	42	England	1683
Bartlett, Edward	39	England	1676
Hillier, John	39	England	1655
Denslow, Elizabeth (widow)	38	1585	1669
Parsons, Thomas	22	England	1680
Buell, Mary (widow)	19	England	1684
Sension, Nicholas	11	England	1690

Second generation

Name	Amount	Birth	Death
Wolcott, Henry	3977	England	1680
Hosford, John	1203	1627	1683
Allyn, Thomas	1174	c. 1626	1696
Porter, John	993	—	1688
Hoskins, Anthony	984	Dorchester	1707
Stoughton, Thomas	941	England	1684
Bissell, Thomas	864	England	1689
Phelps, Samuel	773	c. 1625	1669
Bissell, Nathaniel	655	1640 Windsor	1714
Drake, Job	583	England	1689
Newberry, Benjamin	563	c. 1624	1689
Drake, Jacob	551	England(?)	1689
Terry, John	548	Windsor	1691
Winchell, Nathaniel	540	--	1700
Strong, John	483	1626	1697
Holcombe, Joshua	474	1640	1690
Phelps, Joseph	473	c. 1629	1695
Phelps, William	472	England	1682
Hoskins, Thomas	450	England(?)	1666
Gaylord, William	423	England(?)	1656
Grant, John	424	1642 Windsor	1684
Browne, Peter	408	—	1691
Strong, Return	392	1641(?)	1726
Drake, Mary (widow)	388	1651 Windsor	1693
Loomis, Thomas	377	England	1689
Wolcott, Christopher	372	England	1662

Bissell, John	301	England	1688
Grant, Tahan	300	1633 Dorchester	1680
Gaylord, John	293	England(?)	1689
Loomis, Joseph	281	England	1687
Eglestone, James	275	England	1679
Gaylord, Samuel	239	—	1689
Drake, John	223	England	1689
Pinney, Nathaniel	221	1641 Windsor	1676
Wolcott, George	207	England	1662
Rockwell, Simon	206	England	1665
Wolcott, Sarah	191	c. 1622	1684
Rockwell, John	186	1627	1673
Baker, Joseph	179	1655 Windsor	1691
Buckland, Timothy	167	—	1689
Hayward, Ephraim	142	1657	1690
Randall, Abraham	140	England(?)	1690
Winchell, Thomas	138	—	1697
Hayden, Daniel	134	1640 Windsor	1713
Marshall, Mary (widow)	130	—	1683
Hoyte, Nicholas	114	c. 1620	1665
Pinney, John	107	1651	1697
Buckland, Temperance	99	1642 Windsor	1681
Stiles, John	96	England	1683
Pond, Nathaniel	66	1650 Windsor	1675
Dibble, Ebenezar	65	1641 Windsor	1676
Clarke, Joseph	44	—	1659
Buckland, Thomas	36	—	1676

Note: The lists in Appendix II should be used with considerable caution and in terms of orders of magnitude only. A few inventories include some land as well as chattels; there are one or two – Matthew Allyn is an example – the bulk of whose possessions lie outside Windsor; and allowance must be made for those, usually elderly, who have already deeded the bulk of their property to children before their death; but even in its raw state the lists reveal the concentration of possessions, if not 'wealth', in the hands of a minority of families and predictable families at that. They bear comparison with the list of grants from the plantation in Appendix I.

NOTES ON SOURCES

These notes are not a comprehensive bibliography. They are concerned with the primary sources on which this book is based together with such secondary works as have special relevance to the story.

INTRODUCTION: THE EARL OF WARWICK AND THE COLONIZING OF AMERICA
1600-35

As a general introduction this draws heavily upon the wealth of secondary material relating to the late Tudor and early Stuart perid. Worthy of special note, however, is A.P. Newton, *The Colonizing Activities of the English Puritans* (1913). For the Rich family see J. Sargeaunt, *History of Felsted School* (1889); for the Earl of Warwick see especially W.F. Craven, 'The Earl of Warwick, a Speculator in Piracy' in *The Hispanic-American Historical Review*, vol. X (1930); also references in J.G. Palfrey, *History of New England* (1858); Alexander Brown, *Genesis of the United States* (1890); J.A. Doyle, *The English in America* (1882); see the *Dictionary of Natural Biography* for good accounts of the first Lord Rich, Lord Chancellor, Lady Penelope Rich and for Warwick himself. For contemporary accounts see J. Nichols, ed., *Progresses, Processions and Magnificent Festivities of King James I* (1828); Arthur Wilson, *History of the Reign of James I* (1653); Edmund Calamy's funeral sermon on Warwick, *A Pattern for All, especially for Noble Persons* (1658); Edward Hyde, Earl of Clarendon, *History of the Great Rebellion* (1702).

CHAPTER 1: JOHN WHITE AND THE WEST COUNTRY'S ATLANTIC HORIZON 1629–20

Central to this chapter is the pioneer work of Frances Rose-Troup on John White and his times, especially, *John White, the Patriarch of Dorchester (Dorset) and the Founder of Massachusetts* (1930) and *The Massachusetts Bay Company and its Predecessors* (1930); see also the essay by S.E. Morison in *Builders of the Bay Colony* (1930); for Dorset, see John Hutchins, *History and Antiquities of the County of Dorset* (3rd ed. 1863); *Victoria County History of Dorset* (1908); R. Hine, *The History of Beaminster* (1944); William Stevenson, *A General View of the Agriculture of the County of Dorset* (1812); Report on the Newfoundland Trade, *Parliamentary Papers* (1793); John Reeves, *History of the Government of the Island of Newfoundland* (1793); F.W. Mathews, *Poole and Newfoundland* (1936); of contemporary accounts, 'The Lamentable and Fearful Burning of the Towne of Dorchester', British Museum Tract C.27; C.H. Mayo, ed., *The Municipal Records of the Borough of Dorchester* (1908); Thomas D. Murphy, ed., *The Diary of William Whiteway of Dorchester, County Dorset from the year 1618 to the year 1635* (PhD thesis, Yale, 1939); see also W.M. Barnes, ed., 'The Diary of William Whiteway 1618-1634', *Dorset Natural History and Antiquarian Field Club Proc.*, vol. xiii (1892; selections only); J. Leland, *Itinerary of England and Wales* (1744 ed.); Thomas Gerard, *Survey of Dorsetshire* (c.1630, publ. 1732); *ibid.*, 'A Particular Description of the County of Somerset' (1633) in *Somerset Record Society Publications*, xv (1900); Edward Leigh, *England Described* (1659); William Camden, *Britannia* (1695 ed.); John White, *The Planters Plea* (1630) in S. Mitchell, ed., 'The Founding of Massachusetts 1628-31', *Massachusetts Historical Society, Proceedings*, vol. lxii (1930); White, *A Humble Request*, printed in A. Young, *Chronicles of the First Planters of Massachusetts* (1846); Rose-Troup *op. cit.* pp. 204-5; Roger Clap, *Memoirs of Roger Clap* (1731), reprinted in Young *op. cit.*; Clarendon, *op. cit.*

CHAPTER 2: THE UPROOTING 1603–1635

For the topography of this chapter see the titles listed for Chapter 1. For local conditions see especially Whiteway, *op. cit.* and Walter Yonge, 'Diary, written at Colyton and Axminster, Devon from 1604-1628' ed. G Roberts, *Camden Society Misecllany*, xli (1848).

Knowledge of the family origins of individual emigrants has been obtained from Dorset parish registers, Dorset Record Office, Dorchester; E. and T.W. Dwelly (eds.) *Bishop's Transcripts of Somerset Parish Registers*; W.P.W. Phillimore and E. Neville, eds., *Somerset Parish Registers, Marriages*; T.L. Stoate, ed., *Dorset Tudor Muster Rolls* (1978); *Visitation of Devon* (1620),

Dorset (1623) and Somerset (1623), Harleian Society publications; *Protestation Returns for Dorset* (1641) in Dorset County Museum and Library; A.J. Howard and T.L. Stoate, eds., *Protestation Returns for Somerset, 1641-2* (1975); C.A.F. Meekings, *Dorset Hearth Tax Assessments 1662-4* (1951); R. Holworthy, *Hearth Tax for Somerset 1664-5.*

For genealogical references, of varying degrees of accuracy: C.E. Banks, *The Winthrop Fleet* (1930); *ibid., The Planters of the Commonwealth* (1930); *ibid., Topographical Dictionary of 2885 English Emigrants to New England 1620-50* (1937); J.C. Hotten, ed., *Original List of Persons of Quality . . . Who Went from Great Britain to the American Plantations* (1874); J. Savage, *A Genealogical Dictionary of the First Settlers of New England* (1860-62); C.H. Pope, *The Pioneers of Massachusetts* (1900); H.R. Stiles, *The History and Genealogies of Ancient Windsor, Conn.* (revised ed. 1891); H.F. Waters, *Gleanings from English Records about New England families* (1880). There are very many individual genealogies, compiled mostly by settlers' descendants, of mixed quality and too numerous to list here. For the principal families see the notes to Chapters 10 and 11. A valuable, comprehensive source for the *Mary and John* passengers is to be found in the publications of The Mary and John Clearing House, ed. Burton W. Spear, Toledo, Ohio. See also A.N. Hansen, *The English Origins of the 'Mary and John' Passengers* (1985).

For the Puritan clergy and their attitudes to planting in New England see John White, *Planters Plea* and *A Humble Request*; R. Eburne, *A Plain Pathway to Plantations* (1624) ed. L.B. Wright, 1962; T. Fuller, *The Worthies of England* (1952 ed.); Clarendon, *op. cit.*; Archbishop Laud, *A Remembrance of the Church of Sarum* (the account of his visitation to Dorset in 1634), Report IV, *Historical Manuscripts Commission*, Appendix 131; Dr. R. Skinner, Bishop of Bristol, *Speech at a visitation at Dorchester 18 Sept. 1637* (1744). See *Somerset and Dorset Notes and Queries*, xi, for the penance of the church wardens over Warham's farewell sermon; for the lampoon on Warham see Calendar of State Papers, Colonial, American and West India 1571-1669.

Secondary works include R. Hine, *op. cit.*; A.L. Clegg, *A History of Dorchester, Dorset* (1972); Joan Thirsk, 'The Farming Regions of England', vol. iv of *The Agrarian History of England an Wales 1500-1640*; G.E. Fussell, 'Four Centuries of Farming Systems in Dorset', *Dorset Natural History and Archeological Society Proceedings*, vol. 73 (1952); G.D. Ramsay, *The Wiltshire Woollen Industry in the 16th and 17th Centuries* (1943); T.G. Barnes, *Somerset 1625-1640* (1961); D.G.C. Allen, 'The Rising of the West, 1628-31, *Economic History Review*, 2nd Series, v (1952); D.E. Underdown, *Somerset in the Civil War and Interregnum* (1973). Rachel Lloyd, *Dorset Elizabethans At Home and*

Abroad (1967); Dorset Natural History and Antiquarian Field Club, *Proceedings* (after 1938 continued as Dorset Natural History and Archaeological Society); Somerset Archaeological and Natural History Society, *Proceedings; Notes and Queries for Somerset and Dorset; Victoria County History of Dorset, passim*; A.N. Hansen, *The Dorchester Group: Puritanism and Revolution* (1987) covers some of the same material as this chapter.

CHAPTER 3: THE VOYAGE

The only documentary evidence recording the voyage of the *Mary and John* is that of Roger Clap, *op. cit.* This chapter is therefore based largely on an amalgam of sources concerning similar voyages, especially that of the *Talbot* of the year before, 1629, as recounted in the diary of Francis Higginson: 'A True Relation of the Last Voyage to New England', ed. Stewart Mitchell, in Massachusetts Historical Society, *Proceedings*, lxii (1930), that of the *Arbella* who sailed the north Atlantic just behind the *Mary and John* in 1630 as recounted by John Winthrop in his *Journal*, ed. J.K. Hosmer (1908), that of the *James*, five years later, in 1635, as recorded by Richard Mather, John Warham's successor as pastor of Dorchester Church, recorded in his 'Diary of a Transatlantic Journey, 1635, in the James of Bristol' in A. Young, *Chronicles of Massachusetts*, vol xxii; and those of John Josselyn in 'A Relation of Two Voyages to New-England' (1638 and 1663) in *Massachusetts Historical Society, Collections*, 3rd series, III (1833).

For the arrival of the *Mary and John* and the landing at Nantasket and then Mattapan, see Clap, *op. cit,*; Winthrop, *op. cit.*; William Bradford, *Of Plymouth Plantation, 1620-47*, ed. S.E. Morison 1952; T. Prince, *A Chronological History of New England in the form of Annals* (1735); J. Blake, *Annals of the Town of Dorchester* (1750) reprinted in *Dorchester Antiquarian and Historical Collections*, No. 2 (1846); C.F. Adams, *Three Episodes of Massachussetts History* (1892).

Other useful secondary works include: E.K. Chatterton, *English Seamen and the Colonization of America* (1930); R.G. Marsden, 'English Ships in the Reign of James I', *Transactions of the Royal Historical Society* (new series) xix (1915), and 'An Atlantic Crossing of the 17th Century' in *American Neptune*, xi (1951); Horace Ware, 'Winthrop's Voyage', Colonial Society of Massachusetts, *Transactions*, xii (1908); A.N. Hansen, 'Ships of the Puritan Migration to Massachusetts Bay', in *American Neptune*, vol. xxiii (1963); W.H. Baker, 'Notes on a Shallop', *American Neptune* (1957); D.R. McManis, *European Impressions of the New England Coast, 1497-1620* (1972).

CHAPTER 4: SOJOURN AT DORCHESTER ON MASSACHUSETTS BAY 1630–36

The documentary sources for the founding of Dorchester, Massachusetts start with N.B. Shurtleff, ed., *Records of the Governor and Company of the Massachusetts Bay in New England*, vol. i (1853) from which much may be gleaned, not least the standing and at least putative dates of arrival, from the lists of admission as freemen; also Winthrop *op. cit.* The Dorchester town records are contained in two *Reports of the Record Commissioners of the City of Boston*: the 4th Report (1880) comprises the town records proper, the 21st Report (1890) births, marriages and deaths down to 1825. The town records themselves are incomplete, starting only in 1633; but thereafter they are detailed enough to enable one to reconstruct the pattern of land grants and settlement, highways and waterways, and other early decisions of town government; see also W.M. Trask, 'Grantees of Meadow Lands in Dorchester (*New England Historical and Genealogical Register*, January 1881); 'Allotments of Land, Dorchester, Massachusetts 1660' (map), C.O. Paullin, *Atlas of the Historical Geography of the United States* (1932); D. Clapp; *The Ancient Proprietors of Jones's Hill, Dorchester* (1883); J.A. Fowle, *Old Dorchester Burying Ground 1634* (Dorchester Historical Society 1901); T.M. Harris, *Memorials of the First Church in Dorchester* (1830) and *Records of the First Church at Dorchester in New England 1636-1734* (1891); also R. Clapp, *op. cit.* Other contemporary accounts with references to Dorchester include W. Wood, *New England's Prospect* (1635) ed. A.T. Vaughan, 1977; T. Lechford, 'Notebook kept in Boston 1638-41', American Antiquarian Society, *Transactions*, vol. vii (1885); E. Johnson, *Wonder Working Providence*, ed. J.F. Jameson, 1910.

Early histories are: J. Blake, *op. cit.*; T.M. Harris, 'Chronological and Topographical Account of Dorchester', *Massachusetts Historical Society, Collections*, 1st Series, vol. ix (1804); *History of the Town of Dorchester, Massachusetts, by a Committee of the Dorchester Antiquarian and Historical Society*, (1859); S.J. Barrows, 'Dorchester in the Colonial Period' in J. Winsor, ed., *Memorial History of Boston, Including Suffolk County* (1881-6). See also W. Hubbard, 'A General History of New England from the Discovery to 1680', *Massachusetts Historical Society, Collections*, 2nd Series, vols. v, vi (1815).

Among the wealth of secondary works dealing with the settlement of Massachusetts Bay the following have been found especially valuable for Dorchester or are quoted. For government: A.B. McClear, *Early New England Towns, a Comparative Study of their Development* (1908); R. Akagi, *The Town Proprietors of the New England Colonies* (1924); W. Haller, *The Puritan*

Frontier: Town-planning in New England Colonial Development 1630-60 (1951); G.L. Haskins, *Law and Authority in Early Massachusetts* (1960); D.G. Allen, *In English Ways: the Movement of Societies and the transferal of English Local Law and Custom to Massachusetts Bay, 1606-1690* (1981); T.H. Breen and S. Foster, 'Moving to the New World: the character of Early Massachusetts Immigration' *William and Mary Quarterly*, 3rd Series, vol. xxx (1973). On religion: P. Miller, *Orthodoxy in Massachusets* (1933); the works of E.S. Morgan especially *Visible Saints* (1963); D. Rutman, *American Puritanism* (1977). On military matters: L. Boynton, *The Elizabethan Militia 1558-1638* (1967); Underdown, *op. cit.*; T.H. Breen, 'English Origins and New World Development: the Case of the Covenanted Militia in 17th Century Massachusetts', *Past and Present* (1972); D.E. Leach, 'The Military System of Plymouth Colony', *New England Quarterly*, vol. 24 (1951); H. Telfer Mook, 'Training Day in New England', *New England Quarterly*, vol. 11 (1938); H.L. Peterson: 'The Militery Equipment of the Plymouth and Bay colonies 1620-1690', *New England Quarterly*, vol. 20 (1974); J.S. Radabaugh, 'The Militia of Colonial Massachusetts, *Military Affairs*, vol xviii (1954); J.W. Shy, 'A New Look at the Colonial Militia', *William and Mary Quarterly*, 3rd Series, vol xx (1963); M. Sharp: 'Leadership and Democracy in Early New England Defence', *American Historical Review*, vol. 1 (1945). On economic and social affairs see R.R. Walcott, 'Husbandry in Colonial New England', *New England Quarterly*, vol. 9 (1936); D. Rutman, 'Governor Winthrop's Garden Crop', *William and Mary Quarterly*, 3rd Series, vol. xx (1963); W.B. Weeden, *Economic and Social History of New England* (1891); G.F. Dow, *Every Day life in the Massachusetts Bay Colony* (1935); A.M. Earle, *Two Centuries of Costume in America* (1903); H.R. Shurtleff, *The Log Cabin Myth* (1939); W. Cronon, *Changes in the Land; Indians, Colonists and the Ecology of New England* (1983).

CHAPTER 5: ROGER LUDLOW AND THE TREK TO THE CONNECTICUT RIVER

1635–36

For Roger Ludlow see N.B. Shurtleff, *op. cit.*, vol. I *passin*; J.A. Taylor, *Roger Ludlow, the Colonial Lawmaker* (1900); R.V. Coleman, *Roger Ludlow in Chancery* (1934); entries in both *Dictionary of National Biography* and *Dictionary of American Biography*; for the trek itself, H. Ayres, *The Great Trail of New England* (1940); also Winthrop, *op. cit.*; Bradford, *op. cit*; Hubbard, *op. cit*; K.M. Abbott, *Old Paths and Legends of the New England Border* (1907); *Connecticut circa 1625: its Indian Trails, Villages and Sachemdoms*, National Society of Colonial Dames of America (1934); A.T. Vaughan: *The New England Frontier: Puritans and Indians 1620-75* (1818); W. Cronon, *op. cit.* For the Palisado see A.N.B. Garvan, *Architecture and Town Planning in Colonial Connecticut* (1951). The population figures for the Dorchester exodus are based on Dorchester town records, *loc, cit.*, and *History of the town of Dorchester, loc. cit.* The figures in William Haller, *The Puritan Frontier: Town Planning in New England 1630-60* (1951) are comparable but computed somewhat differently. For standard references, J.H. Trumbull, ed., *Public Records of the Colony of Connecticut*, Vol. 1 (1850); C.M. Andrews, *The Colonial Period of American History*, vol. i (1934).

CHAPTER 6: CAPTAIN MASON AND THE MYSTIC FORT FIGHT

Principal sources are the accounts written by three of the chief English protagonists. John Mason wrote *A Brief History of the War with the Pequot Indians in New England* at the general court's invitation in 1656; the ms. was probably given by John Allyn, secretary of the colony, to Increase Mather who printed it in 1677 in his *A relation of Troubles which have happened in New-England by reason of the Indians there*, ed. S. Drake (1864, reprinted 1972). Mather's version lacks Mason's own preface; but this was printed by Thomas Prince in 1736 with a streamlined version of the text (with occasional paragraphs written in the third person); reprinted in *Massachusetts Historical Society, Collections*, 2nd Series, viii (1819). Mason also appears to have written a separate, shorter version which was incorporated by William Hubbard in his *A Narrative of the Troubles with the Indians in New England*, also published in 1677. John Underhill's *News from America containing a True Relation of their Warlike Proceedings* was published in the year following the war, 1638 (reprinted Massachusetts Historical Society, Collections, 3rd Series vi, 1837). Lion Gardiner's 'Lieft Lion Gardiner his Relation of the Pequot Warres', is to be found in *Massachusetts Historical Society, Collections*, 3rd Series iii (1833); for his correspondence see 'Winthrop Papers', *Massachusetts Historical Society, Collections*, 4th Series vii (1865); another immediately contemporary account, published in London in 1638, is Philip Vincent's 'A True Relation of the Late Battel Fought in New England between the English and the Pequet Salvages', reprinted *Massachusetts Historical Society, Collections*, 3rd Series vi, 1837. Mather *op. cit.*, also includes further anecdotes of the Fort Fight and preceding incidents culled from an anonymous mss found 'in the library of a learned and worthy person deceased'. See also S. Niles, 'A Summary Historical Narrative of the Wars in New-England with the French and Indians in several parts of the Country', ms. 1760 (*Massachusetts Historical Society, Proceedings*, vol. vi, Series 3); B. Trumbull, *op. cit.*; J.W. de Forest: *History of*

the Indians of Connecticut from the earliest Known Period to 1850 (1852,
reprinted 1970). Useful modern works are H.C. Shelley: *John Underhill,
Captain of New England and New Netherland* (1932); L.E. and A.L. de Forest,
Captain John Underhill: Gentlemen Soldier of Fortune (1934); H. Bradstreet,
'The Story of the War with the Pequots Re-told', *Ter. Comm. of Conn. Publ.*,
No. 5 (1933-5).

CHAPTER 7: THE PLANTING OF WINDSOR 1635–1641

The greater part of this chapter is based on an analysis of the records of the
initial allotment of land to Windsor settlers, either as 'grants from the
plantation' or purchases. These are to be found in *Windsor Town Records
1640-1749*, 8 vols in 9, in the Connecticut Colony Archives, Connecticut
State Library, Hartford, Connecticut. Vol I covers the period 1640-1682.
Vol. Ia is a transcript of Vol. I down to the retirement of Matthew Grant as
town clerk and recorder in 1877-8; it was made by Grant's successor but
one as town clerk, Timothy Loomis, about 1722-3; it is an accurate
transcription and the script is far easier to read than Grant's crabbed hand.
From it I have compiled data for people allotted grants from the Plantation
down to the end of 1641 (see Appendix I). These are a homogoneous group
comprising virtually all the first settlers. Therafter, grants are more
spasmodic and made to later arrivals. For my purpose I have excluded
purchases, as opposed to grants, since the former are extra to the original
allotments and their successive conveyances are difficult to follow. Each of
these entries is itemized for home lot, meadow, upland, wood lot and land
across the Great River, in terms of acreage or linear rods of measurement.
From this data I have constructed a table showing the total acreage per
family head. Taken in conjunction with a parallel list of inventories (see
Appendix II and the note for Chapter 8), this is a fair general index of family
wealth and standing in the town. For most of the entries the actual lot is
identified topographically so that it is possible to construct a town map with
home lots and other holdings individually identified. This task has been
simplified by the painstaking work of two 19th-century antiquarians. In his
'Early Windsor Families', *Memorial History of Hartford County*, ed. J.H.
Trumbull, Vol. ii, J.H. Hayden accurately plotted the original settlement on
a detailed map and his superior knowledge was incorporated by H.R. Stiles
in the revised edition of his *History and Genealogies of Windsor, Connecticut*
(1891).

For individual settler families see the genealogical notes for Chapters 2,
10 and 11; Stiles *op. cit. passim*; also J.W. Barbour, 'Early Windsor Families

1624-1792', genealogical collection, Connecticut State Library. For their topography of settlement see Hayden *op. cit.* For architecture, N.M. Isham and A. Brown, *Early Connecticut Houses* (1900); J.F. Kelly, *Early Domestic Architecture of Connecticut* (1927) and Garvan, *op. cit.*, F.S.M. Crofut, *A Guide to the History and Historic Sites of Connecticut 1639-1703* (1937). For the general history of Windsor's planting see Stiles *op. cit.* and Hayden *op. cit., passim.*

CHAPTER 8: MATTHEW GRANT AND WINDSOR'S SECOND GENERATION 1641–1662

Basic sources for this chapter are: J.H. Trumbull: *The Public Records of the Colony of Connecticut*, Vol. I, 1636-1665 (printed 1850); *Records of the Particular Court of Connecticut 1639-1663*, printed, *Connecticut Historical Society, Collections*, vol. xxii (1928). The following mss collections in the Connecticut Colony Archives, (State Library, Hartford) contain useful fugitive material: *Town and Lands*, 1st Series, *Private Controversies and Court Papers*, I and II; *Militia* 1st Series.

Manuscript inventories are to be found in the probate records, Hartford County Court, Connecticut Colonial Archives, *loc, cit.* Inventories transcribed for the court record are to be found in bound volumes titled: Vol. I *1636-49 Records of the Colony of Connecticut*; Vols II and III *County Court 1649-63* and *1663-77*; Vols IV, V, VI *County Court 1677-1706*. I have transcribed 172 such inventories for Windsor settlers who died between 1636 and 1726. The itemized details vary according to the competence and diligence of the townsmen or neighbours charged with conducting the inventory; but for the most part they are comprehensive lists of goods and chattels, in many cases itemized room by room and including farm stock and implements. They are an invaluable source for the early history of the Windsor settlement. A list of inventories for 127 Windsor people of the first and second generation only, arranged in order of the total value of personal estate in pounds sterling, is attached as Appendix II. A select number of inventories are printed as an appendix to Vol. I of the *Colonial Records of Connecticut*. The records for wills are less comprehensive, many people having died intestate; but for these see also C.W. Manwaring: *A Digest of the Early Connecticut Probate Records*, Vol. I, Hartford District 1635-1700, which also lists total valuations for inventories.

Apart from the volumes recording land grants and a few early town acts in Matthew Grant's *Old Church Record* (see below), Windsor's town records are only extant from 1650 onwards in *Windsor, Town Acts 1650-1714*, Vol. 1; these are in Matthew Grant's hand until his retirement in 1677 (a pertinent selection of them is conveniently to be found in the relevant chapter of Stiles, *op. cit.*). The Connecticut Historical Society, *Some Early Records and Documents of and relating to the Town of Windsor, Connecticut, 1639-1703* (1930) consists largely of Matthew Grant's own records kept as town clerk under the title of *Old Church Record* (itemized in the text). This contains, among other matters, a wealth of vital statistics including the list of birhs, marriages and deaths which, as town clerk, he returned to the General Court and which are separately reproduced form the court records in E.S. Welles, transcribed and ed., *Births, Marriages and Deaths* etc., Hartford, 1898. Matthew Grant's mss *Diary, 1637-1654* is to be found in the Connecticut State Archives. For Matthew Grant see also A.H. Grant, *The Grant Family: a Genealogical History* (1898).

Stiles, *op. cit.* and Hayden *op. cit.* continue to be central to the story, as are the other genealogical sources quoted elsewhere. A valuable modern demographic study of Windsor in this period is L.A. Bissell, 'From One Generation to Another: Mobility in 17th Century Windsor, Connecticut', *William and Mary Quarterly*, Jan. 1974, following on her 'Family, Friends and Neighbours: Social Interaction in Seventeenth Century Windsor, Conn', PhD dissertation, Brandeis, 1973. Also relevant are: M.J.A. Jones, *Congregational Commonwealth: Connecticut, 1630-1662* (1968); B.C. Daniels, *The Connecticut Town, Growth and Development* (1979); D.H. Fowler, 'Connecticut's Freemen: the First Forty Years', *William and Mary Quarterly*, 3rd Series, vol. xv (1958); A.E. Van Dusen, *Puritans against the Wilderness: Connecticut History to 1763* (1975).

CHAPTER 9: JOHN WARHAM AND WINDSOR CHURCH 1635–1670

The mss records of Windsor's first Congregational church (1636-1932, 17 vols in 16) are to be found in the Connecticut Colony Archive; see also Colony Archive, *Ecclesiastical Affairs*, 1st Series. For church affairs see Grant, *Old Church Record loc. cit*, and Stiles, Chapter IV, 'The Religious Organisation of Windsor', Chapter VIII, 'Extracts from Town Acts' and Chapter IX, 'An Episode of Ecclesiastical History'. For Warham: Roger Clap, *op. cit.*; Bradford, *op. cit.*; Cotton Mather, *Magnali Christi* (1702, reprinted 1853); for Huitt and the building of Windsor Church see 'Wyllys Papers', *Connecticut Historical Society Collections*, vol. xxi (1924). For William Hosford's sermon see D.H. Shepard, 'The Wolcott Shorthand Notebook Transcribed', PhD dissertation, University of Iowa, 1957; for all these persons see also genealogical sources previously cited.

CHAPTER 10: A TROOP OF HORSE 1658

For the proceedings at the session of the General Court, 11 May 1658, see *Colonial Records of Connecticut*, vol. i, pp.308-313. For Governor Winthrop: R.C. Black, *The Younger John Winthrop* (1966).

The sketches of the troopers and the interrelationships of their families are based on a variety of genealogical and historical sources which, for individuals concerned, are separately listed. All draw on the following common authorities: C.E. Banks *op. cit.*; J. Savage, *op. cit.*; Waters, *op. cit.*; Stiles, *op. cit.*; Hayden, *op. cit.*; L.B. Barber, *op. cit.*; M. Grant, *Old Church Record*; the author's transcripts of grants from the plantation taken from *Windsor Land Records* Vols I and Ia (see notes to Chapter 7 above) and of inventories taken from Hartford County Probate Records (see notes to Chapter 8 above); *Colonial Records of Connecticut* vols I and II (see indexes of names) and *Records of the Particular Court, passim.*

For the Allyn family: O.P. Allen, *The Allen Memorial: Descendants of Samuel Allen of Windsor, Conn. 1640-1907* (1907); for the Newberry family: Helen B.J. Lee, *The Newberry Genealogy* (1975); F.F. Starr and J.J. Goodwin, *The Newberry Family of Windsor, Conn. 1634-1866* (1898); for the Cook family: R.G. Cook, *Cook Family Genealogy* (1922), typescript in Connecticut State Library; for the Phelpses: A.H. Phelps, *Genealogy of the family of George Phelps* (1897); for the Terrys: Rose-Troup, *White*; Mayo, *op. cit.*; Whiteway, *op. cit.*; for the Hosford family: Beaminster parish records; Whiteway, *op. cit.*; Shepard, *op. cit.*; M.A. Green, *Spring field 1636-1886* (1887); H.M. Burt, *The First Century of the History of Springfield* (1898); for William Hosford's deed and wills see Colonial Archives; for Jane Hosford's will and subsequent controversy see *ibid. Ecclesiastical Affairs*, 1st Series, *Private Controversies*, 1st Series and Hartford *Probate Records*, vol. iii; also *Colonial Records of Connecticut*, vols II and III. For the earlier John Hosford and the Netherbury free school see Hutchins, *op. cit.*, vol. ii.

CHAPTER 11: THE WOLCOTT FAMILY

For the Wolcott family see the following: S. Wolcott, *Memorial of Henry Wolcott* (1881); C. Wolcott, *Wolcott Genealogy* (1912); O. Wolcott, 'Memoir', *New England Geneaological and Historical Register*, vol. xxvi (1872); Star and Goodwin, *op. cit.*

Much of this chapter is based on the Wolcott family mss collection and Roger Wolcott papers, Connecticut Historical Society, Hartford, Conn, and papers of the Allyn and Wolcott families, Connecticut State Library. For Henry Wolcott's sermon transcriptions see Shepherd, *op. cit.*; J.H. Trumbull,

Early Apples and Old Cider: a Windsor Orchard in 1650, based on Henry Wolcott Jr's shorthand account book (Connecticut Historical Society – now missing) printed in Stiles, *op. cit.*; for Henry Wolcott's original investment in his New England enterprise see B. Trumbull, *op. cit.*; Young Henry Wolcott's fellow passenger in 1672 was John Josselyn, 'An Account of Two Voyages to New England', *Massachusetts Historical Society, Collections*, 3rd Series vol. iii (1833).

CHAPTER 12: THE SECOND GENERATION IN WINDSOR 1662–1675

The references for this chapter are largely those quoted for earlier chapters, namely *Colonial Records of Connecticut*, Vol. II; Stiles; Grant, *loc, cit.*; 'Wyllys Papers', *loc. cit.*; author's inventory lists; see R.G. Pope, *op. cit.* for the half-way covenant and the second church. For Simsbury: N.A. Phelps, *History of Simsbury, Granby and Canton 1642-1845* (1845); L.I. Barber, *A Record and Documentary History of Simsbury 1643-1888* (1931); J. Ellsworth, *Simsbury, being a brief Historical Sketch of Ancient and Modern Simsbury 1642-1935* (1935); W.M. Vibert, *Three Centuries of Simsbury* (1970). For those who migrated and those who stayed see also Bissell, *op. cit.*, and Hansen *op. cit.*

CHAPTER 13: CAPTAIN NEWBERRY AND KING PHILIP'S WAR 1675

Most of this chapter was written from the minutes of the Standing (War), Council printed complete from 1 July 1675 to 9 October 1677 in *Colonial Records of Connecticut*, II, pp.331-509 and from the minutes of the General Court (by this time renamed 'Assembly') in the same volume. I have supplemented these sources with the invaluable and definitive account of D.E. Leach, *Flintlock and Tomahawk: New England in King Philip's War* (1958); see also R.C. Black, *op. cit.*; G.M. Bodge, 'The Narragansett Fort Fight 19 Dec. 1675', *New England Historical and Genealogical Register, 1886* and *Soldiers in King Philip's War* (1906); J.W. de Forest, *op. cit.*; W. Hubbard, *op. cit.*; A.T. Vaughan, *op. cit.* and other titles under military affairs in notes for Chapter 4. For Benjamin Newberry and his family see notes to Chapter 10.

INDEX